HARVESTING THE BAY

I say, Quohog, blast ye!
—Moby Dick

quahog: [kwaw-hawg] the hard-shelled clam, Mercenaria mercenaria.
Narragansett, poquauhock: "drilled shell," or "shell that we drill."

HARVESTING THE BAY

Fathers, Sons, and the Last of the Wild Shellfishermen

RAY HULING

LYONS PRESS
Guilford, Connecticut
An imprint of Globe Pequot Press

To my wife

Lyons Press is an imprint of Globe Pequot Press.

Project editors: Kristen Mellitt and Meredith Dias
Layout: Sue Murray

Library of Congress Cataloging-in-Publication Data is available on file.

ISBN 978-0-7627-7042-7

Printed in the United States of America

10 9 8 7 6 5 4 3 2 1

Contents

A Bullraker's Portrait

Anyway, the fact is that the song of the real and genuine hero of the sea has never yet been sung. Why? Because the true song would be too cruel and too strange for the people who like ballads.

—B. Traven, *The Death Ship*

My father hung a picture on the parlor wall, and everyone mistook it for a photograph of a planet.

The photo hung on the east wall, perpendicular to the front door. You would see it out of the corner of your right eye as you walked into the house. A framed picture, about a foot and a half high by a foot wide, it consisted of nothing but an oblate spheroid of a few deep colors.

In its northern hemisphere, the orb was blue-green, oceanic, hued in clines, obscured in places by white and rust-brown clouds; south, it was Martian orange, shot through with canyons of red, thin and ramulose; and in between squiggled a purplish equator.

"What's that—Neptune?" asked a good friend of mine during our freshman year of high school, when my father first put up the picture. Everyone who saw it for the first time asked much the same thing—*Is that a planet? Is it Neptune?* No, no, it was not a planet; but still these guesses were getting a little warm, because Neptune connotes the sea, and the photograph did have a maritime theme.

The picture formed half of a diptych. Its counterpart hung kitty-corner to it, on the front wall. This second photo—really, a framed clipping from the local paper's Sunday magazine—showed a huge, black Coast Guard tugboat, the *Tow Line*, breaking ice in Greenwich Cove, where my father docks his quahog skiff. In the winter of 1970, when Rhode Island endured a legendary blizzard and a nigh-legendary ice storm, the waters of the cove froze over, sealing in its small fleet of fishing boats.

The Coast Guard sailed up Narragansett Bay, over Greenwich Bay, and into Greenwich Cove, powering through the ice, then towed the men's skiffs over the remaining, impenetrable floes to open water. In the photograph, shellfishermen surround the *Tow Line.* They stand on the ice, wielding picks, shovels, axes, and hooks. My father is one of them. He is at the center of that picture, just as he is of the other.

The picture of fishermen on the ice pairs with the picture of the orb, because what people mistook for a planet was actually my father's eye. During surgery to repair his detached and torn retinas, his surgeons photographed his partially exorbitated eyes. This operation ended his career as a full-time shellfisherman, a bullraker, a harvester of the hard-shelled clam, the quahog. His doctors told him that the physical stress of his work—the pounding of the waves, the strain of digging and hauling in the catch—had damaged his congenitally weak retinas. They said that to continue working as a full-timer would likely blind him.

My mother told me he wept at these words. In all my life, I'd never heard of such a thing as my father crying—not from his parents, not from his four sisters, not from his childhood friends. He was simply one of those men who did not cry. But this news collapsed one of the great arcs of his life: He had started digging quahogs for commercial sale—on his own, from a wooden skiff, with wooden clamming tongs—at the age of ten. The weakness of his eyes had cost him the trade that had defined him for thirty years. And so he hung on the wall a photograph of one of these eyes, in the midst of its weakest moment.

The story of my father's eye has an unusual character, both modern and premodern. It harks back to unrecorded days, even though its events took place just a couple of decades ago.

A bullraker digs quahogs from the mud in deep water, using a long-handled tool called a bullrake, from a one-man skiff. He hauls them up from the bottom and sells them at market. The bullraker is a hunter-gatherer.

While my father let go of this identity more than twenty years ago, others retain it today. At its heart, in the essential character of the work (if not in actual history), bullraking precedes agriculture, yet men still bullrake in the twenty-first century. Today, there are a few hundred men who make a living as quahoggers on Narragansett Bay.

These men, the bullrakers, who now live in a so-called postindustrial age, tell stories that a prehistoric man could have told. My father hunted and gathered until the work broke his body down so badly that he had to quit his trade. That's a tale older than the taming of fire. In ancient times, an old, worn-out hunter might have placed his hand, no longer useful for hunting, against a slab of stone and spat a spray of vegetable dye over and around it. Such a stencil painting of a ruined hand would fit nicely in a gallery with the photograph of my father's eye. They function in a similar way. The art of these images comes more from the act of putting them on a wall than from the measure of beauty in their forms. They are poetic statements, not intrinsically beautiful things—poetry in poor handwriting, conceptual art. My father and this hypothetical hunter both want desperately to express something essential about themselves—or, rather, the loss of something essential to them. They want to say that they are no longer who they used to be. This vital expression has value enough in itself to merit notice and care, but the bullraker has an even more exalted status due him, because of the strange position he holds in such strange times.

The bullraker connects our forebears with us, and he may yet connect us to our descendants. He may prove himself not an anachronism, but a precognition, a vision of the future. The bullraker may persist through time because he works sustainably. The context of his work and its outcome—the fact that he feeds people at a time when farming and fishing have edged up on crisis—make him important. Narrowly speaking, by plying his prehistoric trade in a postindustrial world, the bullraker produces food sustainably. Broadly speaking, he is a sane man in an insane world.

American food production has gone crazy over the past couple of centuries. A succession of technological and sociological changes has all but done away with the small farm and the small fishing operation. The advent of capitalism in the late seventeenth century and the rise of industrialism in the nineteenth flooded the food system with money and machines. Machine-intensive, chemical-intensive, highly centralized, and highly subsidized farming and fishing operations became the norm. Family farms shrank into the shadows of the American landscape, just as working fishing docks dissolved from the seaside. The industrialization and capitalization of agriculture turned food wealth into capital and used that capital to further industrialize food. Americans replaced the food calories that powered human labor with coal and oil calories that powered machines. An industrial energy cycle replaced an agricultural energy cycle. Farming and fishing communities collapsed and crawled off to the mills. Food became strange—heavily processed, dirty, infused with laboratory reagents. Food production became centralized and food distribution diffused. Food traveled longer and longer roads, and it became extremely abundant.

Population figures in the United States increased almost as quickly as the abundance of the food supply, but the health of Americans swung wildly. Americans have eaten some filth in their time, and they have paid a price for it. They have cleaned up their food in certain ways and infused it with new toxins in others. They have traded one type of malnourishment for another. As population in general grew, the number of food producers shrank. This was a worldwide phenomenon. By the time of my birth, in 1974, more than half of humanity had given up farming or fishing or hunting or gathering as their trade—for the first time in all of human history. In the United States, 98 percent of the population enjoys the luxury of pursuing some kind of work other than primary food production. In round figures, no one in America produces any food. To put it another way, the American food system enables a tiny portion of the population (virtually no one) not just to feed, but to *overfeed* everyone. Naturally, the complexities of the new food system caused all manner of economic turmoil, including the flight from rural areas to urban ones.

All of these volatilities continue to this day. The American food system is unhealthy, unsafe, and environmentally and economically unstable, and, because of its reliance on long-distance transport, insecure. Taken together, these troubles presage a crisis, a genuine existential threat, and Americans now face the interesting choice of whether to deal with it. A society can always choose whether it wants to live or die, after all—at least, on the matter of destroying itself through its diet.

People have faced just this sort of decision since prehistoric times: They could choose to wipe out all of their game, their fish, their fruit of the vine, and so commit a slow auto-extermination, or they could control themselves. They could regulate their hunting and gathering efforts, plan for the future, and ensure, with regard to food, the continuation of their societies. It's a choice, and some societies in the past have chosen to die—the Mayans, several Mesopotamian civilizations, even a few North American Neolithic cultures. Some may do so now. Certain people of the modern age may well wish to carry the practices of modern farming and fishing to their inevitable conclusion: collapse.

There's a certain seductiveness to the idea. Americans have always had a taste for apocalyptic fantasy. From Christian fundamentalism to the Cold War, from the Rapture to nuclear Armageddon, Americans often delight in telling narratives about their own society that imagine who might get left behind and what their struggles might be like once the grand edifice of their civilization has collapsed. One could easily understand how huge swaths of the American population could find it fascinating to wonder where all of the terrible practices they see around them—especially on the matter of the environment, and, more especially, on the matter of food—may lead. The American psyche is a tortured and complicated thing, and it is never surprising that, when presented with the possibility that they are poisoning themselves and even setting themselves up for catastrophe, Americans often exhibit not indifference, but a passive sort of morbid curiosity. They are content to see things play out, because dystopia interests them.

Dystopia cometh. Americans waste about 40 percent of the food they produce. They throw it away or they let it rot where it lies. It's like sacrificing a bull to no gods. Of the other 60 percent, much of it goes into the creation of deposits of fatty tissue, which hang in great abundance from American bodies today. Obesity is just another kind of waste, which means that perhaps most American food is wasted. But even moderation in one's caloric intake won't necessarily save you. Strange chemicals added to American foods cause cancers. Antibiotics fed to and injected into cattle contribute to the evolution of hardy, new, harmful bacteria, which, the president of the World Health Organization has warned, could return the world to the state it was in before the discovery of penicillin. Hormones used in the same way foul up the human body more immediately, as do pesticides. Fertilizers deaden soils, rivers, lakes, and oceans as they bring temporary bounty to the farm. The great machines of farming and fishing participate in all of the evils of the oil industry. Just-in-time food delivery balances famine on an insecure infrastructure. These things amount to a sort of generalized sado-masochism, a cruelty Americans inflict upon themselves.

Then there's torturing animals: mutilating swine and fowl, swamping cattle in their own excrement, caging and crowding actual living creatures to the point of asphyxia. Immanuel Kant may not have the final word on the justice of such practices, but, by taking his direction—to judge them by the effect they have on the society that approves of them—it becomes clear very quickly that, with regard to its domesticated animals, Americans also suffer from a generalized sadism unmitigated by masochism.

The depravities of modern food result in bodily diseases, too: diabetes, heart disease, and their ilk, but also more exotic stuff. It helps to reformulate the euphemistic etiologies of these pathogens, in order to get at the truth of what the American food system does. No one gets Creutzfeldt-Jakob disease by eating tissue from a cow infected with bovine spongiform encephalopathy. No; this disease—among the most horrifying of them all—doesn't come from prions, little bits of protein that can warp the workings of the brain. These are proximal causes. Ultimately, the disease comes from the enormous crime of forcing cattle to cannibalize one another. Similarly, no one gets sick by ingesting some brand of *Escherichia coli*. People get sick with *E. coli* because they have eaten shit.

Americans choose to live this way—and may very well continue to do so. This situation should not be euphemized either: The madness of modern food amounts to a massive suicide pact.

There's nothing shocking in this. Scholars of societal collapse have long claimed that civilizations sometimes choose to destroy themselves through unsustainable practices; they've said this for decades, for centuries, if you count Malthus's ideas about population growth and Gibbon's theories on the role of spiritual decadence in the fall of Rome. There is so much in the American food system that is abhorrent, disgusting, and outright mad that it is easy to find classical parallels with it. In American food, torture, cannibalism, plagues, and useless sacrifice occur on a biblical scale. There's something Roman, Babylonian, even Assyrian, about the way Americans not only indulge in gluttony, but actually celebrate it. There are also modern aspects to these excesses. Here, a celebrity chef can inject syringes filled with insulin into her thigh with one hand, shove doughnut-bun burgers into her mouth with the other, and offer the whole performance as an advertisement for a lifestyle—which pretty well captures the death spiral Americans have gotten themselves into.

But there remains another course to take. The path of sustainability turns away from the disasters of conventional food. This other path has the advantage of leading toward life rather than death. The modern food system cannot reverse itself, and should not try to, but it can become more sustainable. The choice exists. What's more, it doesn't require any innovation. The bullrakers of Narragansett Bay, those few hundred neo-primitives, work sustainably. Their system shows the way forward, as does their character. They are not normal people—not these days, anyway. The thing that my father's photograph expresses—a bond with a trade, with the living action of a trade, the actual doing of the work—resides in all bullrakers. It is their animating spirit. They must feel their work in their hands. They are driven to confront a force as chaotic as the sea. The difference between them and the main body of the American workforce is essential. They have a rare essence—though not a unique one.

Millions of people feel a need to work as my father did, as the bullrakers do. The profession of bullraking has its peculiarities, no doubt, but it stands with other ways of working the land and the sea—of working with one's hands rather than through machines. Bullrakers commingle with all other farmers and fishermen and hunters and gatherers who find themselves compelled to draw sustenance from the earth and the water by hard, physical labor.

This doesn't mean that bullrakers have achieved an ideal balance in the midst of an imbalanced world. They haven't. They rely on machines, too—on gasoline engines in their boats, and in the trucks that ship their products. Refrigeration has transformed the industry. So has charting technology. Their work can be compared with other kinds of food production in terms of sustainability, but it is far from perfect. Not that the bullrakers necessarily care. The long-term economic and environmental viability of bullraking may or may not appeal to the individual bullraker. A guy may find his calling in the job because of the sheer physical joy it brings him. He might like how tough it makes him feel. He might enjoy exercising his will, his self-mastery. Or he may take pride in the rightness and social justice of his labor. It doesn't matter: The bullraker works sustainably. There's no way around it.

Sustainability is now a popular idea, which means that even casual analysis can problematize it. What is sustainability, really? Economic and environmental sustainability—what do these notions really mean? For all of the confusion, sustainability can be expressed in simple, pragmatic terms: Sustainable work is labor that can remain the same forever—or at least, for a very long time.

This is a radical position. Modern farming and fishing operations are alien to those of a hundred years ago, and they continue to change rapidly. Modern farmers and fishermen—the capital-intensive kind, the unsustainable kind—want change. They want more-productive operations; they want the work of the future to be easier than the work of today.

The sustainable shellfisherman, the quahogger of Narragansett Bay, wants his work to be as it always has been, which is not an immediately comprehensible position because it calls for modern guys to work just as hard as their contemporaries of a century ago. That is sustainability: to manage a resource—the quahog—in such a way that men can make a decent living harvesting it, forever. Such management takes considerable forethought, continuous efforts on multiple fronts of the industry, and, perhaps most difficult of all, a committed workforce.

The standard approach to advocating for sustainable food falls back on patterns of thought developed during the transition to unsustainable farming and fishing, meaning, people think about sustainable food as if no one actually produces it—as if it will simply appear, ready to be consumed. If three hundred million people suddenly decide they want sustainable food, who will provide it? Who wants to do that kind of work? Even when a proponent of sustainable food counsels you to get to know your farmer, the hedge around thinking cultivated by industrial food production remains. First: What farmer? Sustainable farming reduces productivity per acre, which means a sustainable farm needs more workers and more land than does an unsustainable one. Any significant shift from unsustainable to sustainable food will require a significant increase in the number of farmers. Where are they? Second: Does your farmer want to know you? Is he there to be known, at your pleasure? In Rhode Island terms, you could ask: Who is the quahogger? Do I really want to get to know him? Does he want to get to know me? In order to have its sustainable shellfishery, Narragansett Bay must have its bullrakers, but the bullrakers—lots of them—like to think of themselves as standing apart from the other people who live around the bay. The quahogger—like the sustainable farmer—is not merely another product to be consumed by the person who wants to live sustainably. The quahogger is someone to be partnered with, largely on his terms.

Fortunately, the bullraker needs a partnership with his neighbors if he wants to keep his identity. Only the fact that the bullraker feeds people other than himself gives him the status of tradesman. Without a community to benefit from his work, he would be a mere hobbyist. The same holds true for all of his farming and fishing brethren. Without a community of people who do not feed themselves, these farmers and fishermen wouldn't be able to be who they are.

This symbiotic relationship could occur on a larger scale if Americans made the choice to live sustainably. But choosing sustainability has consequences. A sustainable food system is more complex than an unsustainable one, and it incurs new costs in human suffering. The way of the quahogger is difficult. That is the exchange: giving up a familiar and easy (but ultimately doomed) food system for an unfamiliar and difficult—yet sustainable—one. Americans would do away with much illness and inefficiency and perversion by turning toward sustainability, but they wouldn't rid themselves of oddity. They would trade the unhealthy strangeness of industrial food for the healthy strangeness of the quahogger and others like him. This is not a small thing, and Americans must prepare for it by learning how sustainable farmers and fishermen really work, what they suffer, and what they value.

The shift to a sustainable food system would be gargantuan. Millions of bullrakish folk would suddenly come to prominence. A new class of hunter-gatherer and a new class of peasant would emerge, and their mentality would be quite different from that of their neighbors. America's ruinous food system did not arise through happenstance; it arose in accordance with a set of principles, a field of values. Americans wanted their food to be the way it is, and they have gotten what they deserved. The task of transforming the system will require bringing new values and new expectations to bear on the work of food production. This truth holds all the way down the line of transformation, from the people who merely eat the food to the people who grow and catch it. New values must guide the development and implementation of new practices—values already held dear by quahoggers.

This is mostly good news, because you can find in quahogging a crystallization of the mind-set necessary to make sustainability viable; however, sharing the moral world of the quahogger can also be an upsetting experience, both on its face, and for what it implies about actual sustainable food production. Quahoggers have their own ideas about what is best in life, and what they think is best may seem alien, weird, and dangerous to others.

Take the suicide of William Benoit, a very well-known quahogger on Narragansett Bay.

I knew him only as Cap'n Bill. On the water, it happens that you may know someone only by his nickname even after years of docking near him. I never took up quahogging, so I had very little chance of learning the full names of the men my father worked with. For me, the work is something to be reflected upon in writing, not something to be lived.

All of the quahoggers on Greenwich Bay knew Cap'n Bill. For years he captained the *Beacon,* a buy-boat for Greenwich Bay Clam, the largest shellfish dealer in Rhode Island. Cap'n Bill would pilot the boat onto the water in the very early morning, towing his own quahog skiff behind. Before his work on the big boat started, he would take the cash box, set out on his little boat, dig his own quahogs for a few hours, then come back to the *Beacon* and open it for business. Around ten or eleven o'clock, the quahoggers would pull up to sell out. I vaguely remember him from my childhood, when I would go out on the water with my father. Bill was a brawler, with the archetypal huge forearms of the fisherman. A navy man, Bill had piloted tugboats in New York Harbor during World War II—thus, his honorific.

Cap'n Bill kept his skiff one dock over from my father's, at the ruins of a red shanty owned by Warren Finn, proprietor of Greenwich Bay Clam and another towering figure in Rhode Island shellfishing. Over the years, Finn lost interest in the shanty, and the *Beacon* became too expensive to maintain. Cap'n Bill quit captaining in the early eighties. He went back to merely digging, while the shanty deteriorated. The town finally condemned the building, but the dock remains in operation, extending from a small patch of grass. It was on this dock that Bill committed suicide, and

The *Beacon* in the morning, circa 1980. BRUCE EASTMAN

it was in talking with the guys down the shore after his death that I first
learned his full name.

A long time before he died, Cap'n Bill told my father a story about
an old-timer who'd gotten caught in a storm. With the waves as high as
they were and his boat as small as it was, the old man knew he wasn't
going to make it back to shore, so he tied his anchor line around his feet.
He wanted the search parties who would come looking for him after the
storm to find his body. He would drown, but the anchor would prevent
his body from washing out to sea.

Many years later, Billy Benoit was deep in old age. He had cancer and
couldn't work anymore, so, very early one morning, he went down to his
boat at the dock, tied his anchor line around his legs, threw his anchor in,
and himself after it. Two people found him in the water a few hours later.
One was the owner of the neighboring dock; the other was Cap'n Bill's
son. That morning, Bill had left a note on his son's kitchen table that read:
"You know where to find me."

This, too, is a consequence of the work. Billy Benoit's death is perfectly congruent with quahogging culture. Now, some quahoggers might
say that Cap'n Bill was wrong to do what he did, while others might

think he wrought an honorable end for himself, but none of them would think for even an instant that his act was alien or incomprehensible. The same holds true for my father's photograph. It makes perfect, immediate sense to other quahoggers. What my father expressed through art, Billy Benoit expressed through suicide. It is one passion—a love for life on the water, for the entirety of that life. The shore, the bay, the sun, the motion of the water, the camaraderie among the fishermen, the satisfaction of a good catch, the difficulty of attaining that satisfaction, the empowerment that comes from working alone. The paradox of their feeling for this way of life is that it led them to a confrontation with death—symbolically, in my father's case; actually, in Billy Benoit's. The work they do fosters this manner of thinking about life and death. Everyone around them must contend with the bullrakers' way—family, friends, neighbors, and even the community of bullrakers. While it's not so hard to contend with my father's handling of things, it's very difficult to contend with Cap'n Bill's. Nonetheless, they are both natural consequences; to accept quahogging means accepting the suicide of Cap'n Bill.

Bullrakers constitute an extreme, of course. Any sustainable food system is going to be something like the quahog shellfishery of Narragansett Bay, with all of its imperfections, difficulties, controversies, and turmoil, and with its host of peculiar characters. But even among other sustainable operations and other farmers and fishermen who work sustainably, quahogging and quahoggers stand out. They are vanguards. They are radicals. They are extremists. But they are not beyond the pale. Few sustainable practices will rely as heavily on intense physical labor as quahogging does, but all of them will become the focus of just such hard passions. It is impossible for quahogging to exist as an industry without people who feel about the work the way my father does, and Cap'n Bill did, and the same is true for any sustainable farm or fishery: Only men and women who share this passion will do the work. Sustainability requires more than a trip to the farmers' market or a few well-placed votes. It requires accepting people who have values that are radically different from those of the American mainstream.

There is a stark choice to be made here: the suicide of a nation, or the suicide of a man. By eating the fruits of the conventional American food system, one assents to its present horrors and future disasters. By turning to sustainability, one assents to the suffering of people like my father and to the suicide of people like Cap'n Bill. The American way of feeding itself cannot continue, and so it will stop—either by collapsing catastrophically, or by transforming prudently into something better. The prudent choice will consign a great number of people to backbreaking labor, and will require everyone to understand food and work in new ways. These are enormous demands for people to make of themselves, and facing these demands squarely is the only way to take sustainability seriously.

This is why it pays to explore the world of the quahogger, an extremist in the matter of sustainable food. Through him, we can see the limits of the challenges we might face, and the challenges we might impose on each other, if we are to live sustainably.

CHAPTER ONE

Cove, Bay, and Bay

If I forget thee, O Jerusalem, may my right hand forget its skill.
—PSALMS 137:5

GREENWICH COVE, GREENWICH BAY, NARRAGANSETT BAY. I LEARNED my father's workplace in this order, the order we head out in today. My father and I are scouting locations for an oyster aquaculture operation, an oyster farm, the sort of part-time work he can handle. He's gotten old, and his body's broken down. He's had both of his hips done, and one knee. His back and hands are shot through with rheumatism.

After quitting bullraking in 1988, he found work at Rhode Island's adult correctional facility, the state prison. He got a job as manager of the prison's greenhouses and worked his way up to grounds main-tenance supervisor. He had to work with teams of inmates, and so he belonged to the guards' union, the Brotherhood of Correctional Officers, which came in handy when he wrecked his knee on the job one winter. The union had secured him good benefits—benefits almost halfway equal to the difficulty of working in a prison. He received decent health care at the time, enough to keep him walking, if little else. Now he's retired and disabled, a crutch-walker, a handicapped-parker, a man inches shorter than his height in his prime. But he wants to be on the water. He would like to have some oysters to tend, a small retirement patch where he can work and earn some money and enjoy himself on a boat.

This means we have to put his quahog skiff back in the water, where it hasn't been for a few years. We clean it out, hitch its trailer to my father's truck, and tow it down to the shore, to the cove.

Greenwich Cove is the eastern boundary of the town of East Greenwich, which lies in the middle of the State of Rhode Island. The cove spikes south, splitting the land into two parts, much as Narragansett Bay itself, driving northward, does to the main body of the state. The west side of the cove is the mainland; the east is Potowomut Neck, a bulb of land extending into Narragansett Bay. Though not contiguous with it, Potowomut belongs to the town of Warwick, which lies north of East Greenwich. The Neck has two sections: Goddard Park on the western half, and a smattering of rich people's houses on the eastern half. Thus, Greenwich Cove has a crowd of docks and buildings on one side and woods on the other, a portentous, if artificial, opposition.

Greenwich Cove begins with muddy, reedy shallows, called the Dish. A stream empties into the cove here, draining Bleachery Pond, where textile mills used to stand. Today's old-timers say that the old-timers of yesteryear claimed the mills polluted the cove so badly that its waters would turn the colors of the dyes used on the textiles. You'd come in from work to find the waters turned yellow or red or blue. Clean now, the Dish provides some of the best eeling in the state. Just up from the shallows, on the western bank, bulges the mound of Scalloptown Park, a hill crowned with patchy grass, as inviting for a stroll as a mangy dog is for petting. A sign at the top of the hill proudly declares that the park was "developed and reclaimed from the old town landfill"—and so it was. Rhode Island's Department of Environmental Management (DEM) and the federal government's Natural Resources Conservation Service collaborated with the town to bury the dump, stitch some grass into the pile of earth, and name it for the stretch of Greenwich Cove that used to be called Scalloptown. It ran from London Street to the Old Jail, at the corner of King and Water Streets, a distance of less than a mile. They called it Scalloptown because of the scalloping business that thrived there from the late nineteenth to the mid-twentieth century. In the early 1940s, my grandfather earned up to two hundred dollars a day scalloping, enough that he could afford to buy a parcel of shoreline and put up a shanty in Scalloptown, which even then was in decline.

Scalloptown proper—as much as an informal locality can be proper—is located a half-mile from the edge of the park. The park's misplacement, its poor manicure, and its misguided hopes embody the failings of

Scalloptown, circa 1930. HOWARD DREW

contemporary East Greenwich. The town is now run by middle-class and upper-middle-class white-collar professionals, participants in and descendants of the White Flight of the seventies. East Greenwich is a typical tax-and-spend Republican town. People move in, raise taxes on each other, use the money to pay for school construction boondoggles, then leave. The town government—and its transient residents—see East Greenwich as little more than a means to an end of educating their children, who will themselves leave town, never to return. Virtually no one gives any thought to the long-term prospects of the community, which is how you get things like Scalloptown Park. Rather than invest in a living fishery, the town memorializes a dead one. They use the memory of Scalloptown as a tarp on a pile of trash, a bit of camouflage meant to draw in more white-collar refugees, and to screen out the fishermen who already reside there. And the fishermen know it. Some claim that, on the darkest nights, you can see a greenish glow emanating from the hump of Scalloptown Park. To many fishermen, the town's little project is a ghost story in which they are the ghosts. The town and its residents eagerly await the moment when the flesh-and-blood fishermen will fade into spirits fit for a monument.

Up from the park is a public boat ramp that my father helped to build in the 1960s, and it is here that my father and I will put in. Normally, we would have launched from a ramp just down the road from where my father rents his slip, but, for some reason, the woman who owns that bit of shore has blocked it off, perhaps illegally. Such unexplained inconveniences happen all the time down here. Rights of access and property have vague and shifting protections down the shore.

We waggle the boat trailer into the water, never an easy thing to do because of the counterintuitive physics of the trailer hitch. The technique is similar to steering a boat with a tiller—lean right to go left—only you're on land and going backwards. We push the skiff back off the trailer and into the water until it starts to float. I pull the chucks out from behind the truck's tires and drive it up to the parking lot, which used to be the site of a grand old house on a hill overlooking the cove. Then we have to get my father into the boat, not an easy task with his bum legs. We draw the boat very close to the water's edge so he can reach for the bow. He slips on the seaweed covering the cement of the ramp. "Ray! Ray!" he calls out in a strange tone—not afraid so much as annoyed, as if he had just stripped a screw or snapped a bolt. I catch him, steady him, and soon he's sitting on the bow so he can swing his legs over the gunwale.

Because it has been so long since the motor has run, we need to handle it gently at first. It's a nearly unused motor, a few years old, a four-stroke—just seventy horsepower, though huge and heavy. My father turns the key and works the throttle, which is secured to starboard in the stern by a plywood mount. When he eases it forward, the throttle, mount and all, comes off in his hand. The plywood is bifurcated—an inner ply rotted out during the boat's long languishing in the yard. We jury-rig the throttle back into place and then start to zip around the cove, trying to get the boat to plane off.

A quahog skiff is small and light—tough because of its layers of fiberglass, and fast because of its absurdly huge motor. When running at full steam, the boat will rise up at the prow, slew, and maybe overturn, unless it planes off—levels on the water. Quahog skiffs have planing hulls, nearly flat-bottomed in the stern, which means they level off well in calm water but tend to buck and pound when the waves become high.

My father needs to learn how the new motor changes the way the boat responds to the water, so we head over to a small lagoon on the Potowomut side of the cove—at ten feet or so, its deepest water, it's a good place to run the boat back and forth. On the way, we pass the waste-treatment facility, an excellent facility, by all accounts, with its cluster of brick buildings and big circular vats. In the early sixties, just to show off, the plant ran treated water to a bubbler ("water fountain" in Rhode Island parlance) that stands on a nearby lawn. A student from the seminary school up the bay worked at the treatment plant one summer, and from time to time, quahoggers would see him sipping from the bubbler. "We called it his Holy Water," says my father.

The lagoon lies across from the working docks and shanties I know best: the Wilsons', the Drews', the ruins of Finn's, right at the bottom of Water Street's steep hill. Several dozen skiffs and a few lobster boats tie up there. The shanties are old and shingled; the docks are wood; the pilings are stripped trees. These days, most piles have caps on them, cones of aluminum or plastic put in place to ward off the seagulls, which would otherwise perch on them and streak the wood with bleaching shit. A long time ago, the men made such caps out of tin, but capping fell out of favor for many years for some reason. I never saw them in my youth, and I think they look silly. Nonetheless, it remains a picturesque shore, with its old skiffs and old working docks.

The cove is quaint and pleasing to look at, but it has some ugly truths to it. Just past the last Drew shanty is a bulge of land called Havens Point. In the 1800s, Havens was a small black neighborhood, and a black boy drowned there. Some of the fishermen called it Nigger Point. The Drews never refer to it that way, but the name persists. It's always a surprise to hear it in casual use. A guy they call Prairie Dog (because he comes from Kansas) used the name when telling me about a photo he'd taken of the docks.

"I got a picture o' your old man's skiff down there," he said. "I went down there one mornin', it was in the fall, October of seventy-eight, and friggin' just, oh, a beautiful sunrise . . . the color of the skiffs back then. I stood down there, behind Pumpkin's at Nigger Point. I took a shot goin' south, just the line o' skiffs . . . you can see 'em all. I stood back where you could see 'em all, instead of linin' 'em all up. That's the oldest picture I got, one of the best of all the skiffs down there."

By "Pumpkin," he meant Arthur Drew, whose shanty stands just before Havens Point.

Arthur was one of the most well-known guys on the bay. His mother called him Pumpkin because of his red hair and freckles; many of the bullrakers called him Pumpkin, too. He held both reputations that have real meaning for shellfishermen: He was a good quahogger, and a nice guy—a good friend. It was never Nigger Point to him. Few of the old-timers would brook that kind of language, though it's also true that few of them had very enlightened views about race. A man like my grandfather disliked the indignity inflicted by cruel words and ill treatment, but this did not mean that interracial marriage sat easily with him. Racism in New England is a many-splendored thing. Whiteness remains a quality hard to come by. An old white person may wish for all of the blacks in America to swim back to Africa, but with an Italian under one arm and a Portuguese under the other and a Jew riding on the back. The French and Irish are suspect, too. It's a WASPy bundle of values, but without Klannish overt violence and with a veneer of politeness, due to the fact that so many Latins and Celts and Semites are their neighbors and good friends.

This etiquette extends to black friends and neighbors as well. I remember one morning down the shore when the men were putting in their coffee orders with Arthur Drew, who always offered to make a Dunkin' Donuts run. Bill wanted his coffee black with sugar. "Black and sweet!" roared one of the guys, almost certainly my uncle Jake, "just how he likes his women!"—because Bill's girlfriend, Mimi, was black. For them, this teasing served to welcome the relationship into the fold. Thus, it would be unseemly to torture the memory of that poor boy who drowned with a place-name like that. Many old-timers felt this way, but enough felt differently that Havens Point's other name got passed down through the years.

This is typical of Rhode Island: the first colony to abolish slavery, and yet for a long, long time, the North's busiest port in the business of smuggling slaves. Few residents of East Greenwich would be so indecorous as to use the racial slur, but the town exists as it does precisely because groups of whites and honorary whites sought to abjure the great bogeyman of American schools, the poor black child. As is true for the American map generally, racism played a big role in drawing the lines of the shore. In other words, it really is a short ride from Scalloptown Park to Nigger Point.

Having gotten the boat to plane off, we circle for a while. My father points out the spot where my grandfather's shanty used to stand, between Tiny Wilson's and David Drew's. My grandfather let a guy by the name of Pep Lorensen live there. Pep had fought in World War II, and on his return, had drunk himself homeless. He lived as a hobo for decades down the shore. I remember him from my childhood, a small, gabbling man, bent over, with a choking cough. Sometime in the seventies, Pep burned down my grandfather's shanty. The guys down the shore called the wreckage the Hotel California.

We slow down to the cove-approved speed of five miles an hour. Heading north, we pass by a smattering of sailboats and yachts tied up at moorings, rather than docks. We pass the shellfish dealership I still think of as Finn's, Rhode Island Clam, formerly Greenwich Bay Clam, the largest shellfish dealer in the State. Bob "Smitty" Smith owns and operates the business now, but the Finn family still owns the land and the restaurant next door, the Harbourside.

The Finns are one of Rhode Island's great shellfishing families. The three Finn brothers, Warren, Walter, and Herbie, came down from Middleborough, Massachusetts, during the Depression. They started their shellfish dealership, prospered, and split up. Warren, known as the

Little necks, circa 1980. BRUCE EASTMAN

Colonel, opened Greenwich Bay Clam, right next door to another well-known dealership, King Gorman's, which also had a restaurant upstairs. The Colonel's son, Warren Jr.—known as Sonny, or, depending upon the mood of the guys, "Pig-Paw," because of his misshapen hand—came into power in the late forties. The two Warrens are gone now, but their reputations still cast long shadows over the bay. On the dealer's side of things, they are the two colossi of Rhode Island quahogging.

The Harbourside is a two-story place, just as it was when King Gorman ran it. Gorman bought the quahogs downstairs and served them upstairs, and he was notoriously finicky about his provender, in both selection and service. He wanted a little neck with a certain kind of shell, a soft gray with a broad white lip. He paid top dollar for the right look. He also didn't serve alcohol in his restaurant—not for reasons of morality or social justice, but for reasons of aesthetics. He thought it ruined the taste of his food. "If you're gonna be drinking, you ain't gonna come and eat my food." That was King Gorman.

Today, both floors of the Harbourside serve food and booze, and East Greenwich has become known for the swarms of young drunks who settle on its shores each weekend and each Thursday in summer, to drink and raise hell. Monday's arrest reports invariably showcase the good times to be had down the cove—and there's something traditional about all of this. Back in the day, it's said that Grandma Rice, a formidable woman who oversaw the caretaking of prisoners at the Old Jail, made such excellent chicken and dumplings that the local drunks—guys like Pep—would get themselves arrested on Friday in order to secure a couple of her meals and a warm bed over the weekend.

Then, as it is now, one of the principal means of achieving arrest was the fistfight. The parking lot across from the Harbourside used to be the site of a warehouse, which used to be the Bayview Cafe, also known as the Bucket of Blood. Bayview Cafe is just the sort of pedestrian, treacly name the good people of twenty-first-century East Greenwich would mistake for tasteful, while Bucket of Blood is just the kind of name the town wants to avoid. Once again, the shellfisherman's colloquialism tells a hard truth about the shore.

"The famous Bucket o' Blood," Arthur Drew said as he slapped down an old photograph of the Bayview, when we got together with him and

David later that day, once my father and I had come in off the water. Guys from other towns would turn up there to show East Greenwich boys which town was boss, he said.

"The Wilson brothers went in there one year," he told us. "There was a bunch of guys from South Kingston or Wakefield or somethin' in there . . . There was no windows in the place! They beat the livin' shit outta every one of 'em! That's no bullshit! Charlie . . . Hub and Tiny . . . and I guess Red come down the next day, and, whoever was left, he beat up."

The Drews got in on the action themselves. Arthur's brother and David's father, Howard, earned himself a story in the Bucket of Blood. "His father emptied it out one day," said Arthur, nodding to David. "He emptied it out . . . he had guys jumpin' out the window, the door. He had Dad's shotgun [Arthur and Howard's father, George, built the Drew docks and shanties]. Somebody teed him off . . . He went home and grabbed Dad's shotgun, went down there. Dad was smart; he kept the bullets somewhere else."

The Bucket of Blood's gone now, but a whole mess of bars stretches northward from Finn's. Boatyards, yacht clubs, a massive infestation of yachts where Finn Bros. used to be. Behind all of that, across Water Street and up Queen Street, just below the train tracks, stands the Fireman's Hall—not a fighting bar, but a quahogging mecca, nonetheless.

Anyone who wants to write about quahogging in Narragansett Bay must, sooner or later, make a pilgrimage to the Fireman's Hall, to sit at the feet of Cap'n Ron—Ron Turgeon, eighty years old, sixty years on the bay, and still digging. He's thin and tall, with a long, weathered, white-bearded, and good-looking face. As often as not he wears a Budweiser baseball cap, this brew being perhaps his nectar and his Golden Apple, the secret of his long career. A long time ago, Cap'n Ron told my father about a dream he'd had, a vision of Heaven, in which *Playboy* centerfolds frolicked in the pools of Budweiser waterfalls. A vision of paradise, except that to get in, the petitioner had to fill an-inch-and-a-quarter bullrake with undersized quahogs. The minimum legal size for a quahog is one inch.

Cap'n Ron is everything you could want in an old fisherman: He's clever; he's eloquent, and says strange things; he has a storied, piratical, hard-drinking past. Cap'n Ron lived at the Bucket of Blood in his youth—literally, he rented a room above it. At times, he lived in

Arthur's shanty, and for a while, out of his car. What else would a bar-room man do?

Down at another shellfishermen's watering hole, The Oaks, on King Street, they have a two-by-three-foot poster of Cap'n Ron hanging on the wall, blown up from a photo of him taken by the State Lottery Commission when Ron did an ad for them. He's had other encounters with the local media. In 1987, the *Providence Journal-Bulletin* ran an article on him. Cap'n Ron took a reporter out on the water one winter to hear the "singing ice," a bunch of nonsense about mysterious sounds made by the ice on the bay. He has never held any military rank or captain's license. Why is he called Cap'n Ron, then? "I don't know," my father shrugs. "He acted like a captain, I guess." Cap'n Ron got his promotion on the merits of pure charm.

Cap'n Ron still goes out on the water with that eighty-year-old body of his, but not simply because he loves it: He must go out. He still needs to earn a living. All the lies he told to avoid paying taxes in his younger days—and it was quite easy to get paid under a false name, even twenty years ago—have left him with very little social security to collect. And, though he is blessed with a constitution virtually unparalleled on the bay, he suffers greatly in his work. When you reach out to shake his hand, you might think he has lost his ring finger; it looks lost from the mid-knuckle, a fisherman's knob. But on shaking his hand, you feel his finger under your palm, curled in on itself, like a wood shaving. Trigger-finger. He has an exactly matching condition on his left hand.

"That's why it was tough this winter," he says. "I can't get my hands in the gloves right. I had gloves with no fingers in 'em, but I can't find 'em. They don't make 'em anymore . . . rubber mittens."

He doesn't bemoan his pains. He has to work hard, but, still, he's been able to go out on the water for sixty years. He's raised hell and he's done what he wanted. Further, he appears quite content, even though he hasn't been outside of East Greenwich by any means other than boat for fifty years. He has a small territory, but he has often reflected on its beauty.

"If you wanna look at this thing and actually bring this thing in perspective," he says, "there's Goddard Park . . . that's really beautiful, right? Now you start up at the head of the cove and work down. I can tell you every story that's come all the way down, about where the hell people lived, down to the shanties that's on the shore, how they worked around, how this was like dead land and everything . . . There was nothing here . . . The jail, that was the jail right there, and it was like nothin'. The yacht club was very little, there was no boats in the cove. I did movies . . . I got the movies with a camera of the whole bay, over and over, I did it for years, and I finish up by sayin' when I come up on that buoy . . . I come up and take pictures, shoot my camera at Goddard Park and I says, 'Look at this right in here, that's God-made,' and I swing around and show the picture of this side that's all man-made . . . That's how I end this film that I got. It's all pretty good, too . . . it's pretty good."

My father and I pass by the buoy. It's red and reads PAST THIS POINT 5 MPH in big white letters. We'd broken the rules in the lagoon. We emerge from the cove into Greenwich Bay. Right at the mouth of the cove, the wind and the light change. The weather becomes stronger. You can feel, as a clear and simple phenomenon, the truth of every cliché about "safe harbor," right there at the border between cove and bay.

Beneath our skiff, five or six feet down, a river of quahogs pours into the bay. Greenwich Cove has perhaps the densest concentration of qua-hogs on the planet, but it is closed to shellfishing, as are all coves on the bay. The State keeps a very close watch on its waters, particularly when it comes to shellfish. The chief biological scientist of the Department of Environmental Management comes down to the cove every month in the summer and every few months in the winter. He takes a hockey stick he has modified with duct tape to have a little cup alongside the blade, into which he fits a small, plastic sampling jar. The biologist, a pleasant, round-faced guy named Joe Migliore—who himself tried his hand at quahogging for six months or so, until his hand said "no more"—dips his jury-rigged sampling apparatus into the waters at the mouth of the cove, in front of the sewer plant, by a fuel dock near the yacht club. He carefully caps his sample jars and sends them off to the Department of Health, which tests them for certain kinds of bacteria. The Food and Drug Administration dictates the standards waters must meet in order to be open to shellfishing. The shellfishing standard is more stringent than that for drinking water, which makes sense: Shellfish are filter feed-ers and so tend to concentrate bacteria within themselves. It's possible to find water legally suitable for drinking (though physically unsuitable on account of salinity), but legally off-limits for quahogging.

These protections establish the trust that makes the shellfish market possible, and explain why so few quahogs—virtually none—cause illness. Quahogs have been far easier on the American stomach than spinach and beef and eggs over the past half-century or so. The closing of the coves also produces the massive population of quahogs in them. The quahogs have no human predators, and they stuff themselves full of the plankton that feed on the flood of nitrates in cove waters. The nitrates come from pollution. While sewage-treatment plants scour bacteria and other harmful pollutants quite effectively from their intake, they have too little success removing the eminently soluble nitrates from their discharge. Further, far too many houses along the shore have no sewer tie-in; their septic tanks leak into the soil, which also allows nitrates to pass through to the water. These failings result in coves well-stocked in quahogs, and the hypothesis of many shellfishermen and state scientists alike is that the coves are the Golden Goose: They seed Greenwich Bay with quahogs. The quahogs pour into the bay just as the streams and rivers of the surrounding lands do. The remarkable fecundity of the bay is due, then, in no small part, to the hordes of houses and shops and bars and restaurants that encrust the shore, the filtered filth of which fertilizes the water. The effluent of the human population becomes nitrates, which feed huge blooms of algae, which feed quahogs, which release thick clouds of quahog seed, which become great sets of quahogs in the bay. Indeed, cove waters sometimes turn milky, not with the dyes of textile mills anymore, but with the spawn of quahogs.

This hypothesis may be false, however. It's not at all clear that cove quahogs do much of anything for the bay. The blurry line of demarcation between healthy and unhealthy quahog populations may lie at the liminal point, the mouth of the cove—right where my father opens up the throttle and heads east into more-open waters. In the extreme density present in the coves, quahogs spawn less frequently and less well; they grow more slowly, and may even smother each other in their piles. The milk of the cove may spill uselessly into the bay. It may be that good management, a good plan for tending to the bay, results in the excellence of Greenwich's fishing grounds, rather than the sexual efforts of clots of overfed quahogs. No one really knows why quahogs do so well in Greenwich Bay; all that is known is that it is rich, and such richness tempers any fervor for experimentation.

We turn east. We ride past Sally Rock—really, a few great boulders, not a single one—between which the knowledgeable boatman may take a shortcut, while the novice gives the whole formation a wide berth. We pass Goddard Park's beach, the site of one of the great adventures in the history of Rhode Island quahogging: the ice-digging transplant of 1979. In the winter of that year, the bay froze over to an extent not seen in decades. Aside from all of the expected difficulties such an influx of ice would present to shellfishermen, the cold also sealed a stretch of water the men had stocked with product the spring before.

The State and the shellfishermen organize a transplant program each year that allows quahoggers to load their rakes with the bounty of the normally off-limit coves. For a few hours a day, a few days a week, for a few weeks a year, the quahoggers cross the line into forbidden territory—waters uncertified for shellfishing—under the watchful and suspicious eyes of the environmental police. The guys harvest hundreds of thousands of pounds of product from a cove each day, for which they receive—in funded transplants—about five dollars per fifty-pound bag. The bags go onto big boats, often lobster boats or quahog buy-boats, which take the tremendous catch out to a predetermined spot where the men dump them. The quahogs clear themselves of cove water in a few days, but the State, with the blessing of the Rhode Island Shell-fishermen's Association, declares them unharvestable for six months, in hopes that they will spawn. This means that, come December, the men will have a mighty cache of clams to draw from, legally and for commercial sale.

In that winter of '79, however, the ice capped the very spot where the guys had stowed their quahogs. So, again, under the supervision of Rhode Island's Department of Environmental Management (DEM) agents, hundreds of guys walked out onto the ice, cut big holes in it, and dug up the clams. It was madness, but it made for a good story.

My father was there on the ice that winter, and he laughs about how absurd and dangerous the whole thing was, as we head out across the water, past the park. Greenwich Bay is a rectangle, with its longer side running west to east for a couple of miles. Its western shore stretches for about a mile and a half. Its mouth opens between two mushrooming necks: Potowomut to the south, and Warwick to the north. The bay is immensely productive of quahogs—in no small part because of its complex management system.

Each year, in May, the DEM issues its closure map—a map of how Rhode Island's waters are managed for shellfish. Different management areas have different visual patterns to indicate their different regimes. Greenwich Bay always ends up looking like a harlequin, with its areas of permanent closure, seasonal conditional closure, spawner sanctuary, and so on. Greenwich Bay's tumultuous history, including a couple years of complete closure in the early 1990s, as well as major fish kills in the 2000s, has resulted in major initiatives to control the influx of pollution into the bay and to control the efforts of shellfishermen to keep its quahog population sustainable. All of this complexity makes the bay unsuitable—or at least unattractive—for the oyster farm we'd been thinking of. An aquaculture operation sells consistency above all else, and we won't find any of that here. My father and I skip over Greenwich Bay and head into Narragansett Bay, that great dart shot by the Atlantic into the heart of Rhode Island.

Narragansett Bay makes little sense, ecologically speaking. It is too young to have developed a full ecological identity. Glaciers formed it just ten thousand years ago, as they retreated to the icy depths of Canada. Man already had cities by then, never mind agriculture. Furthermore, the local climate now familiar to those who live by the bay didn't establish itself until about five thousand years ago. China is older than that. The bay's youth makes it confusing, as the fish kills demonstrate. The kills that occurred in Greenwich Bay were due to hypoxia, a dramatic reduction in oxygen in the water. In the main, scientists believe that it was once again nitrates at work: massive algal blooms grow and die, bacteria feed on the rotting algae, and the bacteria's respiration sucks up oxygen, asphyxiating the fish. At the margins, there are scientists who argue that Narragansett Bay causes hypoxia naturally; the nitrate pollution merely intensifies it. It is likely that this puzzle remains difficult to figure out because Narragansett Bay is adolescent; it doesn't know who it is, or who it wants to be.

Rhode Islanders have a similar problem. It's hard for them to truly understand the place where they live. Rhode Island is not an island, the schoolmarms say. They are wrong about this, as the state's actual name is the State of Rhode Island and Providence Plantations, which refers to

the mainland settlements—Providence and its environs—as well as to
the island of Rhode Island (*Aquidneck* by its Narragansett Indian name),
where Newport is located. When Giovanni da Verrazzano turned up in
Narragansett Bay in 1524, to explore and misidentify the land, he found
that one of the islands in the bay reminded him of the Isle of Rhodes.
When Roger Williams fled the whipping, hanging, and beating religious
persecution of Massachusetts for parts south, he decided da Verrazzano
must have meant Aquidneck.

The bay boasts dozens of islands, many of them now holding European names with a biblical flair. My father and I are heading for Despair
Island, which, unlike Rhode Island, is really not an island. Despair consists of a few big humps of mussel-encrusted rock, just off of Hope Island,
which is fairly large and bristling with trees. In and around Despair—
people have died on these rocks, even as recently as a few years ago—you
can find quahogs. A few weeks before our trip, my father and mother
went out to Despair. My father eased out of the boat into the shallow
water and gathered quahogs with his hands. I came by to visit the next
day. They were redoing their kitchen at the time, and there, in the midst
of the demolition, in a chair that constituted the room's only furniture, sat
my father with a great big bushel of quahogs. He beamed with satisfaction as he shucked them into a bowl for the chowder he would cook up
in an electric wok.

Today, finding quahogs is just what we don't want to do. We want
to find a place devoid of them—a few such places, in fact. Narragansett
Bay is a free and common fishery, a "commons," or "common property
resource" in the economic sense. So says the state constitution, which
derives directly, on this matter, from the Charter of King Charles II,
enacted in 1663. No one may own any part of the bay below the high-
water mark. So it is written. Yet, the State may lease portions of the bay
for private use. It has a long tradition of making such leases available for
oyster aquaculture, closing territory to wild-harvest shellfishermen.

For this reason, long veins of bad blood run between the bay's hunters
and farmers. In the early twentieth century, the oyster barons of Connecticut and New York and, yes, even of Rhode Island, controlled tens of
thousands of acres of bay waters, into which they transplanted tons and
tons of oyster seed. The oysters grew out marvelously in the nutrient-rich

waters of Narragansett Bay. The barons paid local men to dredge up and bushel the oysters. My grandfather was one of these men; at the age of fourteen, in the middle of the Great Depression, he would shovel up to fifteen hundred bushels of oysters a day.

As the oyster industry waned, the barons had the gall to rent time on their leases to men who wanted to dig there for naturally occurring quahogs. The barons rented the bay bottom. Rent, one of the great economic crimes: earning money from owning, rather than producing. The bullrakers and tongers—quahoggers who work with clam tongs, rather than rakes—put an end to that reprehensible practice sixty years ago, through protests, poaching, and outright sabotage. In the last decade and a half, however, Rhode Island has very cautiously permitted the return of oyster leases—and a great part of that caution comes in the form of an application-review process that allows any potential stakeholder in the bay to claim that a potential lessee would interfere with some other purpose special to that water. Aquaculture comes in last out of all the bay priorities. My father and I seek useless waters for this reason. Where better to start than Despair—though we would probably not market our oysters under that name.

My father knows where quahogging is no good around the bay, and we head to a few of these spots in order to test them with a pair of sixteen-foot shellfishing tongs, and to take a latitude and longitude reading on a global positioning system—my wife's GPS, from her car. We're a bit behind the times, electronically speaking, because my father got out of the game before GPS became a common tool of the shellfishing trade. For him, fixing a location means taking a range. He looks to the shore and lines up two landmarks—a church and a water tower, say. He then turns his gaze in a substantial arc, maybe 90 degrees, to find another pair of landmarks. Together the two sightings make up a range, and this is how quahoggers of my father's day recorded the locations of good fishing grounds. Today, we huddle over a tiny screen with a computer-graphic readout. It shows Hope Island as a mustard-colored blob on a field of blue, and it identifies our position with the icon of a car, parked just off the island. The State demands that our application for an oyster lease provide the proposed location of our farm in numbers, not in vectors set by white churches and red towers.

It's all new to my father—to search waters open to shellfishing, but dead to it; to rely on a computer and a satellite, rather than real structures that he can see; to work as a farmer of oysters, rather than a hunter of quahogs. Even to work with his son is new. To get out to Despair Island, we followed a course from Greenwich Cove to Greenwich Bay to Narragansett Bay, which my father has traveled thousands of times before, but with a purpose, an outlook, and limits unfamiliar to him. His battle now is an internal one that consists of accepting that his body is shot—a condition for which quahogging is largely responsible. As an old man, he must now turn his mind, shift his perspective, to the cultivation, tending, and husbanding of shellfish, and he must learn to work his body differently.

There is the minuscule of the American majuscule. America must struggle through a restructuring of its thought process. Americans must come to accept the bodily ills that result from a life of hard work, and they must care for those who suffer them. Similarly, they must learn a new way of working—if not each American personally, then, at least, many of them as a matter of culture. Not everyone needs to become a farmer or fisherman, but all Americans need to become more familiar with them, and more knowledgeable about the practices that enable them to live and work as they do.

To follow the path from Greenwich Cove to Greenwich Bay to Narragansett Bay, and to relearn its intricacies in a new way, is to experience what all paths to sustainability must encompass. It's a wrenching experience for me and my father.

CHAPTER TWO

The Feast of '85

Society is a joint-stock company, in which the members agree, for the better securing of his bread to each shareholder, to surrender the liberty and culture of the eater.

—EMERSON, "SELF-RELIANCE"

IN THE SUMMER OF 1985, RHODE ISLAND'S QUAHOGGERS ENTERED A feeding frenzy. The State opened the Upper Upper Bay for the second year in a row. Called the "North Conditional Area" by Rhode Island's DEM, and "Barrington Beach" by people from the town of Barrington, the Upper Upper Bay consists of a roughly six-square-mile trapezoidal patch of water immediately south of the Providence River. It is the uppermost part of the northern half of Narragansett Bay.

For several years prior to 1985, the State closed and opened this territory on an irregular basis because of varying pollution concerns. Though sporadic, this schedule provided sanctuary to the quahogs bedded there, and they spawned in safety and comfort. When the Upper Upper Bay came open in 1984, the guys rushed in; they concentrated there in numbers never before seen in Rhode Island. The eighties had already witnessed a huge increase in quahog landings, an intensification of a trend that had started several years earlier. Since 1974—the year that many historians now mark as the end of the economic golden age that followed World War II—landings rose steadily, in accord with unemployment—in fact, in near-perfect accord with unemployment. In the eighties, anyone could have predicted a boom time for quahogging. Reagan was busy destroying the American economy at the time, especially its manufacturing sector. Guys left the factories and headed for the water. The price was good, too. In 1984, a good quahogger could make a thousand dollars in a couple of hours in the Upper Upper Bay. By 1985, word had spread.

I had gone out on the water with my father in '84. I'd never seen anything like it. From what I had known, bullrakers often worked together, but "together" meant dozens of yards apart, a respectful distance, not intrusive. For my father, working with his buddies on the water—Zorro or Jake Murray or Bay Fox or Billy Clements or whomever—meant working close enough to holler jokes and gossip, rumors of good spots, word of prices. This practice of clustering goes a long way toward explaining the typical volume of a bullraker's voice—the yell.

Then, the State opened the Upper Upper Bay. Holy shit! Hundreds and hundreds of guys crowded together on the water. Suddenly, their little one-man skiffs looked big and imposing, like the puffed-up chests of roosters. They bumped into each other with the intent of testing guts and temper. Arguments boiled up as rakes and anchor lines crossed and tangled. Though they could have heard each other in conversational tones, still the men hollered.

For me, it was a revelation: At last, I could see what certain guys looked like. I had my first up-close look at Zorro, who worked out of Apponaug Cove. I saw how guys worked differently from my father—different equipment, different arrangements of equipment, different rhythms. The ball-busting intensified, too; provided with a large and captive audience, the wits of the bay put on a performance. My father's a big man, barrel-shaped, like an old-time strong man. The guys used to call him Haystack after Haystacks Calhoun, a professional wrestler of the fifties and sixties, who earned his name not by being shaped like a haystack (though he was), but by tossing bales of hay as a demonstration of his physical strength on *The Art Linkletter Show*. And so, out on the bay, a guy such as Jake Murray, a good friend of my family's as well as my father's, could bide his time, waiting for my father to take off his shirt. "The canvas is comin' off the haystack!" Jake would shout. Clever. A slightly cruel bit of inside jocularity—one of the cornerstones of shellfishermen's humor.

Fun tends to motivate the quahogger as much as earnings. The Upper Upper Bay provided both. The quahogs poured in as the men exchanged their brand of pleasantries. The hauls were immense. "Right up to the bar" is how a bullraker sometimes expresses a perfect haul of quahogs—meaning he has filled the basket of his rake to its brim. They used mainly burlap onion bags to secure their catch back then, much as they use plastic ones now. "Sinking the boat" means piling bags high enough that the boat lowers visibly in the water. Though it was rare for water to actually lap at the gunwales, guys have gotten themselves into trouble, and even sunk their boats, by bringing in too much product in rough water. Thousands of guys came to the docks, nearly sinking their boats. The men rolled wheelbarrows teetering with quahogs into Finn's. On day two of the opening, the price would drop by half, but that still meant they could earn several hundred dollars a day in the mid-eighties. The astoundingly rich stocks of the Upper Upper Bay, combined with the droves of quahoggers, led to the state's highest quahog landings since the 1950s, which were so high in large part because dredging was still legal back then. In my father's day, it was all bullrake, all done by hand.

It's the wild-harvest handwork that makes Rhode Island's shellfishing industry sustainable, and it's the bay's status as a free and common fishery that has enabled shellfishermen to lobby successfully to maintain sustainable practices in the bay. It is the shellfishermen themselves who have relegated themselves to hard labor by way of the laws of the State. In the fifties, the diggers defeated the dredgers in the struggle to determine how the state should harvest quahogs, one of the major battles of a larger conflict known in the papers as The Quahog Wars, an occasionally violent struggle among diggers, dealers, and dredgers. The process of making a commons work properly is never easy, and, in Narragansett Bay, it often leads to swings in the quahog harvest as the industry responds to changes in equipment or environment or market.

In the summer of 1985, the DEM issued several hundred shellfishing licenses in a day, over a thousand in a week—not the best approach to controlling the fishermen's efforts. Still, the State did apply a strict digging regime: The men could work in the Upper Upper Bay only from six to eight in the morning. The early end to the day prevented guys from double-dipping—loading their boat once, going in, selling out, then heading back out to sink their boats again. The early start kept the late-sleepers, those not desperate or dedicated enough to snap awake in the dark, out of the game.

So the State provided me with the pleasure of crawling out of bed at five in the morning to go to work with my father. Even at the age of ten, I liked nothing better than a good, old-fashioned noon wake-up call. There's nothing unusual and perhaps nothing wrong in this preference. Marcus Aurelius himself admitted that he found his warm bed far pleasanter than his duties as emperor. He rose to his responsibilities anyway. But what did such an example mean to the ten-year-old me? I had the charges of neither an emperor, nor a slave. A stoic argument for getting up early couldn't make me look favorably on having to unglue my eyes at four-thirty in the morning. The quahogs were out there, but I didn't have to greet them with temperance.

I viewed my familial responsibilities askance. My father hauled his catches in so fast that it helped him immensely to have me there to cull the quahogs from the crap that came up with them from the bottom, and to separate the quahogs into size categories, from smallest to largest: littlenecks, cherrystones, and chowders. This is also the progression of their value, from most to least valuable. A littleneck is your typical clam on the half shell, a chowder is for chowder, and a cherrystone falls to either side, as taste dictates. In those days there was only one means of getting quahogs: to wild-harvest them, either by dredge or by rake. Before dawn, my father and I got up, loaded the truck, and headed to the shore, all while trying to temper my bad attitude, he with jokes, I with guilt.

The trip from the house to the shanty mirrored the sunrise: We emerged from shadow into light. I grew up in the woods, on the same land where my father had grown up. Our house lay in the midst of a woodland that had sprung up on an old farm. We had a half-mile-long dirt driveway at that time, narrow and canopied with leaves. The town road we lived on—where my parents still live—runs for a mile, comfortably, if not completely, enclosed by trees overhead. The larger road of which it is a tributary, Frenchtown Road (named for Huguenots who mistook East Greenwich for asylum), opens up a fair strip of sky, and it points east, toward the bay and the light. The trip down Frenchtown remained cool enough that I would keep the window rolled up, possibly even drawing my bare legs up under my sweatshirt. Frenchtown hits South County Trail, Route 2, after a few miles. Route 2 unfurls wide and barren, a great plane of asphalt, hideous and lesioned with strip malls, open to the sun. At this corner, it is suddenly hot and homely.

A portrait of East Greenwich amounts to a beautiful picture with its center burned out. On its west side, very close to the towns of Exeter and West Greenwich, a few rural corners persist: a few old farms, a few old houses, big lots of woods and brush, crisscrossed with New England bones—stone walls, ungainly and pale-green with lichen, laid down by farmers hundreds of years ago. On its eastern extreme, East Greenwich has its picturesque shoreline. Between the two borders lies the most repellent suburban wasteland an aesthetic masochist could desire. A bleak devastation wrought by the wildfire of White Flight; the blasted heath of suburban neighborhoods, called "plats" in Rhode Island, which brambled up from the ashes. We drove through the woefully (but not interestingly) disfigured landscape that forms the main body of the town, but, showing mercy to ourselves, we kept to the largest roads, which offer little view of the scabrous plats that outlie them. Better blankness than hideousness.

We turned from Frenchtown onto the Old Post Road, a paved Narragansett trail, and from Post Road we turned toward the shore, avoiding Main Street, a strip maintained as quaint by the town's wise leadership, for whom the word means "not as immediately offensive as the development of Rhode Island's poorer towns." East Greenwich permits very few fast-food franchises within its borders.

By this time, I'd usually rolled the window down and hung out my arm. We stopped at Cumberland Farms, a popular convenience store in Rhode Island. My father and I would make the mistake of allowing me to pick out some delicacies from the sweets rack for a breakfast and lunchtime treat, to be washed down with a soda. Only a child's stomach wouldn't cringe at the prospect of digesting that pseudo-chocolate, pseudo-cream-filled mung. This breakfast always instigated a blood-sugar cascade an hour or so into the workday, but it was a gustatory delight for an irritable ten-year-old.

At the shanty, we gathered our shit together. The shanty always provided a respite between stages in the journey to the bay. I could pause and inhale the air of the cove, which is always bracing. It is redolent with the scent of the tide and often with the scent of work: gasoline and sweat. There is the salt to smell, of course, and, at low tide, seaweed and cove mud. It's the lobstermen who concentrate the miasma to a superb intensity, as they use rotten fish to bait their lobster traps. From time to time,

I'd find a barrel of fish heads, fish tails, and fish guts fermenting on the dock. I always found these congeries of mutilated fishes irresistible. There's nothing like looking into that hellish mass of hacked-up, putrescent flesh and inhaling its stench. A real gut-wrenching gross-out. Lobstermen say that after baiting their traps, their hands reek so badly that soap won't do; they have to resort to the old Indian trick of washing up with brake fluid.

But there was little time to fool around with such pleasant diversions. There was equipment to move—gas tanks, burlap bags, rakes, coolers, five-gallon plastic buckets, maybe fishing poles. It was at that moment I first started getting dirty. Quahogging is considered a clean fishery because it doesn't deal with fin fish and their fish slime. A smashed quahog might impart a slight scent, and there is mud and man-sweat enough to demand a shower at the end of the day, but it's all easily cleaned off without resort to petrochemicals. Still, the dirtying starts straightaway—or it did back then. Most bullrakes are stainless-steel now, which helps them keep their shine and smoothness. My father's rakes were plain steel and so bore the color and crust of corrosion. By the time I had put the rakes in the boat, I had orange palms and fingers and streaks of rust on my legs. Usually, I'd rinse my hands in the green cove water, leaving them sticky with salt. Though I had learned to swim early, I'd learned in freshwater ponds. At the age of ten, I remained averse to salt water, and, even today, I have to force the right perspective on myself—one that appreciates a good bout of stickiness—to enjoy bathing in the water of the bay.

Everything into the boat, we started the long trip north. On the way, the sunlight that reflected from the water slowly intensified, until it became a harsh, burning white. Eventually, the great mass of men would shimmer into view.

Bullraking looks strange. From afar, an observer of a bullraker sees a man standing in a skiff, holding a metal T-bar that descends into the water—the handle or splice, as the bullrakers call it. The bullraker pulls at the handle in an odd, jerking way, up and down, back and forth. After a time, he reaches for the down pole and hauls it out of the water. He hauls for a surprisingly long time. A long length of pole emerges—aluminum tubing. The bullraker raises it way overhead, then lets it fall back, the pole curving as it falls. The pole actually consists of several linked poles, called stales by the bullrakers—an ancient word for pole, related to *stylus*. The bullraker fastens the stales together with bolts and collars. He keeps an extensive assortment of lengths of stale in his skiff in order to adapt to changes in the depth of the water and the quality of the bottom.

At the end of the stale is a semi-cylindrical basket, lined with teeth on one side, the bullrake proper. It comes up dark and dripping with mud, laden with shells, seaweed, and various live animals. The quahogger gives the catch a few shakes in the water to rinse it clean. Then, the stuff goes onto the culling board, a shallow box, with one end balanced on the gunwale and the other set on a pair of wooden legs to keep it level. Then, the whole operation goes back into the water. When thousands of bullrakers work together on a small field of water, they resemble a particularly uncoordinated phalanx of spearmen, their implements rising, falling, weaving arrythmically, crossing from boat to boat, a horde of barbarians sacking the bay floor.

But even in this close formation each fisherman enjoys a real barrier from the other: their little boats. The quahog skiff is simple, but perfectly shaped to accommodate the peculiar job of quahogging. My father's boat is twenty feet, six inches long. In the eighties, most boats ran about that length; today, they average a couple of feet longer. The skiff is formed mainly from two-by-fours and marine plywood, all slathered over with fiberglass. In 1985, my father had a big outboard motor, a Johnson, 115 horsepower—big for the time. Nowadays, guys mount motors of up to 225 horsepower. At the stern, he had a tiny cabin, two windowed walls, a front door, and a rear wall that amounted to little more than wooden webbing left over from the hole he'd punched out for the motor. The cabin had a sunroof, a common feature. Shellfishermen with such accommodations very much enjoy piloting their craft while standing upright in the cabin, head and shoulders through the sunroof, like a soldier in the turret of a tank, only more ridiculous.

Skiffs differ in style, size, color, and the arrangement of their constituent elements. These differences are the principal means by which quahoggers identify each other out on the water—and often the sole means by which they know each other at all. Aside from their use in marking identity—and perhaps expressing personality—the skiffs are all essentially the same, as they must serve the same narrow purposes: fast transport, and a stable and serviceable platform for quahogging.

The skiff makes deepwater quahogging, by bullrake and by tong, possible, but not easy. It is brutal work. The shellfisherman acts as a flesh-and-blood hinge connecting the boat and the rake. He binds them together, even as the boat rocks and bobs in the water and the rake scrapes the bottom. It's like operating a jackhammer while standing on a trampoline—only the jackhammer has no motor, and it's thirty feet long.

The bullraker endures stress from head to toe—literally to the toe, in my father's case. Bullrakes function as a kind of manual dredge: While the bullraker digs the rake into the bottom to dislodge the quahogs from their bed, he wants his skiff to drift backwards, to bring the rake over new ground. Controlling the speed of this drift is key to the work of bullraking, and it's difficult to do. Much of the mental labor of bullraking comes from determining how to arrive at the proper drift, given the forces of the tide, the wind, and the quahogger's own digging. When the wind blows against the tide, the bullraker finds himself in unfortunate circumstances: The tide and the wind may cancel each other out, leaving him stuck in place, if not becalmed. He ends up digging a hole. Ask a guy how he made out on such a day, and he might complain, "Ah, the wind was against the tide ... I was goin' to China." Anchors play a large role in controlling drift, and my father's technique is to control the running of his anchor line with his foot. He throws his anchor out in front of him and his boat drifts back from it. The line runs through a cleat on the gunwale, but he traps it under his foot. As he works, he raises his foot from time to time, releasing more line from the coil, in a rhythm suited to the running of the tide and the gusting of the wind. It's like he's a pianist working the pedals of a piano that someone else is playing.

Bullraking is an all-body effort, but, in the main, it is an upper-body job. The rake can weigh as much as twenty pounds. In the section of the Upper Upper Bay, where most of the men were working that summer, near Barrington Beach, the water reaches a depth of fifteen to twenty feet, which requires thirty to forty feet of stale. Crazy bullrakers sometimes hit quite deep waters in the bay, swinging eighty feet of stale. I have heard of true madmen working a hundred feet of pipe. The weight of the operation isn't the only problem; the stale also transmits all the strange stresses of the twisting waters of the bay into the body of the bullraker.

For a long time, especially in Rhode Island, quahoggers worked with tongs, cleaving to this tool for far longer than men in other places did. Shellfishing tongs are double levers, like scissors, with wooden handles and a metal head, which consists of a basket cut in half, with each half fitted to one handle. The tonger works the two halves of the basket together through the mud, trapping quahogs in the unified basket. The motion of working tongs is similar to that used in the operation of an old-fashioned chest exerciser, consisting of two handles connected by rows of springs, except that tongs also require some downward pressure. The longest tongs run about twenty feet, good for fifteen feet of water or so. Rhode Island has an immense amount of shallows, and so tongs remained productive for years after the introduction of the bullrake.

But, once introduced, the bullrake never left. In the early days, stales were made of wood. Born in 1947, my father is old enough to have started his career with wooden stales. Though the wooden splice tends to tear up guys' hands even worse than aluminum does, wooden stales were, in a way, kinder to the bullraker. He had to treat wooden stales gently, work them gingerly, so they wouldn't bust on him, consigning his catch and his rake to the bottom. Today, aluminum allows the bullraker to use his full strength, which, in the end, may lead him to tear his body apart.

It is super-masculine work. A bullraker's body develops a horseshoe of hard muscle from the back of the neck, running down the trapezius muscles, through the arms, and into the hands. The hands of a bullraker are sculpted by work, his fingers and palms swollen with muscle and calloused to monstrous proportions. Aluminum has a roughness to it, and the connecting point between all that stale and all that boat is where the bar and the pads of the hands meet, two small cylindrical areas of stale and skin. The effects of that friction on the human hand are remarkable. Some quahoggers—a very few, really—mix up their labor by going out on fishing trawlers. If they spend enough time fin-fishing, working nets or lines, they find that their hands blister when they come back to quahogging. A job as hard as trawler fishing softens their hands. It's like lotion to them.

This phenomenon speaks to the particular physical capacity quahogging rewards—the kind of men it attracts. Bullrakers tend not to be the biggest guys. My father is an exception, as was my grandfather. Just as my father's colleagues likened him to a pro wrestler, so my grandfather's working buddies said he resembled Tarzan, with Johnny Weissmuller's portrayal in mind. My grandfather stood about six feet tall, was blue-eyed, and had dark blond hair. My father, in his prime (which was about that summer of '85), stood maybe five-nine and had black curly hair and a black curly beard. He had skin dark enough that my sister once asked my mother if her daddy was black. He wore eyeglasses secured to his head with an elastic band, and he smoked a corncob pipe. Big guys like my father and grandfather pop up from time to time on the water. You might find a guy they call Hercules or one they call Terminator, and these men do look the part, but it's not strength that most benefits a quahogger. Nor is it simply toughness. It's ruggedness, a quality that combines the two, but is strictly neither.

My grandfather's father died when my grandfather was just three. When he was five or six, his mother's mother rented a room in her house to a man named Frank Kaeton. Kaeton used to take my grandfather to work with him sometimes, woodcutting or scalloping. He became, per-haps, my grandfather's earliest male role model. My grandfather spoke admiringly of him. He remembered Kaeton carrying him on his shoulders down to the shore to gather scallops. When they'd gathered two bushels, they'd head back, only instead of bearing my grandfather, Kaeton carried the two brimming bushel baskets of scallops on his shoulders. What's more, Kaeton had a bum knee, causing him to limp. My grandfather never learned what had happened to Kaeton's knee; he just remembered that it was swollen up like a softball. "He was the ruggedest man I ever knew," my grandfather said.

It is ruggedness that most benefits the quahogger physically. To be rugged is to enjoy a combination of toughness and strength in just the right measure. A rugged man can tough it out through intense pain, and can perform feats of abnormal—though not necessarily incredible—strength over extended periods of time.

My grandfather was rugged, as was my father. While working out on the water, sometime in the forties, my grandfather spotted a young man digging on his ranges. My grandfather drove his boat right up to the interloper, circled him a couple of times, then butted up against his boat. He reached one hand over to the young fellow, grabbed him by the collar, and hauled him off of his feet.

"What are you doin' workin' on my ranges?!" he hollered. Then he laughed, set the guy down, and said, "I'm just jokin', kid . . . Work here all you want!" Later in his life, when my grandfather was working as a welder, a short Italian guy mouthed off to him one too many times, so my grandfather picked the little man up and hung him by his belt from a coat hook, where he would have to stay, "until he learned how to behave." My grandfather was big and strong and inarguably tough. He'd broken his back in a train accident when he was eighteen. He and two of his friends were in a truck that got hit by a train. All of them survived; none of them ever told who had been driving. My family knows only that my grandfather's friends folded him up—that's the term everyone uses when telling the story, *folded*—put him in a basket (or maybe a fishing pram), and carried him to the hospital. His injuries did not prevent him from becoming not only a manual laborer, but a sort of local Stakhanovite. That's ruggedness.

My father's buddies say similar things about him.

Zorro, one of his quahogging friends, is a short guy, round-featured, an Italian who talks in a nasal Providence accent. His real name's Matthew. One day, about forty years ago, he wore a big, floppy black hat to keep the sun off of his head. One day was all it took. Somebody decided his hat looked like Zorro's, and he became Zorro forever.

Zorro and my father and lots of the other guys used to move their boats out of the Greenwich Bay coves and down to more-open harbors in the winter, to prevent their being trapped in the ice. Sometimes they didn't know their new dockage well enough to avoid calamity. Somebody would sink a boat just about every winter. This particular winter, it happened to my father and Cap'n Ron.

"Over Quonset, there's a gutway in there," Zorro says. "What the hell they call it? Anyway, it's in Quonset. Your father, he was one of the guys that sunk, him and Cap'n Ron. Wind came up northeast, and we ain't used to stayin' there. We stood there in the winter, and the wind had come in a certain way, big rolls." The rolls sank their boats.

The men had to raise their skiffs from the bottom, flip them, salvage what equipment they could, and unhook their motors to bring them down to a shop and have them flushed. My father had waded into the water to get his motor.

"Your father carried his Mercury motor walkin' through the water," Zorro says, and then, in disbelief, starts to shout. "He carried it outta the shallow water!"

"It wasn't that heavy," my father says. "I just unhooked it and brought it on shore and they helped me put it in the truck."

It wasn't that heavy. When I was about twenty-one, my appendix ruptured. After the operation, the surgeon informed me that I had two or three very slight tears in my abdominal wall. He diagnosed them as hernias, but said there was no point in operating unless they tore more deeply. My suspicion is that the tears formed when I tried to pick up things that my father had described as "not all that heavy," and when he had encouraged me to do so with the words "What's the matter—wimp?" I believe that my father has a voice inside of him that has always teased him in the same way, but, because of his capability, he's usually been able to accede to his inner cajoling—to his own detriment, one more serious than mine.

One time, about twelve years ago, I went up to my grandfather's house for a visit. He asked how my father was holding up after getting his knee replaced. I told him that he wasn't holding up that well. My father reacts poorly to anesthesia, and he has thickly clotting blood that complicates his surgeries. My grandfather shook his head and sucked his teeth in disapproval. He'd never wanted his son to work on the water, and had actively discouraged him from quahogging. He blamed my father's ill health on his stubbornness in the matter of bullraking and in all physical labor.

"It's no wonder!" he barked. "He goes around lifting up every damn thing in the world! I remember one time we were down at the gravel bank gettin' stones . . . I couldn't believe the stones he was liftin' up and puttin' in the truck! Jesus Christ!" My grandfather spoke English in a way that emphasized the language's Germanic roots: *Djeezus Greidz!* is how his dialect takes the Lord's name in vain. Plus, he was half deaf and shouted to hear himself. He punctuated nearly everything he said with a sardonic laugh. He reverberated with stentorian disapproval and muttering, black-humored resignation. "I don't know," he said, shaking his head again. "Heh heh."

Other guys have also blamed my father's troubles on his own abuse of his too-powerful body. Even Cap'n Ron.

"I remember when your father hurt his eyes," he told me. "I'll never forget that. He got underneath the boat in Jake's yard—he was a strong man, your father was—he got underneath that thing and lifted it on his back. He popped his damn eye, but he lifted the whole damn boat right up, cuz we wanted to move this boat up on its side, and that's what he did, y'know. 'Course, he was awful strong, but he whacked his eyes out."

That's Cap'n Ron's deduction: He figures my father tore and detached his retinas in that one memorable effort. It's not true, but it does get at the bullraker's reflexive suspicion of excessive strength. In their view, too much raw power can be a disadvantage, especially in the long term. Strength is still admired, of course, but cautiously. Toughness and endurance are respected with much less mitigation, and, just as my grandfather did, my father earned admiration on these counts, too.

"When we used to work outta Wickford in the winter," said Zorro, "me and Shotty'd be sittin' in the truck. Your father'd come down with his green Chevy pickup . . . He'd get outta the door and close it, and then he'd say, 'Watch this.' He'd go in this pail in the back for his gloves and put 'em on—it's fifteen degrees or ten—and he'd stick his hand in these gloves, all fulla ice! Look at that! Here I am warmin' up by the heater! Tough as nails."

In winter, my father used to dry out his gloves with an old hair-dryer. Each night, he'd set them by the woodstove in the kitchen and stuff the dryer's hose into one, then the other. The process stank up the place with the stench of sweaty rubber. On the day Zorro remembers, my father had completely forgotten about his gloves. He'd left them in a bucket in the back of his truck overnight. They had frozen stiff; ice glazed them over, inside and out. But he had to wear them. His skin would stick to the aluminum stale otherwise.

"Oh, I put 'em on the heater, and they warmed up eventually," my father says.

This is half bullshit. Back in those days, the men used small heaters cobbled together out of Coleman gas tanks meant for camp lanterns and steel grills jury-rigged into radiators. They called them "angel makers" because they expected them to blow up and kill somebody someday. The heater would have melted off a good portion of the ice on the outside of my father's gloves, but he would have had to melt the interior ice with the heat from his working hands.

Thus, both my father and grandfather could claim ruggedness—and what good did it do them? They earned a living wage binnually, and then their ruggedness ran out. By their mid-fifties, both men were disabled; by their mid-sixties, both could hardly walk. Their work had crippled them, and it's likely that their own ruggedness tricked them into doing more than they should have done. They believed they had higher physical limits than other men, and they repeatedly tested their own limits, rather than accept them. Quahogging is ultimately a stone no man can lift, but they kept trying, with the results being physical ruination.

This should be celebrated. It's a happy thing for a son to hear stories of his father's physical prowess, but, even more, a community—a society—ought to take pride in the excesses of its working people. My father and my grandfather and many other men gave up their bodies and sometimes their lives out of passion and, in so doing, they fed their neighbors and countrymen in a just and sustainable way. Destruction of wealth, passion, food, and the good keeping of a bay—these should elicit celebration from the society that has benefited from them, and so, in Rhode Island, they have. The shellfishermen have their Scalloptown Park; they even have a statue in Warwick, a bullraker in bronze, by the public library. Rhode Islanders enjoy commemorating the living embodiment of tradition found in their small fleet of quahoggers, especially if this commemoration takes the form of inanimate objects, rather than festivities, because they can then celebrate bullrakers while avoiding any interaction with them.

The problem for Rhode Islanders is that they perceive the bullrakers mainly as storied men, as romantic figures—as if bullraking were some kind of achievement in the humanities. Because there are so few quahoggers, they are seen more as a wellspring of amusing tales, like the ones about my father and grandfather, than as an economic force or as a model of sustainability. When the State approves something more than mere statues to celebrate quahogging—when they actually express support for it—their justifications sound patronizing, like a family trying to appease a drunken uncle. In turn, the quahoggers often find themselves playing a role, perorating about tradition and nature and whatnot. This may help to explain why the summer of '85 proved so traumatic for Rhode Island, and why both the State and the shellfishermen made so many mistakes afterwards. Both were frightened by the number of hungry men who had turned out for the feast.

Quahoggers make fine distinctions about themselves. A good quahogger can be a "bull"—a strong but unsophisticated digger, a man who can pull rakes quickly and raise huge hauls of quahogs. When it comes to working a bonanza such as the one provided by the Upper Upper Bay in the mid-eighties, it helps to be a bull—or to have a bull's strength. I remember that, as my father was dumping another big catch onto the culling board, a guy on a nearby boat—a guy my father knew vaguely as a man from the town of Warren on the East Bay—cried out, "Don't you ever miss?!" "I guess not!" my father said. My father had certain working preferences, as many bullrakers do. He found that he had a knack for working banks—the sides of holes in the bay floor. Not many guys like digging at such steep angles, but my father sought out these places. He used to pore over charts, looking for holes. In other words, he brought a certain skill to his work. Other guys do, too, in different ways, but my father could also work like a bull. Good for him in 1985—and good for many of the unskilled part-timers who had just bought their licenses the week before, or even that day. The new guys didn't know what the hell they were doing, but many of them could bull through to a day's pay. Their success panicked both the State and the full-timers, the guys who had always had, and would always have, their licenses.

DEM clamped down on licensing. They enforced a moratorium for a while, then a cap expressed as a ratio: Three licenses had to expire in order for the State to issue a new one. The Shellfishermen's Association supported these measures, and the regime worked. By 1990, landings had dropped from two thousand metric tons of meat weight to barely more than a thousand. Then, from 1992, when the State closed Greenwich Bay on account of pollution, landings plummeted. They have never recovered.

Not all of this was unwarranted. The resource—the quahogs—did need protection. Rhode Island could not have continued to record such huge landings within the confines of its certified waters without depleting the quahogs to perilously low numbers, and the State was not prepared to take the environmental initiatives that would have cleaned up the bay, thereby expanding the water open to shellfishing. The State could justify its panicked policies with the consequences of its own indolence. On the fishermen's side, the perceived problem was division of resources: The old hands thought that the new guys were digging up all of their profits. What supported three thousand guys for a few years could have supported several hundred guys for a decade, was their thinking. Time for a freak-out. Together, the State and the quahoggers succeeded in reducing the population of shellfishermen dramatically.

But Rhode Island needed to keep production up and steady, and it needed to infuse new blood into the industry. The licensing scare led to policies that not only reduced the population of quahoggers, but aged them as well. Young guys couldn't get into the game. Now, the average age of the shellfisherman is a little over fifty. There are a considerable number of guys in their forties and sixties, virtually none in their thirties, and a handful in their twenties. The bulk of the workforce is gray and winding down. The response to the gold rush of '85 left the industry underpopulated, and thus unprepared for the advent of pollution troubles and, more important, the advent of quahog aquaculture. When the big quahog farms of the South flooded the market in the 1990s, Rhode Island had neither the workforce nor enough certified waters to compete on quantity or consistency. At just the moment when guys my age reached their maturity, the missing demographic of thirty-somethings, the price was no good, licenses were unavailable, and waters were frequently closed. The young men of the '90s were discouraged from taking up the rake.

I can't pretend I was among the discouraged, however; I never liked the work. There were good times to be had on the boat. My father has a well-formed sense of country humor; all his friends say so. He's a gentle giant, good-tempered, but with an undertone of cruelty in his funning. He is a paragon of the witty workingman. One of the most frequent bycatches of quahogging is the spider crab, a viciously ugly creature, a mud-dweller, and a much-hated predator of quahogs. Spider crabs have the worst kind of olive-drab color when they come out of the bottom. They have an acarine shape, a tick-like teardrop body, with long, thin limbs. Their features come to a point in that worst aspect of all crustaceans: a hairy, thousand-part set of waving mandibles. Overall, the spider crab looks like a venereal parasite that has crawled up to the bay floor from the crotch of Hell.

Further, divers have attested that, when feeding on the quahog, the spider crab doesn't pry apart its valves with its claws, as any civilized hunter would do; instead, it crushes its prey against its underside and tears at it with several legs at once. Naturally, shellfishermen often kill or mortally wound the foul things when the opportunity arises. A guy might take the crab by its legs and, with a flick of his wrist, crack its shell against a cleat, before tossing it into the water, where, upon its settling to the bottom, other predators, including its fellows, will devour it. With a bit more time to spare, a man might leisurely rip off or partially rip off its claws, and then back into the depths it goes.

Libinia emarginata can also serve a humorous purpose. When I least expected it, my father would grab one up and surreptitiously aim its pincers at my back or ass or thigh. What a funny prank—a solid pinching from a benthic monstrosity. In turn, I would wait for my moment: When my father's digging exertions caused his jeans to drop down enough to expose his crack, I'd toss in an undesirable shellfish, a decker or birdseed clam. A good pinch deserves a good shellfish down the pants.

It can be fun to work on the water, and one can certainly make money. One time in '85, after we'd quit on the Upper Upper Bay, when my father had already made his day's pay, we drove into Greene's River to have me try bullraking for a while, before going into the cove to sell out. Greene's River splits the southern half of Potowomut Neck. It is one of the most beautiful rivers in the world, and has the potential to be even more beautiful. (Its banks bear a number of houses, the removal of which would contribute greatly to the river's charm.) Greene's River is closed to shellfishing now, because the houses there have no sewer tie-ins, the people in them feed the birds that come there, and Hunt's River, which drains into Greene's, takes in water that overflows from neighborhoods too irresponsible to install storm sewers.

In 1985, Greene's River offered one of the most placid and sheltered places to quahog in all of the bay. My father had me bullrake there for an hour or so. I made thirteen dollars and change. Thirteen dollars an hour as an eleven-year-old in 1985; not bad. But I just didn't like the work. About the only thing that could have drawn me into it would have been the challenge of its hardships, the opportunity to ruin my body the same way my father and grandfather had, to participate in the traditional family misery. I became far too angry an adolescent even to consider such challenges, much less to permit them to overcome my dislike for the business. Then, too, things looked dismal for the industry as a whole—the decline of which, by virtue of its difficulty, could also have proved another temptation for me, if only I'd had any love for the bullrake. As it was, I had no foundational pleasure to make the hardships of bullraking not just palatable, but desirable. Other men do have such a foundation, however, and this mixture of pleasure and noble, dignified pain is the source of their passion for their work.

Bullraking makes men mad—crazed for the water. That's what the job does. My meager forays into quahogging left me only half-mad, at least with regard to my understanding of work in general. Most bullrakers deal with both inferiority and superiority complexes. They often feel as though they could not have held any other job, as if they've failed in life by resorting to quahogging. Conversely, they know that they work harder than just about anybody they know, and that their profession has an immediately recognizable social purpose. They bring home meat—just the thing that brought God Almighty to favor Abel over Cain. The bullraker's lofty sense of his own importance is unassailable. Furthermore, in Rhode Island, they do the job the right way. No dredges, no farms. My father and my grandfather and their colleagues imprinted me with these attitudes, but, because I never took up bullraking myself, I developed neither the passion they felt, nor the work ethic they followed. No one's so-called hard work impresses me, but that doesn't mean that I know how to work hard myself. In fact, the very concept of hard work is problematic for me.

The phrase *hard work* has weakened over time; it used to mean "physically strenuous," exclusively. Today, it can have a different sense. White-collar workers, people of mental toil, can be said to work hard. Ask a working man if he works hard, and he'll hold out his claw, that horn-hard talon into which his hand has been shaped by years of abuse. Ask a white-collar man if he works hard, and he'll tell you how much he works, usually in hours per week. There is something imprecise about this usage; it ignores boundaries that have real importance. It is more accurate and more respectful of their respective sacrifices to say that men and women of letters—for that is really what they are—may work *a lot*, which is not the same thing as working *hard*. They spend a lot of time at the office;

they spend a great deal of time doing work and work-like things. They *forgo leisure.* Or, anyway, they transform their leisure into something like work, through meetings and lunches and such. They do not *work hard.* On this point, because of the understanding of hard work I grew up with, I find it difficult to take pride in working a lot, rather than working hard. There are no heroics in pushing papers, tapping keys, in having discussions. The end result of these things may become a source of pride, but the activity itself is an embarrassment to me.

My father and grandfather also trained me to regret the loss of large numbers of hours to work, another dissuasion from my professional activities. One of the great attractions of quahogging is the trade-off it provides: You work hard so you don't have to work a lot. There's an adage for this: Quahoggers ain't lazy, but they don't want to work. This is something they say about themselves. It's an idea virtually unknown to the community of people outside the quahogging fold. The sentiment resides in me, but I am no quahogger, which, again, leaves me ill-prepared for the wonderful opportunities afforded me by a life of mental labor. This doesn't mean that I myself am motivated to do the right thing. I am caught between the bullraker and the world he righteously derides. If my position were grander, it would be tragic: I have all of the bullraker's scorn and none of his discipline.

There's an advantage to this unfortunate character of mine, however: It makes it easy to listen to bullrakers with an unromantic ear. It's hard enough merely to understand them, because they have their own way of speaking, and because they have concerns that are alien to larger society, but to listen to them without romanticizing them is much more difficult. And it is crucial not to make the bullraker into something he is not— especially not into something idealized. A romanticized understanding of him would lead inevitably to the destruction of the system that makes his work possible. A free and common fishery cannot justify itself through romantic ballads alone. Getting to know the bullraker means listening to his true voice without being seduced by it—or using it to seduce oneself.

CHAPTER THREE

Their Hardship, in Their Own Words

. . . and here, for the first time, I grew proud of the enemy
who had killed my brothers . . . They were glorious.
—T. E. LAWRENCE, *SEVEN PILLARS OF WISDOM*

LINGUISTS USE A HANDFUL OF CONCEPTS TO TYPOLOGIZE LANGUAGE.
Phonology, for example, describes the sounds each language recognizes;
morphology, how a language forms words; syntax, how speakers of a language chain words together. These three are standard, inarguable elements;
all linguists accept them. But there are other elements that some (or even
most) linguists dispute. The concept of rhythm is one of the disputed.

For those who subscribe to the notion, rhythm refers to the way native
speakers of a language time their syllables with respect to each other.
Rhythm is the beat of a spoken language. The layman detects rhythm
easily: When he encounters someone who speaks his language perfectly
well in all respects other than rhythm, he immediately detects the musi-
cal oddity, the foreignness of his interlocutor's speech. Likewise, a person
who exhibits an exquisiteness of timing in his spoken rhythm might be
regarded as an excellent orator, a natural poet, a good talker, even if, in his
vocabulary or accent, he is barbaric.

The linguist has a harder time discerning rhythm because his dis-
cernment requires rigor and codification. The linguistic theory of rhythm
recognizes just two broad categories into which all languages fall (this
dichotomy already a sign that the theory has problems): stress-timed and
syllable-timed languages. A stress-timed language separates speech into
groups of syllables—essentially, what poetics calls "feet." In English, an
exemplar of stress-timed rhythm, the following sentence has three feet:

"The bay, at least so it seems to me, works in cycles." To punctuate it another way: //The bay/at least so it seems to me/works in cycles//. In stress-timed languages, each foot has roughly the same duration in speech. When a guy utters the sentence above, it will take him just as long to say "The bay" as it will for him to say "at least so it seems to me." This timing means that he has to crunch up the syllables of the second foot and extend the syllables of the first foot—or add a pause to them: "The bay . . . atleastsoitseemstome." You could find the rhythm of the whole sentence by snapping your fingers at each stressed word: ". . . bay . . . least . . . works." The count between each snap is roughly the same, although the number of syllables between them is not. That is a stress-timed language.

On the other hand, a syllable-timed language ignores feet; it finds its rhythm by establishing in each utterance a standard duration for a syllable and then maintaining that duration throughout an utterance. Again, the rhythm is quite difficult to analyze, but easy to hear. French is categorized as a typical syllable-timed language, as is Japanese. In these languages, the feet of the example sentence do not have the same length, because the syllables maintain their duration with respect to each other. They refuse to be stretched or crushed. English speakers may change their enunciation in the direction of syllable-timing, but usually to impart an emotional meaning. This is why, to English ears, native speakers of French often sound annoyed and native speakers of Japanese sound angry.

It is extremely difficult to acquire a foreign language's rhythm— perhaps uniquely difficult. Rhythm runs deep, literally; the process of native language acquisition doesn't merely impart acceptable sounds and proper grammar to a child; it also trains the intercostal respiratory muscles to work in a certain rhythm during speech. Picking up the cadence of a foreign language with a different rhythm requires retraining the little-thought-of muscles between the ribs. Likewise, it may be the case that a person with exceptional rhythm has trained his intercostals particularly well, perhaps even athletically.

If this is true, then many bullrakers should be considered athletes of English. The English pulse booms in their lungs. They know it, too. They know that their speech continues the traditions of the fisherman's lie, the sailor's story, even the pirate's tale, all of which owe their effect in large part to the vocal rhythm of the waterman who tells them. Bullrakers wouldn't put it in linguistic terms, necessarily, but they happily declare that they enjoy hearing themselves talk. Yet, they don't get off on any old subject; it's their work that inspires them to poetical heights. In other words, they talk best when talking about what they do. They flaunt their specialized vocabulary, their technical terms, their place-names, and the wavy rhythm they use to enunciate them. They take pride in narrating situations particular to quahogging—things having to do with the rake, the skiff, the keeping of the bay, and the quahog itself. And among all of the many subtopics that fall under the rubric of quahogging, nothing moves them more than the subject of their own suffering.

Ray Wyss is an old-timer who has hung up his bullrake. He's in his eighties now, retired to an old farm in rural Rhode Island, a quiet and neat place, which he tends with a bent back. He's a big man—big in body and features. For a time, he was maybe one of the best two or three quahoggers on the bay. He took up bullraking in the late 1940s as a teenager who knew nothing about fishing, or even boating. "When I started, I was workin' another job full-time, five days, so I was only bullrakin' weekends," he says. "I think I worked eighteen or twenty days when I started that fall, and the last day I think I made twenty-one bucks . . . and I was makin' forty-two dollars up to Lloyd's for five days, so that was half a week's pay.

"That followin' spring, I built a seventeen-foot skiff . . . The fella who started me in told me what I had to do and how to do it, and I took little notes. I bought the stuff over in Barbour's, over in Pontiac . . . They sold cars there, but in the back they used to sell oak. A lotta guys went there; he knew exactly what I wanted. I told him what I was doin' . . . He cut 'em, rough boards, planed 'em up, sliced 'em for the chine and the ribs and stuff like that, and I built that skiff and I gave my notice, I think, in about the middle of June, gave 'em two weeks' notice and struck in that summer. Never looked back . . . the first year I actually made more than a teacher in school."

A competitive, aggressive, and inquisitive man, Ray Wyss looked to the older guys to learn how to do things right. "The guy that was like my mentor," he says, "or that I really watched was Nick Carcieri . . . you know that name." Nick Carcieri was a teacher and a football coach at East Greenwich High, as well as a much-admired bullraker. He was a good dozen years older than Ray Wyss. My father played football for Nick, and my grandfather sometimes dug alongside of him. Nick's son, Don, served two terms as governor of Rhode Island, and during his tenure, Governor Carcieri hung two oil paintings of quahoggers at work on the walls of the governor's office. One of the paintings depicted two men in the mid-ground, digging next to each other. Don and his wife, whose father also worked as a bullraker, liked to imagine the two men in the painting as their two fathers, together on the water.

"I watched Nick," says Ray Wyss. "He was top man . . . when I struck in, he was top man. I said, 'Why is he the top man? What does he know?' He worked hard . . . I don't want to call it furiously, but he worked as hard as he could, and when I started doin' the same, I started doin' well, and after maybe . . . how many years? Probably when I was about twenty-eight or thirty, then I started givin' Nick a hard time. One time I said, 'Nick! I've gotcha!' I saw the veins on his neck sticking out."

Ray Wyss stretches up from working on his old truck in his old barn. He stretches up as far as he can, which is inches shorter than he stood thirty years ago. Still, in late winter, he's just gotten back from a vacation in New Hampshire, where he skied a little. "The guys who are successful," he says, "there are really four things that you gotta have: First, you gotta have the knowledge of what to do. There's places you work in the summer, you don't work in winter. Second, you need the skill to catch them. Your grandpa, he and Lester Arnold, they straightened me out a lotta times: 'You don't have enough stale on,' they said. 'That's why you're not catchin' 'em, y'know?' They'd tell me; a lotta guys wouldn't say boo."

Ray is both pale and red in the March sun. He has few wrinkles, even when he smiles. "Third, you gotta have your health; you gotta be healthy. As I always say, 'Strong back, weak mind—you'll make a good quahogger.' Then, the fourth thing: willpower . . . you gotta have the willpower to go."

It's an interesting formulation and a common one among shellfishermen—to suggest an equivalence between willpower and stupid-ity. Ray Wyss puts the mental component last in his list of the four things essential to succeed as a bullraker, in order to emphasize the importance of one's attitude, and in order to make it a punch line: bay knowledge, skill with a rake, health, and willpower—or weak-mindedness. The reason he makes his joke is to underscore the fact that a bullraker needs to will him-self past physical hardship—a task, so the joke goes, that stupidity would make easier. You can look at a guy who powers through pain and injury, a rugged guy, and observe that he has possession of either a strong will or an obdurate brain, insensitive to the suffering of its own body. These are just two ways of characterizing the same phenomenon, one more charitable than the other. The point is that a quahogger needs a mind suited to the overcoming of the pain that plagues him, and Ray Wyss does not underplay this pain.

"My hands!" he cries. "Brown! Gnurled! In here, believe it or not," he says, pointing to the webbing between forefinger and thumb (a vestige, perhaps, of a time in our evolution when we lived semi-aquatically). "You had a callous about a quarter-inch thick, and it took me a couple of years before they went away, after I quit." This particular callous grows in response to the friction on the hand that comes with hauling the rake out of the water. As the bullraker pulls up the vertical stale, hand over hand, his thumb webbing rolls against the aluminum, which hardens the skin and splits it. "Nick Carcieri, his used to crack. He used to shave 'em with a razor blade, try to shave 'em down thinner. He used to have an awful time, but maybe that's cuz he worked so hard."

Ray Wyss sold insurance during his time as a bullraker. Moonlighting in white-collar environs made him sensitive to the appearance of his hands. He came to wear gloves all of the time when he bullraked, not just in winter. He wore a long-sleeved shirt and a hat to keep from getting too rough and tanned for his clients to bear. He cares for his speech with similar ends in mind. Ray Wyss is a true bullraker, but he's also fit to print. He's ready for National Public Radio. He's polite, network-safe. He gets across the hardship he has suffered with rhythm, with exquisite detail, with a touch of jargon, but without transgressing any standards of decency. This approach has its advantages: Church ladies will listen to him all the way through to the point where he describes Nick Carcieri's shaving of the callous on his thumb web (right at the end of the superficial branch of the radial nerve), at which point the ladies will wince and make that backwards hissing sound that signifies empathy for pain—and that's all for the good. They need to understand, to sympathize with the hardships of the bullraker and, by extension, all those who fish and farm sustainably. But there's a big disadvantage to the generousness of Ray Wyss's speech: By refusing to be impolitic, he allows himself to be romanticized.

When a man communicates with consideration of the fact that his and his audience's mores differ, he allows his audience to assume that he lies within their fold. More specifically: When a fisherman accedes to the taboos of an American audience while speaking of fishing, he lets himself become a symbol of the American dream. The evangelical mind that dreams this dream will quickly romanticize the fisherman and interpret him as the very embodiment of self-reliance. Or as the modern incarnation of the long struggle between the American man and the American wilds. Or as representative of any number of similarly fundamentalist and delusional notions. The problem with the courtliness of Ray Wyss is that it allows his listeners to find themselves—or idealized versions of themselves—within him. His audience becomes like a pack of little Hemingways, projecting their hopes and wishes onto the body and work of the fisherman. They come to believe that he is like they are—or, really, as they wish they were. That is, they believe that they and the fishermen are all alike, because his success seems to come from his own hard work and nothing else, just as they believe theirs does. The whole thing devolves from messianic tendencies.

It is vital to do away with this misperception. It is vital to listen to the bullraker with open ears, to know him as he speaks to himself. Quahogging in Narragansett Bay is not merely interesting; it is also important. In order to keep quahogging sustainable, and in order to replicate the success of Rhode Island's quahogging industry in other sectors, one must recognize the bullraker, the sustainable farmer or fisherman, for who he is. The whole project of sustainability relies on working with special people, abnormal people; the project cannot succeed if their strangeness is in any way ignored. The bullraker must be confronted as a bullraker.

This requires paying attention to the fullness of quahogging talk, which itself requires more than the elimination of censorship; it requires an embracing of the things the old American puritanism would censor. To hear the shellfisherman, one must delight in his profanity.

The shellfishermen themselves certainly do. They make a toy of vulgarity, with happy results—at least for themselves. The word *fucking* has special importance for them; it holds a high position in some wonderful formulations. In English, *fucking* sometimes serves as a rhythmic placeholder. As an emphatic interjection, it replaces a pause or an extended syllable or an "umm." This usage is much more common on the bay. For a bullraker, *fucking* preserves rhythm in a way similar to the word *like* in the speech of suburbanites. A guy might say: "DEM came over and said, 'Oh, I think you're over the line,' and I said, 'Oh, you think?! Fuckin', take a GPS reading, or whatever!'"

To accept—and even adore—this kind of language means recognizing, even if only for an instant, that the quahogger may not be like you. You might even find him repugnant. He might feel the same way about you. In this respect, it becomes quite difficult to use the bullraking way of life to advance an interest. The disingenuous market fundamentalist, to take one example, who hopes to use the bullraker to provide the testimony of a self-made man, in order to argue, incredibly and paradoxically, for the elimination of the inheritance tax, may find that his witness believes all those who inherit wealth to be parasitic sons of bitches. Similarly, the earnest promoter of green jobs (an ingenuous market fundamentalist, in other words), who hopes to pick the quahogger for Team Green, may find that he thinks Whole Foods is for fags. Or the bullraker may agree with the fundamentalists, to their chagrin. He might express his agreement in his own, unacceptable way. Expression matters. The bullraker alienates his neighbors with his words—and critically so. His are the words of a man who cannot lose his job by mouthing off. A man with that kind of power, that kind of freedom, is terrifying. One aspect of the romantic view of the shellfisherman is that he is raw and mean and likely drunk anytime you encounter him. These things are sometimes the case, but what's more important is why this might be so. Quahoggers live in the sun, with no bosses to cast a shadow on them. It is working in the light that darkens their reputation.

"You know," says Ray Wyss, "there's a buncha guys out there, like Jimmy Rice and Lester Arnold and your grandfather . . . They owned their own home; quahogging was a job. But there's also a bunch out there that can't hold a job anywhere, and it's the only thing they can turn to, to make any money . . . and they gave the reputation to everybody else."

He's not alone in his judgment. Lots of people claim that bullrakers are unsuitable for any other work. Quahoggers are men with too much disdain for authority—their own as much as anyone else's—to take on ordinary work. They are not "people people," the argument goes. Or they're big drunks. Drug addicts. Dopes. They're the ones who pour salt on their salty language.

Cap'n Bill, for example—certainly a man who could've taken no other work—was known to have a foul mouth, even by the standards of other quahoggers. It's the men who take advantage of their position, of their bosslessness or who absolutely require it, who make every other bullraker look bad. That's the story some tell.

There's truth in it. To understand these men who can work if and only if they bullrake requires recognizing that they are not alone; not only bullrakers have this attitude. There are people who cannot abide authority. Not all of them can earn a living as a quahogger. Maybe they can't stand the water, or they get seasick; maybe they can't navigate. Maybe they didn't inherit a boat and don't know how to save up for one. At any rate, a good many of this type do hold jobs, and every single day, they make themselves and everyone they come into contact with absolutely miserable. A sizable number of bullrakers, then, constitute a lucky few of this irascible, petulant population who have made their way into a tolerable trade. Some bullrakers have found in bullraking a way to satisfy their antiauthoritarian natures. The same holds true for the drunks: Plenty of drunkards have jobs; quahogging might be a particularly favorable one for them, but not all of them get the chance to take up the rake. A few fortunate ones do.

There can be no doubt that intemperate men are overrepresented in quahogging, but most quahoggers move in and out of the industry, as my father and grandfather did. Or, like Ray Wyss, they moonlighted— or bullraking was moonlighting for them. Some of those bullrakers who change professions are men who can handle the transition; others are not. The crucial point here is that the bullrakers' communities, their neighbors, their society, can choose how to deal with them, and with men and women who are their colleagues in spirit. Rhode Island could speedily do away with its bullrakers by privatizing the bay and permitting dredging or any kind of mechanized harvest. It would be over in an instant, sending all the quahoggers off into another field, adding a significant number of irritable, antiauthoritarians into the normal workforce.

Rhode Island could also expand the number of quahoggers by making it easier to obtain a license and managing the industry to promote its growth, rather than effect its slow decline. Such initiatives would enable other men to take up the work. Similar to the problem of sending

bullrakers under the shadow of bosses, creating more bullrakers would
mean empowering just the sort of guys who give bullrakers their bad
reputation. Suddenly, Rhode Island would find itself blessed with an even
stronger force of shellfishermen more than happy to tell the state that
made their jobs possible in the first place to go fuck itself—which, done
right, is a glorious thing.

Now, on the other hand, all of the sprung-rhythm fuck-speech down
the shore shouldn't ring in another bout of romanticization, although it
easily could. The siren song of the quahogger lies at the heart of all efforts
to romanticize him. Enjoy his swearing too much, and you'll find yourself
coming right around to the dismissive, insulting, impractical misperception of him that setting his tongue loose should have disallowed. You'll
think that the bullraker speaks as he does because of his independence,
or because he contends with the sea. The rhythm of his voice comes from
the waves; the harshness of his language comes from the salt. To hear
him musically call someone a fucking asshole is akin to putting one's
ear to a shell. It seems vital that the bullraker works alone. He has neither employer, nor employees. He has no masters and no servants. In this
regard, he is unlike other manual laborers, and even unlike other fishermen, who are either captains or captained. That's why *fuck* is a mark of
social status. The king may use the royal "we," but can he refer to his sub-
jects as a pack of assholes? The bullraker is so free that he lies beyond the
pale of all verbal law, and he is free because he commands only himself.

It's so very hard to get past this romantic enchantment with the shellfisherman's speech and to really listen to what he has to say, because the
romantic view of him is largely true. When Jean-Jacques Rousseau romanticized the cultures that European colonization had revealed, he didn't
find nobility in the savage; he imbued him with it. Rousseau found the
realization of Enlightenment ideals in primitive man because primitive
man was neither primitive nor enlightened. Bullrakers actually do possess
the qualities their romanticizers attribute to them. They are self-reliant,
Emersonially so. They do have a special connection to the natural world.
But "self-reliance" and "nature" are complicated concepts. One should not
trust them. That's one thing. The other thing is that, by elevating these vir-
tues, the bullraker's panegyrists, of whom there are many in Rhode Island,
ignore his most important virtue, the one most crucial for society.

Rhode Islanders tend to speak of the bullraker as if he harvests quahogs for no reason at all. They speak of Tradition, Hard Work, Confrontation with Nature, a stand against the march of History and Technology. It's as if the bullrakers are out there re-creating, digging for fun, or doing some kind of performance art, as if it would make no difference to anyone if the catches they sold were tossed right back into the water. You might even say that Rhode Islanders blow right past romanticism and run smack into decadence. The aesthetics of A. C. Swinburne and Oscar Wilde have taken hold of the local appreciation of the bullraker. Rhode Islanders find the bullraker beautiful because they think he is useless. They want him to be a curiosity, and he indulges them: He is curious! Curious in manner, curious in speech.

Behaving curiously does not make him virtuous, however. He has virtue because he feeds his society while taking good care of the bay. That's the real reason he counts: He works at the most essential of occupations, and he does so righteously. This truth reveals one of the great dangers of making farming and fishing sustainable: Sustainability means giving millions of people a power similar to the one that bullrakers have. It's just like the problem Rhode Island would face if it grew the population of bullrakers, only on a much larger scale. The new farmers and fishermen will have voices nearly as free as that of the bullraker, and their neighbors will hear them. Some of them will turn out to speak like Ray Wyss; others will not. In the end, the way Americans speak to themselves—and, thus, the way Americans establish their consciousness of themselves as Americans—will change. This consequence is the proper thing to keep in mind when listening to the bullraker speak. Beneath everything he says is this great danger to American identity.

The threat to the modern American posed by a man who produces food without a boss comes across nowhere more powerfully than it does in the words of "Tim Trim" Moynihan. Over by Apponaug Cove, in the northwest corner of Greenwich Bay, lives a whole tribe of fishing families. The Bennetts, the Coles, the Chases, and the Rayhills are just a few of the families in this circle. Tim Trim is related to nearly all of them. Just about every old-timer in the cove is somehow his uncle.

He got his nickname from two sources: He painted a nice trim on his boat when he was young; and, when he bullrakes, he trims—meaning, he does better than—the guys working around him. Guys do say he's a good quahogger, which, among these men (who tend to think expressions of admiration demean oneself) means that he's a superb quahogger. Tim's no big man. He's shorter than average, lean, with big, knobby hands. In his mid-forties, he's shot with wrinkles in the fisherman's way, all from work. He moves carefully, efficiently. You can see what makes him a remarkable bullraker in his every gesture. There's not a lick of fat to carve off of his movement.

He's also the kind of guy who has arrived at his grace after long years of tempering himself. He seems to be restraining an inner storm of energy. He must be burning fuel at an extraordinary rate, after all. He does all manner of fishing, as well as myriad other jobs. "Lobsterin', sharkin', tunerin'," he says. Quahogging in the summer. Snowplowing in the winter. And, during theater season, he does "show business"—working on sets, handling curtains and theatrical machinery, mostly up in Providence—a union job that provides his health care. He also builds boats. Tim is not a man of small spirit. When he's juggling several kinds of work at once, he sleeps in snatched moments, two, three, four hours at a time. He has worked this way since he was a teenager, when he first started quahogging.

Tim also took up a bit of quahog pirating—digging quahogs from uncertified waters. By the time he was sixteen, he'd already outfoxed DEM a bunch of times; he'd even stranded an agent who'd been chasing him on a sandbar. That kind of thing can be sweet for a teenager, but before long, Tim had to let it go.

"When I quit piratin'," he says, "it wasn't cuz I wasn't havin' enough fun. I quit because of my dad . . . and my uncle. My uncle didn't like it, my uncle Tom. I didn't want him to think bad about me, after what he's done for me growin' up, bein' like a father to me. I felt bad cuz he looked down on it. And my father . . . God. Jesus Christ—if I ever had gotten caught, he would've been very upset. I was doin' drugs, y'know. I was snortin' coke. I didn't drink a lot, but I had some friends, guys doin' all kinds o' drugs and smokin' weed and doin' all that, and I said, 'Man, I better get outta this. I'm gonna end up in the ACI, in fuckin' Cranston.' And my fuckin' father, Jesus Christ. So I joined the service to get out of it."

Tim put himself through the Marine Corps to straighten out, but he came back to quahogging. He has always come back to quahogging, and he really knows how to talk about it. Tim is a poet of bullraking. A natural poet? Who knows? He might study and practice storytelling. He certainly has enough elders to learn from. In any case, he's the Robert Burns of Apponaug Cove. When it comes to telling his stories, Tim Trim has no restraints—other than self-imposed, formal ones. Perhaps because he's still quahogging, perhaps because he lives on Highliner Row, a street occupied by Bennetts and Coles and various other shellfishermen of note, a street that ends at a dock and even has a shellfish dealer right at its corner. Tim is immersed. When he tells a story about the suffering of bullraking, he accedes to nothing.

"You're gonna wanna write this down, cuz this is the truth," he says. "I used to get up, four-thirty in the mornin' . . . My cousin is piratin', right? My cousin went straight for a while; next thing you know, he started doin' cocaine or whatever the hell he's doin'. I don't care. He starts piratin' . . . A guy on my dock used to be there, four-thirty, every mornin'. He had a skiff, and he was a terrible quahogger. He just . . . I don't know, he doesn't quahog anymore; he hasn't quahogged since then.

"And one mornin' I get down there, I saw my cousin comin' in, fuckin' loaded down, and I just can't believe it. And it was botherin' this guy: 'Aw, yer cousin's keepin' the price down'—and this and that. 'You can get people sick with them quahogs . . .' And you know, 'I don't know what to tell ya . . . he's not gonna listen to me.' I go down the next mornin', he's got a patch o' white hair, right here, big around as that on the side of his head. Next mornin' I see him, he's gettin' ready to go out, same thing, right here—a patch of pure white hair. Within seven days, he was completely white. This guy's forty years old, brown hair, Frenchman, right? Next day, I see him again, he's got a patch right here, no hair on it, bald—that size—where that white patch was, the first one. Next mornin', I see him, he goes, 'Look! Now this side!' Another one!

"Within two days he was completely bald. The hair was fallin' out in his bed. He'd wake up, it's just gone. Within two or three weeks, he had a full head of hair again, all brown . . . Stress . . . stress did this to him. He quit quahoggin' soon after that . . ."

Here are all kinds of things that no one who works in sustainable food wants anyone to say, but Tim has no boss. He has no one to answer to—and certainly no movement to be a good face for. He is an excellent quahogger and knows that he feeds people. For him, the only concern is that another quahogger would respect the truth about what he is saying, even if it's ugly. The story's about failure, which is bad enough, but it's also about wrongdoing. Tim casually mentions both drugs and piracy, both of which are common tropes in bullraker tales. Pirating among quahoggers means working in areas the state has set out-of-bounds—"dirty digging" usually, harvesting from areas deemed polluted. The practice is scarce today, largely due to the severe fines and punishments imposed over the past twenty years, but it persisted for a long time, because shellfishermen simply didn't believe that the law had correctly determined what safe water really is. The pirates may have had a point, in that quahogs from such areas are often safe to eat, but the law won the argument by confiscating their boats. Today, pirating means clean pirating: harvesting from waters the state has declared clean, but has set as off-limits for resource-management purposes. Dirty or clean, quahog pirates are like all pirates: They are romantic figures who perform exciting stunts like stranding lawmen on sandbars, and they are embarrassments to clean-working guys, and even the industry as a whole.

But embarrassment is what you get when bossless folk speak the truth. The crimes of industrial food are enormous and revolting, but sustainable food has its crimes, too. Worse, while capitalist farmers and fishermen and food conglomerates struggle mightily and juridically to conceal the truth of their crimes, sustainable-working men and women, new peasants—certain of them, anyway—will not shrink from discussing, opining on, laughing at, and sometimes even celebrating the crimes of their peers. You could interpret such insouciance as contempt for social norms or as a respectful assumption that all men can handle a deviation from the norms they adhere to. However it is viewed, it will not stop. What is more threatening is the fact that they will tell these tales in their enchanting way. The bullraker's rhythm, his liberated lexicon, and his strange moral wisdom will seduce his audience. He will gain converts. If enough people take up sustainable work, Americans will find their dreams and delusions mocked and undermined by the people who feed them, and many Americans will find themselves all too happy to have awoken from these dreams.

Right there, in that little prose-poem about a man who failed as a bullraker, a man whose mind was either too weak or too strong, is the supreme, sublime truth about the hardships that underlie the keeping of the bay. The bullraker's society may come to glorify his hardships as much as he does.

None of this applies to me, of course. My experience of bullraking ended before I came to hear enough about its hardships to romanticize it. The pain of bullraking is not as real to me as its material aspects, its constituent parts. This too, is important, because they are the physical objects that make the industry possible and sustainable. That is: One cannot know bullraking and the reason it works without knowing the boat and the rake.

CHAPTER FOUR

Water in a Dry Boat

Deep quahogging is a comparatively recent innovation on the Cape—
at least I believe it is. Cape Codders have always raked quahogs, no
doubt the first settlers raked for them along the flats. But when we
were youngsters, we never heard of anyone raking them in deep water.
To go quahogging in a boat would have been a town joke in our youth.
But scores do that very thing now and do it daily.
—JOSEPH CROSBY LINCOLN, 1935

MY FATHER'S BOAT HAD BEEN OUT OF THE WATER FOR THREE YEARS, mounted on its trailer, parked on a path in the woods, when we started getting it ready to go. I'd been away for a long time, and my father had been unhealthy, but now I was near to home and we wanted to go fishing and maybe figure out this oyster-farming thing, and there, under the trees, was the boat. Throughout its period of disuse, my father continued to pay rent on his empty docking slip, just as he had continued to renew his shellfishing license throughout all the years since he'd quit full-time bullraking. From time to time, after his eye operations, he quahogged, and he even brought in significant earnings doing so, but as his responsibilities at the prison grew and his health worsened, his time on the water tapered off to nothing. A boat in the water needs regular attention, which my father couldn't provide, so he'd stranded the boat on the farm, all the while banking on the prospect of getting it back in the water, to do a little digging on the side. Years went by. The boat, much like the farm itself, became part of the woods.

No one has worked our land commercially in decades. It has become overgrown, thick with trees and underbrush. Coils of bullbriers, tough, green vines, bearing stiff thorns every inch or two, choke the ground between the old stone walls, where fields and pastures used to lie. The trees around the boat, mainly oak and maple, shed leaves and twigs into it. Rainwater has blackened the leafy detritus and swamped the deck to a foot deep in places. Salamanders, slugs, and earwigs have swum, slithered, and crawled through the mess. While working on the motor, my father found a tree frog huddled under the casing and a mouse's nest on the starter. The boat had begun to resemble the land around it, riotous with animals and plants and rot.

It was my summer back from New York City, following the completion of my graduate program in journalism, when we started to clean up the boat for fishing—a task that, at first, appeared similar to the process of cleaning up old farmland for farming. We had to impose an order of things: Man before Nature. A farm looks nothing like the wild. On the boat, we had to clear away the overgrowth and get to the stuff that would allow us to force Nature to do what we wanted it to do, just like on the farm. But the farm and the boat are very different. The farm changes everything; Nature cannot survive it. All farms are the site of a massacre. The boat is merely a tiny bulwark against Nature. The area that the boat makes productive is indistinguishable from any other natural place. Fishing grounds necessarily remain wild, but to get to them we needed to scrape the wilderness off of the boat.

I shoveled the swamp-water slurry over the side while my father reached over the gunwales and grabbed up the slimy and rusted tools that surfaced as the water receded. Though he'd been feeling better that year than he had for some time, he still had trouble climbing into the trailered boat. He'd hurt his knee several years earlier at the prison, while coming down from a plowing truck during a snowstorm. Prison security dictates that snow may not cover its internal roads, which meant that the plow crews my father directed had to work continuously, for the full duration of a storm and for a while after it ended, for days and nights sometimes, to ensure that guards could always get to the prisoners. The injury he'd suffered getting down from the truck made it difficult for him to ascend into the boat. Later, when the cleaning had come along and he had space for a landing, he'd clamber up a ladder and swing himself over the side, but at the beginning, he could only set his two canes against one of the trailer's fenders and unbend his back with some effort in order to peek over the gunwales. It troubled him greatly to be denied access to his boat.

The boat is all-important to the modern bullraker, but such was not the case for his ancestors. Years ago, no one used a boat to gather quahogs, and a few people still don't today. Some people, men and women, wade into the shallows to go quahogging. They hook up a short splice with a bullrake, inflate an inner tube around a bushel basket, secure this make-shift floating receptacle to their waists with a short rope, and then head into the water to dig. Sometimes they tow a pram behind them; some-times they use scratch rakes. It all amounts to the same thing. Bullrakers call these people "puddlers," or "short-stickers." There remain very few of them who rake commercially. They are the last stand of the earliest type of European commercial quahogger, who slogged into the water hundreds of years ago with potato rakes and little rafts.

It takes only a small investment to start out as a puddler, and even, relatively speaking, to start out as a bullraker. Considered as a small business, a bullraking enterprise requires minuscule amounts of capital: twenty, thirty thousand dollars for a new boat; ten, twenty grand for a new motor, a few thousand for a full complement of equipment. A qua-hogging license—a license that permits only commercial quahogging and no other commercial fishing—has a negligible fee, but the State makes fewer than twenty available each year. Multipurpose licenses, which allow for endorsements to harvest all sorts of fishes, have severe caps on their issuance: Two current licenses must expire for the State to issue a single new one. A young person hoping to enter into commercial bullraking may purchase an active license from another shellfisherman, but in this case, *active* has the legal sense of "seventy-five sales have been made on it during the past two years." Lots of old-timers who have hung on to their licenses past retirement cannot sell them without going back to work for a couple of years. An active multipurpose license may draw twenty thou-sand dollars in a private transaction.

When a young guy who wants to bullrake for a living sets everything up for himself, it can come to seventy-five thousand dollars. Not too bad in the scheme of start-ups. But bullraking isn't quite the kind of enter-prise a bank's loan officer looks upon with favor. A small-business loan for bullraking would be quite a thing. The business plan itself would be a marvel: "I plan to dig quahogs for money." A guy usually has to accumulate savings in order to put in as a bullraker, and some puddlers do in fact work their way out of their waders and into a skiff.

For a guy who wants to stick to puddling, a boat's a waste of money. For other guys—not just puddlers, but anybody who has worked to save up to become a bullraker—the quahog skiff is prestigious. A good skiff will swell a guy's chest with pride, especially a skiff slowly earned, and a bullraker will find pleasure or pain in the public appreciation of his boat throughout his career. The fitness of a man's boat is the subject of much bullraking gossip. Praising and disparaging skiffs accounts for a considerable percentage of conversation down the shore. One guy might offer, helpfully, to burn his buddy's boat to the water, as the insurance money would allow him to buy a skiff that isn't such a lousy piece of shit. Quahoggers are helpful—and they are aesthetically minded. A fleet of quahog skiffs is a thing of beauty to them, something to be stared at from a pickup truck, with a can of beer. Why, aesthetics alone may stir a man to take up bullraking. In the end, however, the boat must serve the job; the physical and spiritual charm of the quahog skiff, its status as prize and as object of beauty, come from its being designed for working ends. And, just as puddling shows what a serious investment a quahog skiff is, so another kind of boatless bullraking shows what the skiff actually does for the quahogger.

A while back, David Drew loaned my father and me a videotape of guys out bullraking in two different periods: the summer of 1955, and the winter of 1979. Warren Wilcox, an old-timer of my grandfather's generation, used to bring his 16mm film camera out on the water now and again, and, in his very old age, Warren had had some of his films transferred to videotape. The whole thing's in color. It's strange to see the men of '55 that way. I have no actual memory of bullrakers on the water in those days, as I wasn't born yet; I know such scenes only from black-and-white photographs. But there on the video, young and in full color, is David's father, Howard; there's Beebee McDonald and Al Perretta, all of them in wooden skiffs, digging, hauling, picking over from their old-fashioned bullrakes. Warren narrates, his voice whispery, weak with senescence: "There's Beebee, diggin' away."

In '79, Greenwich Bay froze over to an unheard-of extent, and Warren walked out with his camera, way out, hundreds of feet from shore, and

Walking out to the quahogs, 1979. BRUCE EASTMAN

filmed the men digging through the ice. It's there, on David's copy of Warren's film, that you can see what it means to have (and not to have) a boat, because the men on the ice were swinging full bullraking operations—not a puddler's kit—without boats. Deep water, long stales, no boats. That one strange moment in the modern history of quahogging in Narragansett Bay shows the real uses to which quahogging skiffs are put.

The years of 1978 and '79 proved unusually cold for Rhode Island. My father's picture from the Blizzard of '78, the photograph he hung kitty-corner to the image of his eye, shows that, as does Warren's video from the following year, with its soft monologue. "One cold day," says Warren, "the batteries froze up on my camera . . . it was sure cold."

Normally the bay didn't ice over so far from the shore. Greenwich Cove, just a couple of hundred feet across, always got choked solid in its southern half, but Greenwich Bay itself never closed up so much. Then came the depths of February of '79. Ice skinned the water a mile offshore. Several hundred yards, even a half-mile off of Goddard Park, it set in over a foot thick. Beneath the ice, everyone knew, lay half a million pounds of good quahogs. Now, in other years, the guys would have simply left the stuff under the ice, but, in regard to quahogging, Rhode Island had done one thing right and one thing terribly wrong that year.

The wrong thing was that they'd fucked up the Providence sewage-treatment plant. The Providence River was boiling with bacteria because the plant had flushed so much raw sewage into the bay. The State had had to shut down the waters of the North Conditional Area, the opening of which would cause so much commotion in the summers of 1984 and '85. Though the waters of the Upper Upper Bay remained tantalizingly liquid, the quahoggers could not work there.

But Rhode Island had its transplant. During the summer, the shellfishermen had moved several hundred thousand pounds of quahogs from polluted grounds to clean ones. The quahoggers had piled the transplant catch onto the *Beacon,* Cap'n Bill had piloted the boat off of Goddard Park Beach, about a half-mile offshore, and the men had dumped the quahogs overboard. The DEM had declared the area off-limits for six months, scheduling the start of the harvest for the end of January. Rhode Island had provided a winter's cache of food, a victory of the ant over the grasshopper, the very stuff of prudence. It was no one's fault that an unexpected coldness had secured all of those heaps of quahogs under a fat crust of salty ice. The State had done the right thing, in that it had prepared for the lean times of winter; it just turned out that, in order to reap the fruits of that wisdom, the State and the shellfishermen would have to do something foolish.

For a few days a week, quahoggers and DEM enforcement agents trod out onto the ice to bring the transplant to fruition. DEM agents stood around and guarded the labor of the bullrakers, who were permitted only a hundred and fifty pounds of quahogs a day, and could work only from 8:00 a.m. to 2:00 p.m. The shellfishermen chopped and sawed through the ice they and the DEM guys were standing on, slid rakes into the holes they'd made, and dug and hauled up quahogs, slopping water and mud all over the ice beneath their rubber soles. "After a while," says my father, "they were questioning whether they should have ever let us do that, but . . . too late!"

You can see the lunacy of the production in Warren's film—hundreds of bullrakers not only crowded together on the ice, but cutting holes in it. My father used a chain saw to get through it, but a number of guys dusted off antique ice saws. David Drew still has one, a huge affair, three feet long, fifteen pounds, with a blade half an inch thick and teeth an inch and a half long. The handle is a wooden bar perpendicular to the blade. You had to chop a starter hole in the ice, work the saw in, and cut a hole big enough to give the digger access to a worthy strip of bottom, a couple of feet square. As the men worked, often two or three to a hole, they piled up their hauls in dirty, black mounds, stark against the ice. The scene has an irreal quality to it: It looks like and unlike a normal quahogging scene, like the paintings on the wall of the governor's office, but it's as if both the boats and the water have been erased, leaving just the men, their rakes, and the quahogs on a bare white canvas. The guys seem both at ease—not at all tentative on the ice—and embarrassed, naked without their boats. They have to work in a new, uncomfortable way, and their movements don't have their usual rhythm and decisiveness.

The ice moved up and down as the guys dug. Water slicked the surface. Sometimes, guys paired up and tied themselves together with ropes. If the shellfishermen had cut too many holes, then DEM would close the site down for a few days, to let the openings scab over. Even so, an area tended to rot out from overwork, from both the act of quahogging and the weight of its accoutrements. It was hard getting the tools onto the ice and the product off of it and over to the dealers, who parked their trucks on the shore, set out their scales, and waited for the guys to come in. "You had to drag your stuff out with a sled," my father says. "I probably used yours." The men winnowed their equipment down to the bare minimum: one rake, twenty-five feet of stale, burlap bags, water, and a cutting tool. Because they had sown the digging grounds, they usually got good hauls, but that meant dragging a couple of hundred pounds of quahogs, plus their equipment, back to the trucks. "It was cold and miserable, and you had guys in line waiting to sell out," says my father. Often, the buyers would hunker down in the cab, crank up the heat, crack the window, and tell the quahoggers to weigh their own catch. "They didn't really even check what you were selling them," says my father. "They usually trusted people they knew—probably a mistake!"

The quahoggers took the opportunity to fuck over the dealers in a couple of ways. The quahogs went into burlap bags, the bags went on the scale, and the weight was the weight. So the guys laded the burlap with water, which iced up nice and heavy. That trick worked even when the dealers deigned to emerge from their warm trucks to cast a cold eye

Digging through the ice, 1979. BRUCE EASTMAN

on the scales. When the buyers chose to stay cosseted in their trucks, however, the quahoggers did something different and strange. They didn't simply yell out an inflated number to the guy behind the steamed window; they actually put a hand or a foot on the scale, pushed it to a certain weight, and then yelled that number, a number that the needle actually did mark at that moment. There's bullraker psychology for you: It would have been bad form to cheat by simply calling out an extra twenty pounds, by making no more than a verbal effort. A guy had to earn his cheated dollars by exerting precisely the force in pounds that he was screwing the dealer out of. It was the kind of performance the quahoggers like to put on for each other, a display of schoolboy mischievousness.

They live for this juvenile shit. Bullrakers love tales of manly adventure—Arctic exploration, cave diving, pioneering—and, that winter, they got to live one such tale, replete with the pain of severe cold and the thrill of doing something dangerous and new. It was a magnification of the hardships they suffer all of the time, and they were grateful for it, once they never had to do it again. "It was freezin'-ass cold, I remember that," says my father. "Sometimes it would shut off the chain saw, cuz it was so cold . . . It was worse when it snowed . . . but it was still kinda neat doin' it."

He and the other guys had a grand old time figuring things out, braving harsh weather, and muscling their way to a living, just as they did every day, only more so. My father even got another good photograph out of it. The local paper for the town of Warwick sent a photographer down to the site on a day when icicles happened to be hanging from my father's beard. Perfect small-town visual eloquence. OLD MAN WINTER read the caption in the paper, underneath a head shot of my father, mugging a bit, his curly beard spiked with ice. He was thirty-two years old.

On their days off the ice, the men continued to work from their boats, which they'd moved a ways down south, to Wickford Cove, which never froze over in the way the coves of Greenwich Bay did. On those days, the guys could enjoy the flexibility the boat afforded them. They could head out to clear waters and even take breaks in their little cabins to warm themselves over their angel makers. On the ice, they had to guess where Cap'n Bill had dumped their product, maybe calculate what the tide had done to move the quahogs, then choose the spot where they would dig throughout their workday. They did not drift, and they could stand the cold only so long. Plus, the ice in no way changed the status of the bay as a free and common fishery. They could own a hole in the ice no more than they could own a wave. "Once you abandoned a hole," says my father, "somebody else would come over and say, 'Oh! Look what you missed!'" Everyone could see what everyone else caught, and there was nothing anyone could do to stop other guys from working a productive hole someone else had cut.

All of which reveals the essence of the boat. The quahog skiff is the ice, a platform for work. It is a means of reaching quahogs in water over a fathom deep, where the puddlers cannot go. Without the ice, the bullraker, unless he is Jesus H. Christ, needs his boat to stand on, to hold his equipment, to transport his quahogs. The boat also replaces the transplant, in that the bullraker uses the boat to find his product. In this regard, there's a trade-off: Without Cap'n Bill to tell him where the quahogs are, the bullraker must seek them out, make guesses about what lies beneath the bay's greenly opaque waters, but he also gets the chance to try to hide his catches from other guys. The latter is one of the main functions of the quahog skiff, one of the ways it makes itself so superior to the ice: It is a means of preventing other quahoggers from finding the quahogs you have found.

These purposes shaped the evolution of the quahog skiff, from the simple flat-bottomed skiff to what it has become today—an unmistakable icon of the bay. Near to where my father's boat now sits, again on its

An unused quahog skiff, 2010. RAY HULING

trailer, lies a small wooden rowboat, maybe ten feet long. It lies belly-up, exposing a long and wide plank for a sandboard, a flat keel, good for running the boat onto a beach. A few dozen planks cross under it, nailed to the sides of the boat. It's an osseous arrangement, like a rheumatoid old spine hammered down on a triple set of thick ribs. It's made of fir and marine plywood. David Drew's father built it in the late fifties, my grandfather bought it for a hundred bucks or so, and there it has lain for fifty years. It has never touched water.

Men used to work out of skiffs like this. My father did as a child; my grandfather did as a young man. Even when motors first came along, before each man could afford his own, the guys would work out of rowboats towed by a powerboat. The older guys have a touch of nostalgia for those days, when they had to group together, make a team in the old sense, workhorses harnessed to each other. Nick Carcieri started out that way.

"In those days—that was before outboards—there was a family that lived right in the neighborhood with my father," says Governor Carcieri. "There were three brothers . . . they were about yea high." He holds his hand a dwarven four feet off the floor; he's talking about the Maddalena brothers, a family of quahoggers and suppliers of fishing equipment. "And they had a powerboat, probably twenty-eight foot, maybe thirty feet, a wooden powerboat, and in those days the work skiffs were all out of wood, and you rowed 'em . . . So you would stand—they had oarlocks near the center, slightly toward the bow—they would stand and they rowed. You'd row down to the big boat and then they would tow the skiffs out. Then they would anchor and then get in the work skiffs again and then row out to wherever they were gonna work. My father started behind them; they'd tow him out. He started when he was just a kid, thirteen, fourteen years old, he was quahoggin'."

David's uncle Arthur rode out that way for a while. Big John Northup was the guy with the motor. Each guy had to pay a dollar each way for the tow, which, at ten or eleven skiffs at a time, added up for Big John, who also used to sell sodas to the guys. "The only thing I can remember about Big John," says Arthur, "was he'd charge you ten cents for a soda, and he'd open up two sodas for himself, and he'd guzzle the first one and drink the next one."

The guy with the powerboat held a prominent position, naturally. He lorded it over the men, to some extent or another, even if he didn't want to. Yet, the arrangement had something to recommend it—environmentally, of course, because they used little fuel, but also socially.

"My uncle actually was a tonger when he was young," says Tim Trim. The uncle this time is Tommy Cole, known as one of the best quahoggers on the bay, maybe the best there ever was, if such a thing could be known. "He was a tonger . . . He used to have a twenty-two-footer, and he called it the *Pumpkin Seed*. It was a catboat"—this is a small sailboat; it was popular at the time to power catboats with car engines—"and he used to tow five or six boats out, and actually, him and Bunky"—Bunky Bennett, also Tim's uncle, and known as one of the best all-around fishermen ever to work on the bay—"they used to steal wine from their grandfather, who made it, and supposedly it was really good wine . . . But they used to take it out, and if it was bad out, all these little boats would just row back to the catboat and they'd start drinkin', playin' cards, and stuff. They would actually come there for lunch and eat lunch together, four or five boats, and then row back away and go tongin', and my uncle would tow 'em in."

It's a sweet thought, this conviviality. Perhaps the bullrakers of years ago embraced more openly their dependence on one another. Or maybe they resented the guy with the motor, even if they liked him. In any case, technology changed, and the quahogging teams disappeared from the bay.

By 1957, my ten-year-old father had a five-horse outboard motor. That's how he got started. He would stay over at his mother's mother's house—his *mémé*'s, because she was French-Canadian. He would stay on the weekends, get up early, carry the motor—over a hundred pounds—down to the shore, fix it to his little skiff, ride out in front of the house, near the mouth of Apponaug Cove, and tong for a few hours. Then, he'd come back in and carry his catch and his motor back to the house.

Outboard motors opened the bay and changed the boats. A quahog skiff has a wide transom, the board across the stern, to hold the big outboards the guys like to use. They have chined hulls—soft chines, usually, meaning that instead of a round hull consisting of a single curve, the quahog skiff hull consists of angled planes. Where a rowboat would have its stern and bow curving upward—so that both fore and aft, the boat emerges from the water, leaving the midships to provide buoyancy—the quahog boat has a return in the back. It returns to a flat hull, parallel to the water from midships aft. This design allows the boat to plane off at high speeds, to get its lift not from displacing water, but mainly from the hydrodynamic lift created by the movement of the boat through the water. The advent of fiberglass only intensified the quickening of the skiff. Slathering glass all over a wood frame resulted in a strong boat. You could pound the little wooden skiffs to pieces with the big motors, but fiberglass could take the impact of the water at high speeds. Fiberglass also meant that fewer and fewer guys built their own boats, and that even when they did build them, building no longer meant from the keel up, but rather from a glassed shell. Boat companies—Dyer, Midland, Romarine—began selling fiberglass skiffs. The bullraking game got faster.

All of that cheap speed meant that guys no longer had to depend on tows. An era of individual exploration ensued.

"I'll tell you," says Zorro, "I followed Tommy Cole around for about thirty years; he quahogged everywhere. Everybody copied Tommy Cole's boats . . . he had the fastest boats. They used to race. I don't know how many years ago, cuz he's older than me. They used to race for outboard motors; you'd win an outboard motor. They used to have races every year; they'd build a boat just for that, a skiff. He used to do good.

"He used to take me all the way over to Sakonnet River, all under the Mount Hope Bridge and under the other bridges, to Gould Island . . . in the Sakonnet River with a wooden skiff. I always watched him and the Rayhills. He used to try all the spots . . . He'd go down to Newport—he knew all the places, you know? We used to go down below the Jamestown Bridge, and right on the right there's a little beach there, right before the URI thing—there's a URI dock—we went over the side of it, digging."

Guys didn't just zoom around randomly, however, hoping that their splices would dip like a dowsing rod when they ran over a bed of quahogs. They'd prospect—and they'd go about it with as much caution, as much paranoia, as any miner in the Sierra Madre. Guys would hook up their rakes, dig, examine the haul, toss it, and pull up stakes to head somewhere else—all in order to keep their discoveries for themselves. That's how Ray Wyss did it.

"It was like an adventure every day," he says. "I didn't know where I was goin' . . . I kinda had an idea, and I was one who always looked. I can remember, I'd make a haul, pull it up, man, just have that damn thing from guard to guard, loaded up with quahogs, shake it back and forth and, whoosh, right back overboard. Take ranges, start the outboard, just buzz right off somewhere else, try again—the days nobody was out there, or when everybody went home."

My father's use of charts served a similar purpose, but with certain advantages. When he unrolled a chart on the kitchen table and looked for abrupt changes in depth—holes, submerged hills, channels—he could scour the entire bay, confident that his boat could take him to any promising spot and get him home in time for a nap before supper. Plus, no one could see him or the spots he marked. Working from charts conferred these advantages, but my father could not have cared less about them. For one thing, few other guys wanted to work banks. For another, he never bothered to try to hide a spot, which was something of a rare position among quahoggers.

Guys can become covetous of good catches, and, thus, protective of good spots. There's no formal way to stake a claim on the water, however.

There are no legislated property rights on the bay. There are informal practices that respect a claim on a patch of water, but they require enforcement by the individual claimant. The bullrakers call the claims "ranges," after the old-fashioned method of recording a location on the bay. Even when a guy marks his site on his touch-screen GPS, he calls it his range. Holding on to a hot spot requires a guy either to conceal its location (or even its existence), or to ward off his fellows. In the latter case, you have to let guys know when they're working your ranges, and they have to decide whether to give you space.

Some guys do not have the tact necessary for such negotiations. One bullraker earned the name Scott the Screamer, because he used to let loose at the top of his lungs whenever anybody got within a thousand feet of him, which behavior earned him many threats and a couple of beatings. It's a hard thing to know exactly what it means to hold or to violate a range. It's a vague, uncodified etiquette, but it plays a role in maintaining the bay as a commons. A guy needs to feel that he can cash in on his luck and his hard work. That's what keeps him out there looking for stuff, trying out new places. The feeling of ownership over a discovery of quahogs motivates exploration, but it also means that somebody has to scream at somebody else at some point. Further, the mores pertain only to conflicts between individuals. Once a group of guys learns that somebody has found a hot spot, that's the end of any pretense of property rights. They can all head over en masse, and there's no question of any violation of a range. Thus, it becomes more important to be clever about hiding one's ranges than tough about defending them, and, when it comes to cleverness in this regard, no has one surpassed Ray Wyss.

"Duke and I found a place," he says. "That was Irving Windsor. We called him the Duke, but Irving was his right name. Duke used to look with me, we used to go lookin'. . . A lotta guys, the only lookin' they did is, 'Where's Ray Wyss workin'?,' or 'Where's Tommy Cole workin'?,' and that's where they'd go work, where we used to go off lookin' for stuff.

"I can remember we were over to off Bristol, Hog Island, and we found a spot over Hog Island, so we worked it, like part-time. We'd go over, hit it for two hours, and then we'd go somewhere else, cuz we didn't want to come in with too big a day's pay, cuz the guys are lookin' at whatcha got . . . and especially Billy Benoit—he couldn't keep shut. He'd tell guys what you were makin'.

"It finally got to the point where we were workin' over there—we'd get out late, and we'd quit late, hopin' we would miss the boat. In fact, we come in and sat off Patience Island, waiting for the *Beacon* to go. The *Beacon*'d go and we'd give 'em half an hour, and then we'd take off and go into Greenwich. Billy was tied up, *Beacon*'s empty, he's gone home, and then we'd come in and unload . . . and we'd done that a good number of days.

"We hit that spot—I told Duke, I says, 'Duke, I'm gonna hit this damn thing late, late in the afternoon or evenin',' so I'd go down with my fishin' poles and take Ruth with me, my first wife—she died of cancer in eighty-three—I'd take her with me, and we'd take the Coleman stove and supper and a fry pan, whether it was cube steak and maybe some mashed potatoes or some kinda vegetable, and then I'd go out there and I'd hit it for about two hours and then we'd make our supper, and everybody'd think 'Ray Wyss is goin' fishin'.' The next day I had it in the car. I'd come in and back the car into Finn's and unload at the station.

"You had to pull stuff like that," Ray continues. "If you had a spot, you did everything you could to keep it, cuz the guys were watchin' you. We'd go off past Poppasquash, and we'd take out our little spyglasses—I have one here, somewhere—and we'd look back towards Providence Point and see if anybody's followin' us . . . And if we saw anybody, like Nick followed us over one day, we said, Let's just try off the dock, cuz if you go around Poppasquash, there's a big dock there. Jeez, if we didn't land on quahogs. Of course within four or five days there was thirty-five guys workin' there . . . It was good! Wouldn't you know we're tryin' to save our spot and we hit another spot, and Nick comes right in, so it finally got down and they could do better somewhere else, and we just kept goin' there. We kept workin' that, and finally everybody left.and we went to Hog Island.

"But one day, we get there—we'd go by Poppasquash to hang up, cuz it takes a while to hang up—and we're over there, and Duke is only about twenty feet from me. I got my spyglass, and I'm lookin' up back towards Providence Point. Nope, nobody's comin' . . . and I just happened to swing the spyglass down. I swing it down and I swing it over to Hog Island . . . Look! There's Tommy Cole! He's off Hog Island! I says, 'Hey, Duke, get your glasses out. There's Tommy.' And Duke says, 'I'll be damned; what's he doin' over there?' So if this was Hog Island shore, our spot was here and Tommy was here, so we said, Well, Jesus—if he's there, we might as well go over, so we ride over and we worked with Tom. It was just fair workin', not like we had up ahead maybe five, six hundred feet, it was good— where Tommy was, it was just so-so—and so we worked there and just yakked, passed the time of day. And Tommy, well, after about two or three or four days, Tommy disappeared, and we went back on our spot again. And that's how you had to work: If you had a spot, you had to protect it; whatever you had to do to protect your spot, that's what you did."

It seems absurd, like the excesses of paranoid fantasy. Like spy bullshit between the United States and Russia during the Cold War. What are these guys even protecting? A good digger, a skilled digger, will do well over time, hitting good and bad spots, but working them well no matter what. When a skilled digger puts in the extra effort to find a good spot, as Ray Wyss did, or spots particularly suited to him, as my father did, he will do better, on average, but then he has the problem that his catch will draw notice at the dock. Guys will see his success, attribute it to the luck of having come across a trove of quahogs, and then seek out his ranges. This conundrum led Ray Wyss either to hide his catches completely, by selling out in secret, or to disguise his catch by reducing it, by making his catch a blend of hauls from hot spots and so-so spots. In the end, did Ray Wyss really earn more working as he did? More with respect to himself, already a hard, even savage worker? Especially when the time he spent on covert action is factored in? Probably not; but money wasn't the only point of all that activity.

The practice of protecting ranges exposes the gambling heart of the fisherman. Good fishing grounds come and go, and luck cannot save you, but, damned if the bullraker isn't taking the extra dollars he earned from his good spot and buying a stack of scratch tickets. The territoriality bullrakers express through ranges has more to do with establishing a feeling of luckiness than anything else. The illusion of property rights that motivates guys to seek out individual success ultimately benefits the group: Either a guy lets everybody know where the new hot spot is, or he is forced to spend so much time and energy hiding it that he doesn't do any better anyway. This equation doesn't dissuade guys from hiding stuff, because they're not rational economic actors. They're out there screaming and hollering at each other, bumping boats, hiding their catches, sneaking out to their hot spots, because they get a kick out of these things. They're playing games. Ray Wyss's story about Hog Island isn't so much about making money: It's about Nick Carcieri and Tommy Cole; it's a story about three of the Top Men on the Bay at that time crossing paths, and Ray Wyss coming out ahead.

That's what outboards made possible, in addition to opening up new fishing grounds. All these games. You can't fuck around like that out on the ice, where everybody can see if you've hit quahogs and you might have other guys literally tied to you. There's no escape. Much the same situation occurs when a team of quahoggers tow out together. It's only with the modern quahog skiff that you get this simulacrum of independence and competition that allows the industry to prosper while giving the guys a way to mess with each other's heads.

David Drew tells a story of how his father and his father's friend Jimmy Rice stole in on a pile of quahogs that Ray Wyss was trying to hide.

"Ray Wyss was workin' a spot, and, if anybody got near, he'd screw out of there," says David. That's one of the great advantages of having a big motor. Sure, a giant outboard's a big dick to swing around, but it also enables guys to move fast enough that they can get away from would-be range-jumpers. Jimmy and Howard wanted to give ol' Ray a hard time, so they devised a plan to overcome his quick little skiff: "They attacked from this angle, first day," says David. "He screwed . . . Next day, they attacked him from that angle; he screwed. So the third day, they split up . . . Dad ran his range; Jimmy ran his range; and they met." Jimmy and Howard met right on the spot, the intersection of their two attack vectors—and they went out early, because they knew that Wyss often started late, in order to prevent guys from following him. "And when Ray Wyss showed up," says David, " 'Fuckin' son of a bitch!' That was a crowning moment for my father."

Just as intruding on a guy's ranges can let him know how you feel about him, sharing your own can be a way to tell a guy he's all right with you.

"I had a really good summer," says Tim Trim, "but I stayed on the quahogs. I found a little spot, maybe the size of this house, and I stayed on it for a month. I had some visitors, but I did what I could to push 'em away from me, y'know, a little length, so they weren't bumpin' me."

But he didn't dissuade everyone. Donnie Merrill, an older guy about my father's age, who has quahogged successfully for decades, turned up at Tim's spot. "He saw me sell out for a couple weeks straight; I think he got tired of it, so he came and visited me for a couple weeks." That's half the time Tim was on the spot himself. Both guys got something out of recognizing Tim's informal claim on that patch of quahogs. Tim gets to be the guy who was doing well enough to draw the attention of an older bullraker, and he gets to be generous. Donnie gets to be the guy who can intrude on a range, because he's such a good fucking guy, a respected old-timer. It's hard to say who really has the upper hand in that moment, but it's clear that each man thinks well enough of the other.

The outboard motor and the modern quahog skiff did away with some of the power games and some of the conviviality found in the early days of towing, but the bullrakers have figured out how to express social relations through their skiffs. Just as with everything else in quahogging on Narragansett Bay, illusions of independence serve the needs of inter-dependence. The boat's a way for a guy to isolate himself, a means for him to escape other guys, but, in the end, there's no way out: A lone commercial boat cannot survive without the whole fleet. Not every bullraker knows this, or admits to it, but not all of them need to. The material fact of the boat combined with the formal and informal practices of caring for the bay make it so. That's what a boat in action means. That's the view of the boat from the water. There's also the view of the boat on the land, the view for my father and me.

Everything needed to come out of the boat, if we were to clean it. We began with the stale rack. The rack consists of just a few hook-shaped pieces of plywood about a foot and a half long, mounted on the port side. In Rhode Island, nearly everyone fishes off of starboard. There is no reason for this, but anyone who deviates from this convention is considered weird. This means you stow most of your tools portside.

The rack held a dozen pieces of stale in various lengths, a crab net, a wooden oar, a plastic oar, a pair of quahogging tongs, a wooden broom handle, and a plastic hand pump for bailing the boat. Beneath the rack lay a wooden-handled claw hammer with the claw broken off. Usually, my father stowed his gas tank under there as well, but for some reason he had it forward, almost under the bow, a five-gallon, flat, red plastic tank. Next to it, now on the starboard side, an old green plastic bin, insolated pale and weak, all cracked to shit, held a couple of hundred feet of half-inch rope and a five-prong grapnel anchor. David's father and my grandfather made this anchor. Howard learned blacksmithing, built himself a forge out of a cast-iron sink, hammered out the tines, bent them, and brought them to my grandfather, who welded them together. Back farther lay two bullrakes with a plastic dustpan on them. I handed things out to my father or just threw them on the grass. Then, I slowly worked back to the stern, where the water and the mess lay deepest.

The wheel mount is plywood and stands flush to a fiberglass panel that divides the stern from the midships. The mount is very much like the steering-wheel mount and dashboard of a car. It has a white wheel and a black rpm gauge fitted into it. On top lay a small pair of pliers, an 8mm Allen key, and an S-shaped, double-headed Phillips screwdriver. A shelf beneath the wheel held odds and ends: a broom head on a bungee cord; a coffee can with a plastic lid; a rusty, flathead screwdriver; a glass quart jar with several slabs of pork fat in it; a nautical compass; a quart of oil. On the left side of the mount hung a Kidde dry-chemical fire extinguisher. I picked up the coffee can; its bottom had rusted out. Three ballpoint pens fell into the water, but a wad of papers and stickers—license information, boat tags—remained suspended in the can.

Back from the wheel mount, still to starboard, was the throttle mount. Plywood again. My father had bolted the throttle to a square of plywood bolted to the gunwale. This is the piece that would come apart on us in the cove. Underneath the throttle: a blue buoy, lightly crusted with barnacles; a twelve-volt marine battery, free of any crust on its terminals; and a Rule-Mate 750 automated bilge pump, utterly overwhelmed by its circumstances. Two blue cushions and one red floated nearby, and beneath them drowned an Orion Coastal Locator Signal Kit.

All of this junk has some purpose—maintenance or flexibility or safety. You have to have flare guns and various documentation on your boat, per State regulations. We used the salt pork for fish bait, the net to catch crabs. There's bureaucratic necessity; there are different types of fish to catch; and then there's fixing things. Salt water chews right through equipment. So does my father. He's like a mound of salt himself, a huge eroding wave. Equipment almost visibly degrades beneath his ministrations. He can fix things, it's true; but the fixing itself often results in more fixing needing to be done.

This is likely an inherited condition. My grandfather's boat lay out in the yard for all of my life: a white Cape Codder with a center console, a cabin and wheel mount in the middle of the boat, rather than fore or aft. Cape Codders have become a rarity, almost a collector's item. My grandfather took his boat out of the water for the last time in his life sometime in the 1970s. For a time, both of the boats lay on the property, along with a postapocalyptic wasteland's worth of dead machinery—hay rakes, tractors, dump trucks, a graveyard of cars from the 1950s, '60s, and '70s, kitchen appliances, fishing equipment—even an entire 1947 GM school bus. It was all there to be fixed or to be used for fixing. My grandfather bought the school bus to put its motor in one of the dump trucks, which itself has not moved since the early '80s. All of the land is like all of the equipment; rusted metal fits as neatly into the landscape as do the ancient apple trees choked with poison ivy. Overgrown pastures, clots of abandoned grapevines, patches of blackberries lost in the grass—they're all the same as an old Terra Trac, a tank-treaded old bulldozer, rusted in place and shot through with raspberries.

The place is old. The farmhouse my father grew up in, where my grandparents lived when I was growing up, dates from 1795. Older foundations dot the property. Not far from the farmhouse, by a gravel bank my grandfather dug out, stands East Greenwich Cemetery 75, burial place of the Clark family, long extinct by the time my grandfather bought the land from an old man named Pasani in 1956. A quarter-mile east, following one of the dozens of stone walls that crisscross the property, sits the Slave Graveyard, as we've always called it: Exeter Cemetery 143, Unknown. It holds four graves marked only with fieldstones. North of the gravel bank, another hundred yards, heading back toward the farmhouse, is the Old Sheep Barn, its foundation built into a hill on two sides, its roof still mostly intact, but with a few of its beams split, collapsed, and charred. The barn burned in the early 1900s; the fire took a man's life. Even farther north are the ruins of the Old Barn, which Hurricane Gloria brought down in 1985, and which no one has touched since.

That is the boat in my eyes—and all of the things in it, too. Another float in the infinite flotsam, another swirling arm of the storm of junk. A boat can relate a man to other men, separating him from them or bond-ing him to them, a synchronic thing, a phenomenon concerned only with this moment in time, It can also work diachronically. My father's boat binds me to his family's history, which lies scattered all around us. I mean, just look at that patriarchal anchor. Look at our land and the land around our land.

When I was a child, five households of Hulings lived on our street. With the deaths of my grandparents and changes in the layout of the streets, there are now only three. Three Huling brothers, not closely related to us, but descendants of James Huling, of Ipswich, England, who settled in Rhode Island sometime in the early 1670s. The brothers have land much like ours, perhaps even more extreme, with bigger compounds and more crap. A couple of miles away to the southeast runs Huling Lane, a short street named for one of the brothers, who sold the land to devel-opers a few decades ago. Several miles to the southwest lies Huling Road, named for a great-grandfather of mine, Alexander Huling, who bought a big piece of land near there a few centuries ago. Alexander was a wealthy man, and he married into the third family of Rhode Island, the Smiths. He was a captain, a house carpenter, and a churchgoer. He gave a parcel of land for a little Baptist church that still stands on Old Baptist Road, which runs north to end, almost with a flourish, at Devil's Foot Road. Alexander's grave lies in the Old Baptist Meetinghouse Yard, his tomb-stone now 276 years old. This plot lies just a few miles from where I grew up. My family moves at the speed of a mile or so every hundred years. A deep history in a place can make people ponderous, but worse than his-tory can be inheritance.

Remember what Emerson said: "A cultivated man becomes ashamed of his property, out of new respect for his nature. Especially he hates what he has if he see that it is accidental—came to him by inheritance, or gift, or crime; then he feels that it is not having." In this respect, Alexander provided my family with the embarrassment of silver spoons—literally. In the opening of his will, he declares himself: "Expecting at the Resur-rection to Receive the same a Spirituall Body by the Mighty Power of God"—a solidly primitive transactional notion of the afterlife that makes all life—living itself—merely a coin to be paid to Christ. Yet it is a will, after all, a document utterly concerned with the ordering of things in this world, a profoundly anti-Christian document. Alexander first paid his debts, then provided for his "senseless" daughter—not the work of a man deluded by faith. He provided for his wife, and then bequeathed specific possessions to his children. His will is not a simple doling out, however. He doesn't merely give his children a silver spoon each, but "a Silver Spoone marked IH"—iota and heta, jay and aitch, for James Huling, Alexander's father.

This is no joke: I am an American aristocrat. Dozens of my line fought in or contributed to the Revolution against the British. My family is intermixed with that of Nathanael Greene's, greatest general of the War of Independence. William White is the name of my *Mayflower* ancestor. On my mother's side, I descend from Minnetinka Gasesett, daughter of a Narragansett sachem. Yet, neither the silver, nor the exalted bloodline has done me any good.

That is the boat to me: a Silver Spoone marked RH shoved in my mouth. The contents of the boat, for all of the purposes they serve, are the listings of a will and testament, as are all of the machines that weigh on the land, and the land itself. And even the genealogy itself. Alexander's father, James, the first of our line in America, was a mariner.

But it is all so necessary. I look at all of these things that could be useful to me—the boat, the rakes, the screwdrivers, even the jar of pork fat—and sometimes they seem hateful to me, because I haven't earned them. I look on all of the junk and the trash and the overgrown fields, and I feel despondent about how much must be cleared away before things can be made to work again. These are my narcissistic complaints, but the perspective that produces them is a right one. It is necessary to the good keeping of the bay.

The shellfishing industry must look upon itself as if everything it possesses has been passed down to it and will be passed down from it. The commons that is Narragansett Bay must do the same. The society around Narragansett Bay must do the same. These imperatives don't hold for individual bullrakers, however. It's not that my father should have bullraked out of a skiff that James Huling II cobbled together with his father's tools, or that I should fix up my father's boat and take up quahogging so that in a hundred years, my great-grandson can work out of a 1970 Midland. Nor does a guy who worked as a puddler and saved up to become a quahogger need to pretend that he is the bastard prince of an ancient line of bullraker-kings.

Our society does need to assume these things, however. As does the commons. As does the industry. They must ask themselves, "How did they do things years ago?" and "How will we do things years from now?" It is only with the intention of producing some kind of continuity between past and future that we can arrive at sustainable practices now. I am the real inheritor of my father's boat, but I am not the symbolic one, and it's the symbolism that matters. The guys on the water, the bullrakers, they are the real inheritors. By thinking of them as names in a shellfishing geneal-ogy, we can guide them and they can guide themselves to work in a way that will benefit their shellfishing descendants—and these practices will benefit us and them today. All of which means that the genealogies must be done, the wills read.

When the boat was clean enough for my father to climb in and start tinkering with the motor, we moved it to the front yard. He put up a stepladder for himself and soon had a corona of tools, rags, quarts of oil, gas tanks, and motor parts surrounding the boat. We needed to replace the battery, so, from inside the boat, he hefted it up onto the gunwale. He asked me to carry it for him.

Not long after he started work at the prison, the guards—correctional officers, they call themselves—cajoled my father into arm-wrestling them. Everybody says that fishermen are the best arm wrestlers, and everybody is right. My father beat them all, and he let them know it, too. Some of them tried the old over-the-top maneuver, twisting their hands so that the contest would depend more on upper-arm strength than forearm. My father dealt with this in a ball-busting way: He first straightened their wrists back to their initial position, then slowly forced the back of his opponent's hand to the table. Years later, getting the boat back together, he had to have me pick up the battery from the gunwale because his bad shoulder won't let him lift something that heavy from so high a position.

I put the battery in the back of the truck so we could turn it in to get a discount on a new one. Nearby, we had a stack of bullrakes, some of them ages old. My father hobbled over to them.

"These are all illegal now," he said. The oldest of the rakes has three-quarter-inch gaps between its tines; one inch is the current limit. One of the rakes did meet this standard, but my father had wrapped wire around each rod, thereby shrinking the gap between them. He poked his cane at one of the newer rakes, its once three-inch-long teeth worn down a bit.

"The long teeth dig too deep sometimes . . . You can bury a rake if you're not careful," he said. "I made a lot of money with this rake. I took it into a lot of deep water, sometimes fifty, sixty feet of stale." He grinned. "It was a good rake," he said, laughing. "Or maybe it was me!"

What is the rake compared to the hand that digs it? The rake must be something, because it has changed so much over the past sixty years or so. This genealogy, too, must be known, in order to see just what the rake is, how it performs, and how it preserves its line. As it happens, the story of the family of rakes is, in these parts, the story of a family of families.

CHAPTER FIVE

Bullrake Men, Bullrake Women

What is steel compared to the hand that wields it?
—SOLUTION TO THE RIDDLE OF STEEL,
CONAN THE BARBARIAN

DAVID'S SHANTY IS DIFFERENT NOW. IT IS NEAT. IT HAS SPACE. IT HAS decorative lighting—string lights—on the side facing the cove. Sheltering its little deck, also coveside, is a bare trellis. David's wife has considerably more influence over the disposition of the shanty than she did when I was young. On warm nights, she and David and sometimes a few of their friends sit on the deck, sip drinks, nibble on snacks, and look out over the cove. Their younger daughter held her wedding there a couple of years ago. This is not quite the place I remember quahoggers sheltering behind while they pissed into the cove.

My father and I stopped at the shanty after our inspection of potential oyster-farm sites. I drank half of a light beer, David drank a full one, my father had a soda, and Arthur had a coffee. David's grandfather, George, put up the two shanties and their first docks sometime in the 1930s, and he left them to his sons, Howard and Arthur. Howard died a decade ago; Arthur would die a year after we all got together that day at the shanty.

Arthur set a stack of old photographs down on the table and then unrolled a photocopy of an old map of Leased Oyster Ground, from 1922. It showed thousands upon thousands of acres of leases, surveyed into bizarre, blocky shapes, set aside for oyster cultivation, and owned mainly by the oyster barons. The map was crowded with property, even though 1922 was well past the peak of the industry in Rhode Island.

"My father had a lot," said Arthur. We looked through the list of names at the bottom of the map and found George Drew and his lot coordinates: 122-A, a tiny rectangle just off the middle of Prudence Island, about even with the north end of Allen Harbor. There are a few familiar names in the list with George's—Havens, Rice, Northup, Greene, many unfamiliar individuals, and a slew of oyster companies. "I don't know if he had any oysters at it," said Arthur. "I know he used to pirate a lot."

"It was oyster companies from Connecticut and New York," he said. "They controlled so much of the bottom that if you wanted to go quahoggin', years later, they charged you for the quahogs that they didn't put there. You had to pay for them.

"According to Dad, he had the lease to have a reason to be out there, cuz they used to have a night watchman. Dad had a power skiff, and he had a threaded pipe comin' out and put an elbow with a pipe on it, to make an underwater exhaust. He'd paint the boat three times a week to the waterline for a different color, have different numbers on the boat. If he'd get spotted, he'd take them numbers, throw 'em overboard, put the other on.

"Harold Prudeau told me that Dad was comin' up there one night . . . The watchman was bangin' into him, tryin' to drive him ashore, and tellin' him, 'Uncover your numbers!' My old man kept tellin' him to go to hell. Finally he was gettin' close to shore, so he uncovered 'em. When he got up on the other side of Sand Point, he had his other numbers on."

Arthur was a big, redheaded man with a long-boned face. He was unusually adept with quahogging tongs, and even won a King of the Bay contest during a transplant against a guy who was digging with a bullrake. He was also a fireman. His funeral procession drove down Water Street, past his shanty, where a line of young firefighters assembled with a ladder truck. For his viewing, his family placed a baseball cap that read DREW DOCKS and an honest-to-God, Styrofoam Dunkin' Donuts coffee cup, with the cover on, in the casket with him. I have never heard anyone say a bad word about Arthur Drew; he was a good man, with a taste for mischief. While never a pirate or poacher himself, he got a big kick out of their stories. He spent immense amounts of time down the shore, and the oddballs he found there fascinated him.

He held up a photograph of a man on a dock with a catch of quahogs. "You remember Pep? Well, this is before Pep . . . This is Silent Al. All I can remember about him, everything he had—the boat, his clothes, his tongs, and his oars were brown and green. He was shell-shocked from World War Two. He lived across the cove over there"—Arthur waved at the woods on the opposite shore—"sometimes in the summer, in a foxhole. There's always been a character in this town.

"The only funny story I ever heard about your grandfather," he said, "was when they towed a skiff up the road with no trailer." Arthur didn't know who was with my grandfather at the time, probably Lester Arnold. "They said they wanted to go to work, and there was ice in the cove here, so they towed a skiff, no trailer, all the way up Division Street and down Post Road, 'til they hit open water."

"Yeah, he did that," said my father. "It was down at little *Mémé*'s house. It was at that house in the middle of winter. He didn't have a trailer; he had that 1948 pickup, the Dodge, so he tied the boat to it. He wore the keel right off, and the runners." My dad laughed. "I don't know how funny it was," he said, but kept laughing. "Or if it was funny to Grandpa."

That's institutional memory—the living history of the institution of the shanty, of "down the shore," the cove, the bay. You need it to know who the people were who did your job before you, to know how they worked, what they worked with—not just for sentimentality's sake, but for guidance, to know what they did right, what they fucked up. It is not possible to tow a skiff down the road without a trailer. That fact has been determined. It is wrong to rent oyster leases for quahogging. The principle is established.

Above all of the other lessons to be learned from the study of shell-fishing's history is that of the bullrake. It is the spear of the hunt, the tool that gives the bullraker his name, the technology that the bullrakers inherited and that, if they pass it down from working hand to working hand, will aid in the good keeping of Narragansett Bay. The older guys tell the younger ones about the tools they used—and the tools they abandoned. The young guys learn from the older ones how the rake came to be and so how it really works on the bottom. Among the three quahoggers at the table—Arthur, David, my father—David had the least experience quahogging, but he knew the most about making bullrakes.

"My father never wanted me to be a quahogger," said David. Arthur looked at David, folded his big hands, and then turned his eyes north, up the cove. "I was never allowed to be a quahogger . . . He saw the life,

David Drew in Greenwich Cove, 2012. MICHAEL CEVOLI

what it did. A lot of these guys made a ton o' money and some of them could handle it; some of 'em couldn't. Think of it: You get paid every day, in cash. My father was big on that. Kid's a good quahogger? Makin' hundreds o' dollars a day?" David shrugged. "Drugs . . . booze," he said. Arthur laughed a little.

David's nautically handsome—sharp-featured, a touch of ruddiness, a touch of wrinkles. All he needs is a skipper's hat to perfect his look. Over the years, he's grayed and lost a little shape, but he has a straight-backed posture, almost militarily so. When it comes to talking about bullrakes, he takes on a professorial bearing. He enjoys holding forth. For a long time, he worked in a factory, the Bostitch stapler factory, over on Route 2, where my grandmother worked for twenty-five years, assembling staplers, and where my grandfather sometimes worked as a welder. David spent sixteen years indoors, then quit and became a fireman. He did twenty years fighting fires, hit his pension, then got out of the way for the younger guys coming up. Now, in his mid-fifties, he fixes boats, he trains novice firemen now and again, and he works on the water, bullraking.

"I started out tonging as a young man; I worked in the park. I had a sixteen-foot skiff with a five- or ten-horse outboard. I tonged one year, and then I started working in the mud, pulling a bullrake. I was never destined for college; my father, he wanted me to get a job at the mill." That's what David did; he stayed away from working the water full time. But he wanted to be in the mix. In the early eighties, he and his father got into the shellfishing equipment supply business. They went up to Warwick and talked with the Maddalenas, who readily handed over all of their information on wholesalers down in Long Island. David and Howard went down to New York, made their introductions, set up distribution, and opened up shop in Greenwich Cove, right out of the shanty. They did all right for a few years, then thought about expanding in an unusual direction. "We started making our own rakes," David said. "They told us we'd never be able to do it."

The bullrake is a strange-looking, fierce-looking, ungainly device. Though it has had many forms, it has always exhibited this ominous look. The story goes that a man named George Eldridge invented the quahog bullrake in 1863, on the Jersey side of Raritan Bay. His design then spread to other shellfisheries up and down the coast. He developed it from various short-handled clam rakes then in popular use, and his rake took its name from a hay rake, called a bullrake. Ultimately, the bullrake amounts to no more than a substitute for the human hand, and in its early days the resemblance between rake and hand was so strong that the rake actually exhibited some of the hand's weaknesses. The bullrake does the hand's work, after all. If you spread your fingers a little, curl them, and keep your thumb flush to your hand, you've got a rake—a shitty rake, one that doesn't benefit from an opposable thumb, a rake that can't exert too much force on the bottom without tearing itself up, but a rake nonetheless. The earliest bullrakes were little more than steel models of the hand in this shape.

My father and I had brought down a number of rakes for David to take a look at. We wanted to figure out who had made which one. Rakes are everywhere on our land; some of them date back to the twenties. I pulled ancient bullrakes, long and shallow and heavy, from inside the old school bus, from behind the chicken coop, from the wreckage of the old barn. We inspected them, looking for rakes my grandfather might have made and that my father had used. More of our inheritance. A jumble of rakes filled a corner of the deck—rakes of every different era, from the elder days to modern times. Like one of those illustrations of human evolution, only the figures, instead of walking in a line, toward rectitude, lie jumbled, in a pig pile. Each stage in the evolution of the bullrake has its name; the oldest ones we have are called Keyports.

Way back when, a shellfisherman in Rhode Island would send an order by postcard down to Keyport, New Jersey, near to where George Eldridge presumably worked his anvil. A couple of weeks later, the quahogger would head up to the freight company in Providence or Warwick and pick up his rake for $32 cash on delivery. After a while, guys started making their own rakes in the same style, but everybody still called them Keyports.

It's the Keyports that most resemble the human hand and therefore seem the most primitive. They are the rakes with the most obvious weaknesses. First, the Keyport had no sides, just as a hand comported to imitate a rake has no thumb—and, even if one cheats and raises his thumb to catch the quahogs spilling off his palm, he can raise a thumb on only one side, leaving quahogs to spill over the other. The Keyport is just the same: Quahogs spill out of its sides. Second, as with the hand, the digging tool and the basket structure are one thing: The fingers are the tines as well as the basket of the hand. To dig means to lose volume, to lose carrying capacity. As the tines or the fingers sink into the mud to seize the quahogs, the space available to hold the quahogs shrinks. Third, fingers have very little lateral strength. If you spread the fingers of one hand, then take the other hand and use it to squeeze the fingers of the first together, the fingers will be squeezed. It is impossible to resist. The same goes for the tines of a Keyport; they bunch together quite easily, which both leaves gaps through which quahogs may escape and makes clusters of tines that go hard through the mud. As happens with all tools, the Keyport continued to develop in a way that reduced its homology with the human body. It overcame certain of its weaknesses by distinguishing itself from the human hand.

The story of one of the advances is humiliating. Back in the day, a quahogger would cut two sheets of tin to match the curve of the Keyport's tines and then fix these pieces to the sides of the rake with wire. Tin sides—or thumbs, as it were. Of course, the jury-rigged tin contraption would fall apart out on the water, necessitating a lengthy repair session or a glum trip back to shore. David said that a guy from a Warwick mill went out on the water with some of his quahogging buddies and when he saw their rakes with their crummy tin sides, he asked, "Why don't you just weld some sides on?" His buddies stopped what they were doing, tin and tools in hand, and looked at the rake. *Well . . . shit.* "That's how my father used to tell it, anyway," said David.

We had two Keyport rakes in our collection by the shanty. One bore seams where the tines meet the back bar. "This isn't blacksmith-welded," said David, as he gave the rake a look-over. "This might be something your grandfather did up."

"This one is blacksmith-welded," said David, as he hoisted the other Keyport. "But I don't think this came from Keyport," he says. "I think this came from Buster Arnold's."

The Arnolds of Greenwich Cove have as storied a name as the Drews. Lester Arnold, a great friend of my grandfather's, was a big player in the shellfishermen's union. Buster supplied and manufactured shellfishing equipment. If the rake in David's hands came from Buster's, then it's likely that a blacksmith named Ruel Salisbury knocked it together. You can tell the blacksmithed rake apart from the welded one, because it has no seams where the tines meet the bar. It looks organic, but that is deceptive.

"All of that stuff had to be hammered out on a forge," said David. "Somebody had to get you the round rod—they actually had a swagger to make it round—then you had to cut it to length. You didn't have a hacksaw; you had to heat it to cut it. Then you had to flatten it out and have a jig where you start making these bends." He traced the finger-like curve of the tines with a pushing motion, bending them around an imaginary block of metal.

"When you're heating stuff, the fire looks like a volcano, but when you're welding stuff, it looks like a beehive—it has a top on it. It gets hotter; you're sprinkling borax on it, you're hammering it together." He laughed. "So you just think of everything that's involved; think about Ruel Salisbury, down at Buster Arnold's, blacksmithing! He quit and went to work at Bostitch, cuz Buster wouldn't put an exhaust fan in!"

Probably a smart move on Ruel's part, suggested Arthur. "He lived to be almost a hundred."

We looked closely at the Arnold rake. My grandfather had messed with the blacksmithed Keyport; it had side bars, braised on. My father ran a finger over a couple of the joints. He grinned. "A little sloppy," he said.

My father used Keyports as a young man—a wooden skiff, a Keyport, and wooden stales. The men in Warren Wilcox's film from 1955—David's father, Al Perretta, Beebee—they were using Keyports and wooden stales, too. Nick Carcieri used that setup; Arthur, Ray Wyss, Cap'n Ron, all the older guys grew up with it. There remain very few men on the bay who have used such equipment, but the guys who have not, who have never so much as seen a Keyport, still belong to the tradition, in that they are concerned with the same necessity that has always shaped the bullrake: quahogging in deep water.

Cap'n Ron passed by the shanty, on the way home from the Fireman's Hall. He stopped at Arthur's shanty first, Arthur being his great friend, then noticed the party at David's. Fortunately for us, Cap'n Ron knew all about the origins of the bullrake. Right on the spot, he told us how it came to be.

"You know where bullrakes come from?" he asked. "This is true. Everybody was tongin' and they're goin' along the shore, right? So the

Indians come out shootin' arrows, had to keep goin' back, to deep water, didn't want to get hit. So that's when the bullrakes came in. I don't know if this is true or not, but this is what I was told, that's what I heard . . . Makes sense!"

"They were pissed!" said my father.

"Yeah! They used quahogs for money," said Cap'n Ron. "It's like robbin' a fuckin' bank. Hey! He just made a million dollars on our fuckin' land! White motherfucker . . . That's what started all this trouble with the Indians."

For centuries, even professional quahoggers had only treaded and scratched for quahogs. To tread means simply to wade into the water, feel for quahogs with the feet, dislodge the little animals from the mud, and then either bend down to grab them or slide them up one leg with the opposite foot until they are within easy reach. Rhode Islanders who have treaded tend to take great pride in it, especially if they found themselves capable of the clam-up-the-leg trick.

A scratcher uses a rake of some kind to get at the quahog, either a clam rake—one with several thick tines perpendicular to the handle—or a basket scratcher, essentially a basket fixed to a pole, in the manner of a fishnet, with a short fringe of long teeth on the lip of the basket, opposite the pole, angling over the basket. These tools sufficed for a man to make a living—or at least a meal—for a long, long time, but quahogs had always thrived in their greatest numbers in waters over a fathom deep, even at low tide. The Narragansetts themselves used to dive for them. To get at quahogs in great quantity meant working in deep water.

There are two deepwater rakes, the basket rake and bullrake, each developed from one of the two scratch rakes. The basket rake came about simply as an enlarging and a lengthening of the basket scratcher—lengthening especially, from four feet, to twenty, thirty, or forty. Quahoggers took this absurdly long rake and worked it off of a boat. They would throw the rake out in the water, get it set in the mud, rest the end of the pole on one shoulder, grasp the pole with both hands, and work the rake through the mud, toward the boat—a kind of reverse-lever technique.

David, Arthur, and my father had never heard of them. I told them that some rake-makers offer "overboard" models, which are essentially basket rakes. "Overboard," said my father. "That's where they got the name in the *Pendulum*." A couple of months earlier, the local paper had run an article on the transplant program, when the guys were working out of Greenwich Cove. The caption under the obligatory photo of a shell-fisherman digging away identified the man as working with an overboard rake. Nobody knew where the paper had found the term, or what it even meant. It was both wrong and odd, which is typical for that paper. "I never heard of that," said my father. "Seems like it would hurt to use."

The bullrake evolved from the thick-tined scratch rakes, but where the overboard rake amounted simply to an enlargement of the basket scratcher, the bullrake altered its progenitor's form in three ways: in the rake itself, in the shape of the handle, and in the structure of the handle. The bullrake broadened considerably from the scratch rake; it lengthened its tines and curved them to form a basket.

Then came the grip, the handle shape. Quahoggers wanted a tool they could work in deep water, but they also wanted a different way to work the rake. You use a scratch rake in much the same way you would use any garden rake. In the length of a single summer, you can kill a handle. Come fall, the haft of a scratch rake put to professional use tapers to almost nothing in its middle, merely from the rubbing of hands on wood. Bullrakes introduced the T-handle or splice, the crossbar at the end of the pole. Under this arrangement, the bullraker could achieve symmetry in the stresses he applied to his body. Each arm did work equal to the other. He could also keep his body in a more-natural position; he didn't have to have his arms extended awkwardly in front of him.

But moving the stress away from the body and into the handle meant trouble for the splice. The crossbar would snap sometimes. The splice tapered at its end, the better to fit snugly into the hole routed through the middle of the crossbar. A single nail secured the handle, but where the bar ran narrow around the splice, its wood softened and rotted. Eventually, the zealous bull-raker, pulling the rake hard, would hear a snap and find himself stumbling backwards, with half of the crossbar in each hand and the splice slipping down the gunwale, leaving him with no choice but to flail spasmodically in hopes of catching himself before he went ass-first overboard on the opposite side. "I almost went overboard doin' that a couple of times," said my father.

"Not me," said Arthur.

The third thing the bullrake did was to bring about the invention of the multipart stale. The earliest bullrakes had single stales with a crossbar—just a splice, really. Guys wanted to get into ever-deeper water, however, and the splice was fucking everything up—not because guys were snapping their crossbars all of the time, but because the splice made the bullrake finicky. When you rake quahogs—with any kind of rake—you have to maintain the proper angle between the rake and the bottom. As the depth of the bottom changes, so does the angle of the bullrake to it, unless the quahogger changes the length of the stale. An overboard rake with its straight handle can function over a small range of depths. The quahogger can just let more of the pole extend past his shoulder as he moves into shallower waters. He can continue to work the rake, grasping it in his accustomed manner, until it becomes too vertically inclined to dig at all.

Not so with a T-bar. As the quahogger moves into shallower water, the T-bar rises higher and higher, until the quahogger has no recourse but to work the bullrake like a basket rake. Or the quahogger must push the rake forward until it reaches an unusable angle on the bottom. The crossbar handle forced the invention of the adjustable rake. Guys had to invent specialized stales, made just for bullraking.

"You put your operation together with a hammer," said David. He went into the shanty and brought out a hammer, a collar, and a wedge from some cubbyhole, to a chorus of Jesus Christs from Arthur and my father. The collar was bronze, a ribbon of metal about an inch and a half across; the wedge was steel, a couple of inches long. "When I started quahogging," said David, "that's what you had."

He picked up one of the Keyports from the mound and slipped the collar over the Keyport's shank, the prong of metal sticking out at an angle from the middle of the bullrake's bar. The end of the stale would fit in the collar, alongside the shank, and the shellfisherman would put the wedge in, too, then pound it tight into the collar, securing all four pieces together. "In there someplace, I have a twenty-foot wooden main stale," he said, then gestured to where the end of the pole would fit in with the shank.

"Why don't you go find it?" suggested my father, helpfully.

"That would be the main stale," said David. He paused and took up two lengths of wood from a corner, one of which ended in a T-bar. The T-bar had a notch at its other end, making a sort of stunted L-shape. The other pole was notched in the same way, but at both ends. The notches fitted together like the locked hands of a wrestler, and two steel rings would collar the poles, one ring at either side of where the notches mate. "That's the handle or the splice," said David. "And then you have the double-notched pieces, which were called go-betweens. So: the splice, then you had a go-between, then you had a main stale," says David. "And it was all put together with a hammer."

The collar and wedge arrangement and the wooden stales themselves didn't make for the toughest of instruments. The quahoggers used fir wood, mostly, not a timber of the strongest grain. My grandfather was one of the first to take wooden stales into quite deep water off of Patience Island in the bay. He swung over thirty-five feet of stale, and, by Ray Wyss's account, busted about a main stale a week. It was in those days that the bullrake, meaning the rake and the stale, began to become the truly silly implement it is today.

The ridiculousness of the bullrake came into sharp relief when Arthur offered a bit of hyperbole about Nick Carcieri. "They used to say that Nick Carcieri could go up on the roof of any house on Main Street and dig quahogs out of the sidewalk," said Arthur. That's good, folksy humor, and the governor has certainly recounted the joke on a number of occasions, but it's also crazy. If you can dig quahogs out of the sidewalk, why would you go up on the roof of a house to do it? Because you're using a bullrake, and that's how bullrakes are shaped. Otherwise, you wouldn't be a bullraker. There's a logic at work here, and it underscores how strange a tool the bullrake is. Using a bullrake is like going up on a roof with a thirty-foot-long leaf rake, blindfolding yourself, and raking your neighbor's lawn. It's a weird business.

Lengthening out the stale became a major preoccupation of the bullraker, especially for guys like my grandfather, who were looking to reach a length equal to the muscle they could bring to bear on the work. A guy wanted to be able to reach as deep as he could, meaning with a length of rake that he could just lift out of the water with a full haul. When made of wood, the stale would snap before a guy could reach his own physical limit. Aluminum took care of that problem. Aluminum stales fitted bullrakers' needs perfectly, and the guys made a quick transition to them. Where once you used a hammer to hook up, today, you use a screwdriver or a wrench. The collar and wedge are gone, as are the steel rings, and this is for the better. A wedge wears out its collar pretty quickly and rings slip all too frequently. Hose clamps, bolt collars, and three-eighths-inch bolts secure a guy's operation, and these instruments have become standard, ubiquitous equipment for the bullraker. They have become part of his signature accoutrements.

When my family went down to a big reunion one summer, my father's cousin, Joe Greene, a quahogger, had cooked up a huge pot of quahog chowder. The pot was so big that any normal ladle would have quickly disappeared into its ten-gallon depths. So Joe took another ladle, slipped a couple of hose clamps over it, set it end to end with the first one, and clamped the two together. That's the influence of the aluminum stale on the inventive mind of the quahogger.

A few old-timers still prefer a wooden splice—they like the feel of wood under their hands—but once you get past the T-bar, even their rigs are aluminum. The increased durability of hose clamps, bolts, and aluminum stales also allows the digger to work his rake harder, to exert more force through his equipment.

The Keyport didn't take well to such rough handling, just as human fingers do not. Each of its tines moves independently of all the others, like the tines on a hay rake, which is designed for flexibility. A tine will twist, bend, and spring under too much force, either pushing back against the digger or burying itself in the mud or squeezing together with other tines. Shellfishermen needed new, stiffer designs to keep up with the increased power that aluminum gave them.

David hefted another rake from our pile, one quite different from the Keyport. This one no longer resembled a hay rake–cum–rusty lawn ornament. It had a more specialized character; it looked like it was designed for a very narrow purpose.

"A mud rake," said David. "Modern heritage . . . This is a Roy Schultz rake, an Armor Instrument rake, because it's got a stainless-steel pin, where eastern rakes, which were made out on Long Island, had a steel pin." He was referring to a nib sticking perpendicularly out of the end of the shank. The pin fits into a hole in the stale, further stabilizing the connection between stale and rake. The mud rake came around in the 1950s, and it came with little uniformity. The guys also call it a Teardrop, a John

German, a Long Island Bubble, or a Maddalena rake. They're not all really the same thing, but they're close. Where the tines of the Keyport hold a fairly uniform curve, the basket-forming rods of this rake slant straight out at a 45 degree angle from the back bar. They remain straight for a foot or so and then curve in, and when their tips come even with the back bar, they sink into the front bar, rather than taper into digging teeth. The front bar holds the rods rigidly apart, as does another cross-rod that lies across the basket rods at about the point where they begin to curve. Further, the front bar serves as a base for a new kind of teeth, about three and a half inches long, very slim, sharp, and individually welded to the bar. In other words, it's a basket with teeth, but it's different from the overboard rake.

The mud rake maintains the skeleton of the Keyport, rather than ape the basket structure of the overboard. This is the key feature of the bullrake, the feature that makes it indisputably the descendant of the Keyport and an exemplar of a kind of parallel evolution. The Keyport never really made any sense. Why not start out with sides—or with some rods across the tines to keep them rigid? Why not start with a basket? The design of the Keyport seems to be one of those inventions in which the inventor stripped a piece of equipment down to its most elementary components, then slowly built it back up, until it worked even better than the original. Except this process took about eighty years.

When it came around, the mud rake quickly revealed its advantages over the Keyport. The front bar and back bar of the mud rake are parallel; without its teeth, the rake sits perfectly level. The Keyport would sit just as flush, but with the tips of its teeth on the surface. The mud rake's teeth extend through the muddy bottom of the bay without decreasing the volume of its basket. A well-handled bullrake digs with the front and back bars on the bottom and the teeth sunk in the mud. The teeth disturb quahogs from their rest, and, with the proper tooth angle, guide the quahogs into the basket of the rake, which can now fill its basket to its entirety.

The mud rake is more elegant than the Keyport, too. Gas or electric welding holds it together, rather than blacksmithing. It has thinner rods than the Keyport does, and so, even with its greater number of rods and bars, it weighs less. It is stronger, lighter, and more efficient. And it was not merely Roy Schultz and the Maddalenas and John German who were experimenting with these new breeds of rake.

"They were playing; they were learning. The rake was changing from the Keyport," said David. "Guys were doing a lot of different things, and your grandfather and my dad got in on the action." A second mud rake lies in the pile, one unlike every other rake there, because, except for its few remaining teeth, it bears no rust. My grandfather and David's father put together a stainless-steel rake, a great effort back then—so great an effort, in fact, that stainless steel would not become the bullraking norm for another twenty years.

"Your grandfather could weld, but my dad couldn't," said David. "So, my dad, he'd go down in his basement and he'd drill everything and pin it; nothing was welded." At first David's father fashioned working bullrakes with no welds of any kind, neither blacksmith nor gas. But he eventually learned other techniques, too. He took a blacksmithing course; he picked up a Montgomery and Ward buzz box welder, which allowed him to do arc or electric welding. For a couple of decades, he tried things out, making rakes for himself, for Arthur, for his friends. It's hard to tell who came up with what variation when, or how variations disseminated to major manufacturers, but Howard and a few guys like him—Duke Windsor, Ray Wyss, my grandfather—came up with enough innovations that some became standard, brought together in the form of the Rhode Island rake. The Rhode Island is the classic bullrake, in my mind, because it's the kind my father used. My father and I had brought one with us to the shanty, just like he used to do every day.

"The guys call it a Maddalena rake, too, all right?" said David. "And it came from Long Island; down there, they call it a Rhode Island rake, y'know?" The Maddalenas became so well known that shellfishermen, confusingly or confusedly, attributed two different rakes to them, neither of which were actually invented by a Maddalena. But, then, guys sometimes say the Drews invented the bullrake, too, because the Drews made so many rakes in the eighties, and because the Drew family has been a fixture on the cove and on the bay for over a century.

The Rhode Island rake is bigger than the mud rake, and has even more rods. Mainly, its increased utility comes from its increased volume, a result of the deformation of its basket. A mud rake, like the Keyport, shares the same basic form as your curled fingers. The Rhode Island rake has a "kick in the back," as David puts it: a bend in the rods just a few inches above the back bar. Where the mud rake's rods run straight from the back bar, the Rhode Island's upward bend increases its volume, as does a further extension of the portion of its basket that curves. Shellfishermen call the latter part "the bubble," which makes a lot of sense, given that they call the mud rake the bubble rake, not the Rhode Island.

The Rhode Island rake dominated an era of bullraking, roughly the period of my father's prime. These days, it has lost place of primacy to the suitcase rake, which is the kind David and his father used to make most often.

"My father made the jig," said David. "We bent all the rods, the wires, cut 'em to length. My father-in-law had had a stroke, so we set him up at his house, cutting and bending all the wires. My father still drilled the bar, put the teeth in, and I tack-welded them there. He'd load the thing up; I'd weld it, slide the thing off, and it would be the back bar and the wires. We'd put the side pieces all on. By the time I got done putting the side pieces and the tongue on, my father had the jig loaded up. We'd load another rake."

They did it all in a little shanty, which, during those days, was stuffed to the rafters with fishing equipment. They had a good time with their business, especially making rakes, which, right at the time of the Drews' heyday, had entered into a period of considerable chaos, with several different styles of rake in competition. A customer could call on David to make a mud rake, a Rhode Island rake, the new suitcase and pocketbook rakes, or any combination thereof, as well as custom modifications to rakes. Affordability made much of this experimentation possible: a rake cost less than half a day's pay—cheap enough for whimsy. Guys could come in and order this rake or that one, try them all out, toss them if they didn't like them.

"A guy would buy a rake because somebody had a good day with it," said David. "A guy made a ton of money down at Quonset one day—big dollars. The next day, we had a line out the door wanting the exact same rake he had. Because you're working near a guy, he's beating you, and he's beating you consistently—and in your mind you're just as good a digger as he is, so it's gotta be the equipment."

Equipment does make a difference in performance, but so does mental attitude—what David calls the "between-your-ears" problem. Fishing involves gambling; it is extremely difficult to make consistent catches from one day to the next, which is to say that it invites superstition, or, to put it another way, the volatility of fishing requires a good imagination to conquer. To hit the quahogs, you have to reckon with a dizzying number of variables. Naturally, the mind tends to introduce factors without a rational basis.

"A guy broke a tooth in the middle," said David, "and he says, 'I know it's not true, David, but I got a line of quahogs right down the bay, all fallin' out that hole.'" One of the principal jobs David did down the shanty at that time was to re-tooth rakes, replacing teeth that had snapped off or worn down. But just as baseball players have superstitions about their bats and cooks have irrational beliefs about their knives, so shellfishermen can develop notions about their rakes that make no sense, but still affect performance.

"A guy brought in a rake that had a broken tooth," said David. "Guy says, 'Ah, I'm doin' great with this rake.' I said, 'Really?' He says, 'Yeah.' 'Good!' I said. 'It's one of my re-tooths.' He says, 'No; I don't use re-tooths; they don't work right.' I said, 'You can say what you want, but it's welded on the front, not welded in the back. I don't weld it in the back; it's one of my re-tooths.' I said, 'Where'd you get it from?' He said, 'I got it from Crockett.' 'Oh yeah; I re-tooth rakes for them.'"

David laughed. "He came back to me, probably a week later, had to buy a new rake. He said, 'David, the minute you told me that rake was a re-tooth, I never caught another quahog with it.'" The cheap rakes made it possible for the guy to indulge his irrationality. Money makes superstitions go 'round.

It's just the same with the outboards. Prosperity led to new technologies which led to new indulgences. With an outboard, you could play hide-and-seek over the width and breadth of the bay. Cheap steel and a boom time for quahogs meant a bullraker could invent taboos for himself. That's how innovation happened: leisure, materials, a hopping market, flush customers. No pressure, no needs, no necessity.

All three of the men around the table had bought into that program. They took up hard, vital work. Their fathers and often their grandfathers had done the same thing. They put themselves in a position where their work both paid them well enough and satisfied their consciences, which left them at ease to spend their idle hours hammering a forge or welding wire. My grandfather, long dead and gone, did so; Howard, too. They had made those rakes on the deck, and therein lay the pleasures of their lives. They'd been just old rakes to me my whole life, these primitive Keyports, but David and my father pointed out where my grandfather's hands had shaped them. Those side-bars my grandfather had braised on: Why'd he pick that flat steel? Why'd he braise them? Why did any of the men who shaped those rakes make the decisions they did?

Those old bullrakes are almost absurdly useless: rusted steel in the form of a tool with an extremely narrow use. It's inconceivable that anyone will ever work with a Keyport again, but the line of descent matters, the intricacies of the rake matter. They are tools that have kept the bay well. It pays to know them and the men who made them. It pays to see the elements that had to be in place in order for the bullrake to flourish, to see that innovation is simply working made into play.

Sometimes the play gets turned back into work. This reversal happened to Howard and David, who turned a rake-making hobby into paying jobs. Luckily, the sense of fun never left them. What were they selling bullrakes for? To earn a good-enough living that they could take time off to make bullrakes? They did all right with the business, and the guys down the shore gave them shit for it. "We were never gonna get rich selling shellfishing equipment to quahoggers," said David. "But there's Ralph Greene up at The Oaks tellin' everybody that Drew and Son had to loan Warren Finn some money to get through the winter." That's part of the attraction of the water, too; you don't hang around down the shore if you don't want to get wet.

The parallel lines of descent—man and rake—both express the same sort of thing: a sort of excess. It was especially apparent when David and Howard were making rakes together, because lines crossed at that point, lines of family and lines of rake. They crossed and then diverged. Two rake-making families, several new kinds of rake, just at that moment— not bonded by blood but wound together by steel.

Out on Cape Cod, you can find another rake-making family, one of the last manufacturers of shellfishing equipment: the R. A. Ribb Company. Ron Ribb started the business in the early 1980s, and his wife and two daughters run it now. Ron had grown up in Cumberland, a semirural town in Rhode Island. He studied philosophy in college and considered getting a master's in the discipline at the University of Chicago. He was a musician and young and handsome, and, almost of necessity, at loose ends. Then he made his way to the Cape. Though he had no fishing background, he took immediately to working on the water. He became a bullraker.

"I think that he came to Cape Cod and it spoke to him, because with all this philosophy that he had been taking in as a young adult, he found comfort, solace, and truth in working with his hands, getting back to basics, living a life of self-sustenance—all these things he never had in his childhood," says his daughter Greta, now in her early thirties. All of this everyone knew; they thought Ron had found his rightful place in the world. "No one really knew who he was though," Greta says.

Ron had been a bullraker for several years when a friend of his, an old rake-maker who had begun to feel his age, suggested that Ron take up the trade. "Frank said, 'I'm tired of doing this . . . you wanna do it?'" recalls Maggie, Ron's widow. "Frank told him there are three styles of rake; it's easy enough. And Ron said, 'Okay.' I can remember Ron practicing the welding; he was twenty-five years old. We got married, bought a house, and we started the business."

Next thing, the mid-eighties boom in quahogging hit. Narragansett Bay recorded its biggest landings since the fifties. "Ron had to get out of fishing, because he was working in here thirteen hours a day," says Maggie.

Ron started making rakes in his barn; he did his heat-treating there in a forge, judging the temper by the color of the metal. Then he built a workshop dedicated solely to rake-making, and brought in machining equipment. "He had to find a way to automate the tooth-making," says Maggie. "I mean, all the teeth." She sighs. "We hand-made all the teeth; that was my job, cutting the teeth. The kids used to sort them."

Any bullrake can be expressed in terms of six qualities: tang angle, tooth bar or tooth angle, tooth curve, tooth count, basket shape, and throat opening. Tang is the same as the shank, the bar that connects to the stale; when the back bar lies flat, the rake-maker measures the tang angle relative to the flat surface. Tooth angle is measured relative to the front bar. A tooth bar is simply a second bar welded to the front bar. You weld the teeth to the tooth bar, so that you can easily remove the whole

Ron Ribb making a bullrake, circa 1980. RIBB FAMILY

bar from the rake when replacing teeth. Stainless steel makes this con-struction particularly important. Tooth may run straight or have a curve to them. Basket shape is obvious. Throat opening really comes into play with the suitcase and the pocketbook rakes. The throat is the same as the mouth of any basket. Closing the throat is like putting a lid on the basket—a partial lid, to allow the quahogs to come in, but not to fall out. The tooth count measures the width of the rake.

The suitcase rake has a basket shape considerably different from other rakes. Ribb greatly extended the forward bubble but flattened it at the same time. The rake's basket does indeed resemble a piece of vintage lug-gage. The suitcase is blocky, almost willfully inelegant. He also reduced the tooth count, from twenty-four or so to eighteen or so, depending on the customer's preference. Lastly, he closed the throat, which actually added to the effectiveness of the rake, as fewer quahogs would fall free from it during hauling.

Ribb's designs became hot very quickly. David made loads of them. These rakes held terrific amounts of product, but they also required greater skill on the part of the shellfisherman. The suitcase is especially sensitive to changes in digging angle. Its extended basket can bang into the bottom if the quahogger runs too short a stale with it. Old-timers often didn't get along with the suitcase.

"My father hated 'em cuz you can't pick from the rake," said David. The closed throat inhibited the ingress of the bullraker's hands as much as it prevented the quahogs' egress.

Many old-timers stuck with their old rakes, but younger guys took right to the suitcases and pocketbooks. David remembers a guy from Warwick who brought his son into the shop to buy his first rake and set of stales—a young blond kid, maybe twelve or thirteen. David sold the kid a pocketbook—really just a smaller suitcase, fourteen-tooth or so, which Ribb developed with John Linnell, a friend of his—but first David made him promise he would go to college.

The suitcase all but dominates bullraking in Narragansett Bay. We had one down the shanty with us, one of David's manufacture, with all of the trimmings: skids on the side to keep the rake in place while work-ing on hard bottom, and a decker tang—a shank not on the back bar, but extending from the basket itself, which supposedly put the rake at just the right angle to encourage bycatch to fall out of the rake. "It never worked for me," said my father. He splurged on a deluxe rake and didn't like it—which is how invention goes. Even more than the design, however, there was another innovation—more of an investment, really—made by Ron Ribb that would have a bigger impact on the industry: stainless steel.

The rakes are all stainless steel now, even the mud rakes and the Rhode Islands. My father got out of quahogging before the change took hold, and David got out of rake-making not long after.

"They came out with stainless-steel rakes, and the machinery was way too involved, too expensive," he said. "I could weld it, but I couldn't bend it, cut it. All the jigs weren't the same, because the temper is harder. Everything I had, we had to re-tool." He shrugged. "Just wasn't worth it."

Rakes last forever today, and they cost a ton—three or four hundred dollars. Nobody gets rid of a rake instead of getting a re-tooth anymore. That religion has become too costly. Guys remain finicky about their teeth, just not so profligate. The new distribution of wealth becalmed their superstitions, just as it unwound the Drews from the Ribbs. For a time, the two families worked simultaneously, producing rakes of similar design; then they parted ways on the matter of steel. David and his father continued the supply business for a while, but closed it down as Howard got older. They still had the work of their leisure, of course, and this shared time of theirs came to have infinite importance. When Howard was dying of cancer, he and David built a boat together—or started to. They both knew they wouldn't finish it. Yet, they worked.

For the Ribbs, the work continued, too, and with similar significance.

Sixteen years ago, Ron committed suicide. It came out of nowhere. Like Billy Benoit, Ron went down to the shore in the morning to take his own life, but unlike Billy, his act had no comprehensibility to it. He didn't have any cancer; he was not old. For those close to him, confronting his death meant confronting the fact that some part of Ron Ribb—a large, powerful part of the man—had remained hidden from them, and it was likely that this part was the source of immense, insurmountable pain. His family had to reckon with this.

The Ribb women came together about a year after Ron's death to talk about reopening the business themselves, Maggie, Greta, and Kersti, the youngest daughter. Fishermen wanted them to keep the shop going. The women had all the tools and equipment; they had a customer base; they had all the contacts; they even had a little experience making rakes—but still, Christ, the significance of it.

"I remember having discussions," says Greta, "making decisions, because it was not a profitable venture for us to get back into the business after Dad passed away. We had a lot of odds working against us. A lot of the manufacturing techniques weren't even written down; they just passed on with Dad. I remember racking my brain, trying to think back to my childhood, watching him do certain things, operating certain machines. My father let me and my sister play around with the welder and stuff, but it wasn't anything I was interested in doing. I was a musician, I was an artist; I didn't know anything about quahog rakes."

Greta was remembering the man in order to get at the details of the rake. No other evidence could more strongly adduce the connection between family and rake, between past and future—but what a price to pay for that evidence. All of the things that must have come to the fore in the unearthing of memories for that purpose. Recalling those childhood days, searching for clues, could only have aggravated the shock of Ron's death, perhaps joyfully, perhaps hurtfully; either way, it could only be done with immense courage.

And then there was working in the shop. Ron's shop. The R. A. Ribb Company operates out of the backyard of the Ribb home, which is, to all appearances, a tidy, inconspicuous cul-de-sac domicile. Out back reside the workshops and a couple of pickup trucks loaded with odds and ends. One of the trucks bears a Buzzcocks bumper sticker. Inside of an old barn is the rake shop, loaded with machining equipment, bundles of metal rods, racks of rakes, a workspace warmed Franklin-style, by a woodstove in the middle, made of two fifty-five-gallon drums stacked on their sides. Greta's paper coffee cup sits atop the stove. Ron built it all. He shoved all of the machinery in there. He poured the floors. Every bit of their shop and their trade bears the imprint of Ron Ribb's hand—but the women now share everything with him, not he with them. It is theirs first. Alongside the feeling for their work that comes from their remembrance of a husband and a father, they have an equal, if intertwined, feeling for their present life of making rakes.

They themselves delight in the fact of their unusual livelihood, a family of women making rakes. They enjoy the incongruity that they present to themselves. Maggie's an organist; Kersti's a psychiatry student at Yale; Greta's a musician, an artist, a florist (she welds her own wreath frames). You can see the pleasure Maggie takes in complaining about sharpening teeth in the little grinding room on the side of the shop, a room more exposed to the cold: "It's the worst job, the worst job in the shop . . . I usually get it." But it's also clearly a happy thing for her, that she finds herself to be a mom who sharpens bullrake teeth.

The same goes for Greta, when she explains one of the odder and more difficult tasks she has to do. "Some guys have me weld butter knives onto their scratch rakes," she says. "They're back with the things like every other month, because they've worn down so fast—that's commercial guys in Chatham. There's a group of guys that just swear by it. They make me cut the handles off of butter knives and weld the blades to the rakes, literally butter knives. There was this great guy—he recently passed on—he used to hook me up. I don't know if he'd go to junk shops or what, but he had a limitless supply of knives, and whenever I ran into him at the coffee shop, he'd just have a handful there waitin' for me, so I'd never be short on butter knives.

"There was another rake-maker in the neighboring town, named Ben Bach, and he did mainly scratch rakes. He was like the butter-knife king, so when he passed away, then we got saddled with the burden. Whenever I make a butter-knife rake, I'm like, 'It didn't come from this shop.' They're horrible to make, but they just go through the sugar sand so smoothly."

Scratch rakes constitute the majority of the Ribbs' business, which keeps the women busy, as they are the ones who weld up the smaller rakes, while Grant, an old friend of Ron's, welds the larger rakes. Grant can feel the pressure when a big rake order comes in—say, twenty Long Island bubble rakes—but he's philosophical: "It's easy . . . Take a rack full o' stock, cut it up into pieces, throw it in the jig, roll it up, bend it up, box it up—that's it!"

Yet the simple process requires the practiced hands of a knowledgeable craftsman. He can't just follow a pattern. A rake-maker has to know how bullraking works, especially when it comes to suitcase rakes. He even has to instruct guys on their use, from time to time. "A Rhode Island rake is a lot more forgiving as far as fishability," says Grant. "If you're off by a foot in your handle length, you can still catch clams. There's a little more finesse with a suitcase; if we have a rake that comes in and the guy says,

'This thing isn't fishin',' and I look at it and see the whole front end of the back bar is shined, I say, 'You gotta go with a shorter handle,' and then if they come in and say, 'It's not fishin',' and you see no shine at all in here, then I say, 'You need to go with a longer handle.' What you want to see is shine back there; three-quarters to two-thirds should be shined up."

"People don't think of them as precision instruments," says Greta. "But they are . . . and they need to be made with that attitude."

Those who romanticize the bullraker tend to overlook this truth. Even bullrakers don't always pay it heed. When ordinary people take the time to wonder what qualities make a bullraker successful, they usually come up with three of Ray Wyss's four essentials: bay knowledge, health, and will. Lots of bullrakers come to the same conclusion: It's all ruggedness and willpower and knowing the bay. Ray Wyss also marked skill as a requirement, however—skill with the rake. And that's what Greta and Grant are talking about. They make their rakes for use by people who work at the highest level. It's hard to believe that any such person as a highly skilled bullraker could possibly exist, because the bullrake seems so absurd, and because it's fun to think of the bullraker as only a bull. How could anyone use a fifty-foot-long, fifty-pound tool with precision, underwater, out of sight, on a moving boat? But it's true, and the notion shouldn't be all that surprising. All excellence is, at first blush, incredible.

Don Wilcox, one of the Wilcoxes of Wickford—a fishing family that had great rivalries with some of the Apponaug families—spent most of his life working out of big trawlers and dredge boats, but he also worked as a quahogger from time to time. He knew full-timers well, too. Not only did his family rival those from Apponaug, but they also intermarried with them. Don is Tim Trim's uncle; he is uncle or cousin or in-law to half the guys in Apponaug Cove. He worked with many of the best quahoggers on the bay, and he paid attention to them. Don's in his mid-sixties, thin and long-faced. He walks with a limp. His house rests right on Ten Rod Road, in between the two grand plots that belonged to my great-grandfather Alexander, and not far from Wickford Junction, which used to be called Huling Corners. In his small, tidy home, decorated with maritime themes down to a plush lobster on the television stand, he sits in his easy chair and spreads a shawl over his lap.

"You get next to them, you know you're gonna get your ass whipped," he says. He means all of those hard-core guys like Tim Trim, like Tommy Cole, like Bunky Bennett, like Nick Carcieri. "They're very precise and they work like bulls—that's why they call it bullrakin'," he says. "I think that when they get tired, they work harder. Somebody else gets tired, they slow down; instead, bullrakers pour on the second adrenaline. When I get tired, I put a float on my rake, to hold it up a little bit. Timmy! Timmy puts another weight on! He'll put a ten-pound weight on the goddamn rake! I say, 'Holy Christ, I'm puttin' a float on, he's puttin' a ten-pound weight on! Oh, Jesus Christ! They're animals!'"

That's ruggedness and will. That's what Ray Wyss means by the phrase "savage worker." But working like a fool is not the only thing. You can't just shove a rake around in a frenzy and expect to get anything out of it. As is always the case with demonstrations of skill, the best quahoggers bind their savagery with forethought, with finesse, and even with elegance, all in order to direct their energies with precision.

"Everything had to be just right," says Don. "Whether makin' a bullrake, filin' it down, the boat . . . When I say makin' a bullrake, I mean setting things up: stale, whatever. Everything had to be just so. When the tide's droppin' or comin' in, and when they got the right angles on their stale, every fifteen minutes or so, they would adjust the stale a couple inches," says Don. "Their rake was at the right angle all the time. Every fifteen minutes you'd see 'em loosenin' up the stale and changin' the length, about every six inches o' tide, they used to change it."

Don is describing techne—not merely technique—but *techne*, the knowledge of crafts, the so-called mechanical arts, the knowledge of how to apply principles to achieve desired practical consequences. *Techne*, a term from Greek philosophy, connotes an exaltation of craft, which is what Don wants to get across about these bullrakers. When you get certain quahoggers to talk about the guys they admire, guys like Tommy Cole, they'll actually talk in lofty terms.

Walter Scott, the quahogger turned painter whose work graced the governor's office for a time, has an eye for this level of proficiency, and for the habits that help to make it possible. "Tommy Cole, Georgie Fecteau," he says. "There are certain fishermen—Arthur Drew, the Bennetts from Apponaug, Bunky, and there's Doc Haley outta Oakland Beach—these people I'm naming ... It's not that they're fishermen; it's the *type* of fishermen they are. Everything they have has to be perfect; they're like the old-fashioned sea captains. They're the salt of the earth, right as rain ... I'm tryin' to think of all the adjectives that fit them. These are the type of guys, when they went to work, when they came in after an average day's work—and they're highliners, top scorers—they didn't look like they had worked. And they were old men. Their clothes weren't dirty. Their boats were spic-and-span, their trucks—everything was immaculate and custom and done just so. There was just somethin' about their whole demeanor that just set them apart from all the other guys.

"You know both are good fishermen, Tommy Cole, Georgie Fecteau. Tommy, kinda like myself—the boat might get cleaned, it might not. The truck? Ah, more important to get in and get that beer and cigarette, relax after a hard day's work—and I'm not begrudgin' him, he's fully entitled to it. Whereas other fishermen, just the opposite. Everything had to be absolutely perfect, scrubbed down, in its own little place. You could call 'em control freaks, I guess, neatniks, but they were really somethin' to behold ... and Georgie Fecteau was one of those guys."

Not everyone has this appreciation for the niceties of bullraking. There are hierarchies to techne, just as techne itself submits to a hierarchy. The carpenter might think his trade allows for a greater development of skillfulness than does bullraking, just as the old slave-master philosophers of Greece considered episteme, philosophical, or mathematical knowledge superior to techne. It's too bad: Socrates was well respected for his healthy constitution, his physical hardiness, and, of course, his strong will. He was rugged, as well as reflective. He might have made a good quahogger, and perhaps the work would have rid him of his nihilism. As things turned out, the hierarchies of the ancient world remain today: Theoretical knowledge scorns practical knowledge, and there are rankings of techne. Ask any dirt physicist. Ask any carpenter. It's always worthwhile to ignore hierarchies, however, to look at things through the eyes of those who admire them, rather than those who despise them.

"Tommy was good; he was the best quahogger in the bay," says Don. "They used to have bullraking contests. He had trophies—he's still got 'em, I think. He's got trophies he won, over in Bristol, five years in a row.

In fact, he won it so many times, everybody said it was rigged, and so they didn't have it no more."

The trophies attest to Tommy's skill, but what was his actual techne? What did he know how to do? He adjusted his stales ever so carefully, in accord with the tide; there's that. But he also had a way of setting his bull-rake just right on the stale. He used to take washers or even quarters and place them in between the bullrake's shank and the stale. He did this to set the rake at exactly the right angle for digging quahogs on the particular bottom he was working. Little wedges or shims of about a sixteenth of an inch on a rig that could be thirty or forty or fifty feet long, or longer. It's hard to see how such an adjustment could possibly have mattered, but Tommy did win his trophies, and, whether his tang shims put the rake at the proper angle or his mind in the proper attitude, precision absolutely matters to the bullraker.

The techne of bullraking guides the techne of rake-making. When Greta welds up a scratch rake, she does it as if Tommy Cole is going to come out of retirement and start digging up the beach. Each little rake head has its individuality, in the tiny blobs of metal in its seams, but each also conforms to an exacting standard. When the women stack the scratch rakes in stands, one rake over the next, but crosswise, making an "X," the rakes fit together as snugly as machine-pressed silverware. Yet, Greta has no illusions about the use these rakes will see.

"People love to go recreational shellfishing now," says Greta. "People love to be out near the water, and a lot of people can't afford to take their big speedboat out anymore. People can't afford to go deep-sea fishing, but they want to be by the water; they want to be getting exercise and fishing somehow, and those are the people that usually opt to buy a nice, stain-less, fully loaded recreational rake and be what I like to call 'quahog jocks.' People'll be on vacation and they'll have half a dozen guests, and they want rakes for all those people—'Come out, try it, dig your own food.' They can feel alive for a day."

She leans against the woodstove. Greta's tall, thin, brown-haired, and sharply pretty. "It feels real good," she says. "It's like the resurgence of gar-dening, all this resurgence of self-sustenance. I think that the recreational sales go along with that, this whole back-to-nature thing . . . even if a lot of it is false!"

Greta has a discerning eye, almost a cynical one. She has no mercy on herself. The question of what she wants to be true does not enter into her estimation of what the truth actually is. Perhaps she would like for her rakes to be the tool of a genuine self-reliance movement, but that hasn't happened yet, and it's nothing she really needs. All of the care and thought that the Ribb women put into their work responds to the needs of the work and recreation that will be done with them, and to all that could be done with them. The angle of a tooth, the bend of a wire, the thickness of a weld—all of these things have a clear purpose to them. They have a directly observable reality shaping them. And they also have ineffability behind them.

Greta and Maggie and Kersti can never completely untangle what their trade means to them from the meaning it held for Ron, and so the significance of the trade they ply is commingled with a sense of reckoning. They reckon not only with Ron's suicide, but with his passion for life. The fact that Ron died, and the way he died, changes the meaning of each tool, each steel rod in the shop, the work that takes place there—even the shop itself—but all of these things already brimmed with meaning because of Ron's life.

This same phenomenon, with different shades of meaning, happens for David, each time he goes out to work the water, or even when he goes down to the shanties. Not just Howard, but now, Arthur, too, is gone. When the Ribb women build rakes with their own hands, based on the patterns that Ron used, or when David takes ashore the floats of his docks, and Arthur's, they all experience what anyone who has ever built a rake or brought a dock in for the winter has experienced—but they also face uncertainty. That's because no experience is ever fully known without talking about it with other people, and the people with whom they would most want to speak—the people who could best help them to understand what it is that they do when they build a rake, or move a dock—are gone. There will always remain some huge aspect of themselves that they cannot come to know, because the people who could have helped them to know it have died.

This is a hard truth, but it's true nonetheless. It is also fortunate. There are many who do not have the opportunity for this reckoning; or, worse still, they had it and then lost it.

Chapter Six

Eulogies and Secret Codes

And the Lord said to Moses, "The daughters of Zelophehad are right.
You shall give them possession of an inheritance
Among their father's brothers and transfer the inheritance of their
father to them.
And you shall speak to the people of Israel, saying,
"If a man dies and has no son, then you shall transfer his inheritance
to his daughter."

—Numbers 27:6–11

MY FATHER AND I ENROLLED IN AN OYSTER-FARMING CLASS, UP AT Roger Williams University. It started in late October, the classes took place at night, and they were free, though we had to pay for photocopies of the readings. Once a week, I'd take the train down to Providence; my father would pick me up in my mother's car, because trucks are unwieldy in the city, and we'd make the long and winding trip out to Bristol.

Dale Leavitt taught the class. Dale's a tenured professor at Roger Williams University and a major player in shellfish aquaculture in Rhode Island. He's cool; he's got a long ponytail, a full mustache, round eyeglasses, bright eyes, a respectable beer belly, and tattoos up and down his arms—tattoos of fish, an octopus, seaweed. Dale's got a tough hippie look—original hippie, as he's in his early sixties. He's active, too, a scientist who sinks his hands in the mud and who takes pride not only in tying good nautical knots himself, but also in training his PhD students to do the same.

The summer after the oyster class, Dale and I and one of his student workers, a young woman named Kayla, went down to Goose Neck Cove in Newport, to meet a guy from the National Oceanic and Atmospheric Administration (NOAA) who was looking to work with Roger Williams University on an oyster-restoration project. The idea was to see if Goose Neck was a suitable site for planting oysters.

Goose Neck is an odd saltwater pond. It has shrunk considerably over the years, beginning in the 1930s, when the State dug ditches extending from it to lower mosquito populations. We put on hip waders before we went in. It was rotten mud, and deep. We had to wade carefully and stay as close as we could to the grassy shallows. The rest of the group had a better time of it than I did. My 210 pounds of solid muscle drove into the bottom like a steel beam. Surely that was the reason I ended up yards behind everyone, ripping up the long grass that sprouted from the clumps of earth that breached the water in my efforts to haul myself out of the sucking mud. Eventually, we ended up crashing through the reeds, which were mostly some kind of phragmite, and saplings and bushes on the banks, rather than slogging through the mud—which meant that the hip waders quickly became not a way to avoid getting soaked, but armor against the cutting edges of the vegetation.

Dale kept his eyes open for water suitable for oysters. Where we'd gone in and where I'd sunk, the bottom would have oozed right over the poor little mollusks. He needed to find firmer mud, so we stomped through the brush, following the eastern edge of the cove. Then we got kind of lost. Or, really, we found that we could see the road we wanted to get back to, but could not discern any path leading to it, except the long trail behind us. No path led up to the houses perched above the cove, either. We ended up crawling through thirty feet of small trees, over and under branches, to reach Hazard Road, which runs, like an homage to Robert Moses, straight through the upper part of the cove. It's good to see a tenured professor, especially one in his sixties, crawling through damp underbrush, clambering over the branches of small trees, and rolling out onto the road like a trespassing hobo. The guys down the shore groove on Dale for stuff like this—and also because he knows them well enough to speak to their natures when he instructs them on oyster farming.

"Aquaculture is not fishing," said Dale, on the first night of class. "It is not like fishing, other than you get wet when you fall overboard. It requires the discipline of a farmer to do it. We tried many years ago to do a training program for displaced offshore fishermen; that was an abysmal failure. With fishing, you want to work intensively for a week and then take a week off in a drunken stupor; you can't do that as a shellfish farmer, or any kind of farmer; you have to be willing to tend your crop on a fairly regular basis; otherwise, things are gonna get ahead of you. Your oysters are gonna start growing way too fast. They're gonna start overcrowding your bags, which means they're gonna start stunting their growth, which means you're not going to get your product to market when you think you are—or all the fouling organisms are gonna plug up all the meshes in your bags, and there's not going to be any air circulating through your bags, and all your oysters are going to suffocate and they'll never get to market."

The class was a mix. There were several fishermen—my father, a woman from Cape Cod, another father and son from Rhode Island. A few guys from the Natural Resources Conservation Service, a federal program that funds oyster-restoration projects. A guy who thought he might take up oyster farming rather than go to law school. A guy in law school who thought he might take up oyster farming.

Dale had us all introduce ourselves in class. That's how I learned Chelsea Ricciarelli was there. I had attended Chelsea's father's funeral. Lou Ricciarelli had been a quahogger—a diver, not a bullraker—and he had asphyxiated while working the previous summer. He used an air pump, tether, and helmet setup, which allows for hours of work underwater. Something went wrong with the pump, which was old; he probably trusted it for too long. The Warwick Fire Department's dive team found him suspended in the water, the day after he didn't come home.

Lou also farmed oysters, on two leases, one of which lay just past the breakers that shelter the small wharf in Wickford where he docked his boat, the *Chelsea Ann*. His daughter had worked on the oysters with him for several years. After he died, his son, Ross—who had always had a tempestuous relationship with his father—took over the lease with Chelsea.

They're both striking kids. Chelsea's the older, in her late twenties, tall and thin, but rugged-looking, blonde and blue-eyed, very pretty. Ross is handsome, in his early twenties, tall and dark, slathered with tattoos. I met Ross on a rainy day long after I'd met Chelsea. The two of them looked good together, working side by side in the boat, swaying with two- to three-foot swells. Mostly, Chelsea does the dock work,

The *Chelsea Ann* out of the water, 2012. MICHAEL CEVOLI

grading and sorting the oysters, but she goes out to help bring in the cages, sometimes.

Ross showed a lot of spirit as he hauled the oyster cages off the bottom of that prime lease of theirs. The hydraulic hauler wasn't working too well that day, so he had to haul the cages manually from time to time, which he clearly enjoyed doing. They needed to split up the oysters in the bags shelved inside the cages. They brought the cages back to the dock, slid out the bags of oysters from their shelving, sorted the oysters by size, restocked them in the cages by size, and set aside some of the bags to be cleaned. They had to clean the cages a bit, too. Oyster-cage fouling organisms are gorgeous; they're weird algae and plants and animals, loaded with color, twisted into odd shapes, gruesomely textured. It's almost a shame to scrape them off, but there in the rain, that's what Chelsea did.

She had come to the class to learn things her father might have known about oyster farming but had never gotten around to telling her. Chelsea's another woman who made her father's trade her own, as Greta did—who racked her brain to remember her father at work; who took up into her own hands the tools and equipment that brought him always to mind. And, while she was doing this, while she was trying to keep the oysters alive and healthy and marketable, her father's friends—guys he'd worked with, the Shellfishermen's Association, oyster farmers he'd known—all came together to commemorate him. Lou had been both an excellent oyster farmer and a well-liked man. Chelsea inherited both his obligations as a farmer and his legacy as a good friend.

I thought of these things while our class toured the shellfish aquaculture facility at Roger Williams. Dale led us by the tanks and vats, huge ones, where they grow out oyster larvae. We passed tall cylinders stocked with algae, a different color in every cylinder, some of them almost fluorescent. In a trough lay old oysters, harvested carefully from secret spots around the bay and bred with disease-resistant oysters from New Jersey—all in the hope that they could develop an oyster hardy enough to withstand the various pestilences that, it is thought, kill young oysters in Rhode Island waters. Narragansett Bay has never had strong natural oyster populations; no one knows why.

The facility bubbled like a mad scientist's lab, but it was a comforting place. It teemed with life. My father stood beside me, leaning on his crutches. "Remember when we caught a seahorse?" he said, as Dale pointed out a tank with a seahorse in it. Our seahorse had been a tiny green-brown thing in a white plastic bucket. We put it back into the water after a few minutes of looking at it.

In late February, after class, my father paused as we walked slowly uphill to get to the car. It was a gentle hill; we'd only come about twenty yards, and we only had about thirty more to go. He stopped to catch his breath. "Gettin' old," he said. "It's just age." He would have to pause yet again before we got to the car. A week later, he went into the hospital. He would not come home until the day after Christmas. In that time, I would get to know Chelsea. I'd learn about her father from his friends, and I would attend a ceremony to unveil a memorial for him.

The first eulogies for Lou Ricciarelli took place on August 2, 2009, on Gardner's Wharf, a tiny nub of shore in Wickford, an old, nautical, and willfully quaint locality in North Kingstown. Well over a year later, on December 19, he received two more of them: one at Gardner's again, in the morning, by his stone memorial, and another in the afternoon, a few miles down the road, at Duffy's Tavern, where his family hosted a dinner for everyone who had come to the memorial ceremony.

On the day of his first eulogies, a cool, overcast day, on ground paved with gravel and broken chells, a few hundred people stood between Gardner's market and Lou's boat, and listened to an Episcopalian priest who spoke into a microphone on a small, tented stage. Many of the mourners wore casual dress—T-shirts and jeans; a number of them sipped from bottles of Bud Light. The priest spoke of Lou's generosity with his time and his knowledge of the bay and of shellfish farming. As a matter of course, the eulogy hit its crescendo with a recitation of John F. Kennedy's endearing, if not quite true, analysis of man's special affection for the sea:

I really don't know why it is that all of us are so committed to the sea, except I think it is because in addition to the fact that the sea changes and the light changes, and ships change, it is because we all came from the sea. And it is an interesting biological fact that all of us have, in our veins the exact same percentage of salt in our blood that exists in the ocean....

Indeed, after the last bagpipe notes of "Amazing Grace" faded away, Mike McGiveney, president of the Rhode Island Shellfishermen's Association—of which Lou had long been a board member—said, as he walked over to a little knot of guys over by the market, "He was part of the bay"—in that tone of cheering sorrowfulness common among New Englanders when they speak well of the dead.

The timing of this first service was difficult. The Charlestown Seafood Festival would take place the very next weekend—an important event for the Association, and for Lou. Each year, the guys staffed a stand there, the only raw bar in the midst of a cornucopia of fried fish and clams. State law mandates that individual fishermen cannot sell their catches for consumption, but only to a shellfish dealer, so the Association purchases their offerings of quahogs, oysters, and steamers from a dealer, usually Twin Shellfish, owned by Mike's brothers, Tim and Marty. The guys, all volunteers, then spend the weekend working in sleeveless T-shirts, the better to display their thick digging and shucking muscles. They lay open the oysters and quahogs and serve them on the half shell, while they steam the steamers in a marinade of butter, olive oil, garlic, and herbs.

"I don't shuck too well," said Bruce Eastman, secretary of the Association, who stood with Mike and a few other guys by the market, "so I usually get stuck doing the steamers in the back." Bruce is short and stout, with a soft-featured face and whitening hair. He speaks a clipped Rhode Island dialect. Guys say he's a natural for his position, which he has held for many years. His nickname's Auntie. He runs everything by the book, he takes immense pride in his industry, and he delights in the excesses that inevitably occur at the raw bar. "We had a guy one year eat sixty of 'em," he said. "Five dozen littlenecks, one time, in like two hours."

Bruce started telling Festival stories. "It was early in the day," he said, "over in Newport, at the Festival, where the Association used to participate, and they're shuckin' away. These girls come up, you know—big girls," he mimed, holding his arms around a considerable human body, or perhaps a beach ball. "Wide as they were tall. So they came walkin' up, and I think it was Fred—what the hell was his name? This was ten years ago— Fred's shuckin' away, and the girls wanted oysters, so he goes, 'Cleopatra was one of the sexiest women that ever lived in history, and she used to eat a dozen oysters every day.' One of the girls stood right there and said—at this point, Bruce put his hand on his hip and mocked a flounce—'Well, I've been compared to Cleopatra on many an occasion!' He's lookin' over at me, givin' me a look, so he gets the oysters for 'em and they come back. They were celebratin' one of the girls' birthdays. And then they came back again, later in the afternoon.

"So of course it gets dark early. Fred took his boat over from East Greenwich, right? Actually, he was a ship captain, so he's got his boat over to the Black Pearl, which is right next door, and he says, 'Gee, it's getting dark; I gotta get outta here,' you know. So he disappears, and he has his boat around the corner. We look over, and here comes his boat around the corner—he's got the two girls! He's got Cleopatra and her friend with him! They're goin' for a ride! Hey, look at Fred! He's got Cleopatra!"

Lou would have appreciated the telling of this kind of story in a funereal setting. He was a big teller of jokes himself—or, at least, a starter of them. "Half the time, he'd forget the friggin' punch line," says Chelsea. "It would not make sense."

Lou'd had the close calls in life that engender that kind of humor and that kind of insouciance about joke telling. Born in 1953, to a marine and a nurse, both fresh off the boat, Lou took up the pleasures of the counterculture as a young man, aesthetically and entrepreneurially.

"He was a big pot dealer back in the day," says Chelsea. He worked for UPS for several years, and made the most of the advantages such a position affords when it comes to marijuana distribution. Then, in 1983, he got busted. "I was being born, and he was going on trial, facing a lot of jail time," she says. He got out of a prison sentence, but worse for the wear: no jail, but no job, either, with a kid on the way. A couple of his buddies happened to be shell-fishermen, however, and they took him out on the water to give him some work. He decided the job was for him and took it up, but as a diver rather than a digger. This was an odd choice given that he had no prior diving experience, and in those days, diggers and divers did not get along; in fact, they were inflicting harm on each other with increasing frequency and viciousness. He taught himself dive-harvesting and eventually built his own boat.

"That was my present when my brother was born," says Chelsea. "I got the boat named after me."

Much later, during the tumultuous nineties, when the price was tanking and the State had polluted and then shut down large swathes of the bay, Lou tried oyster-farming, then in the very early stages of its renaissance in Narragansett Bay. Again, Lou entered into a business that irked the wild-harvest shellfishermen, who saw each aquaculture lease as an infringement on their territory, and again, he took up work as a sheer novice.

"He watched all these people sink all this money into nice oyster gear," says Chelsea. "A lot of people, even his friends, they put a lot of money into it, and they're not doing it anymore." Lou declined fancy gear; instead, he jury-rigged his own stuff. At the Gardner's Wharf docks, his homemade vats still hang off the floats: plastic bins with their bottoms cut out and replaced with mesh screens suited for—and a few actually cut from—storm doors.

None of this means to say that Lou went it alone. He asked for advice from the few guys who had started raising oysters ahead of him—Bob "Skid" Rheault, Jeff Gardner, Billy Blank. And, in his turn, Lou kept no secrets. Perhaps the most common theme in all of his many eulogies was Lou's generosity with his expertise.

So, he had negotiated difficult moments, prospered, and helped others to prosper. He'd faced a drug bust in the days of Nancy Reagan's despicable and clueless campaign against drugs; he'd dived when certain combative diggers would sometimes toss cherry bombs into the water, the poor man's depth charge, hoping for a good eardrum rupture or two; he'd farmed oysters when diggers and divers alike might tear up a man's oyster gear or poach his product, or both. Lou wended his way with both even-tempered argument and his odd personal charm.

McGiveney recalled, in the eulogy he'd prepared, a meeting of the Marine Fisheries Council that Lou attended as a member of the Shellfish Advisory Panel. Lou had been offering his usual temperate opinion, which tended to cool hot heads, when a woman came in with a dog trailing behind her. It was Rocco, Lou's Chihuahua, who used to—quite literally—live in Lou's truck. When he parked down the shore, Lou'd leave the doors open for Rocco, who'd wait patiently through the day for Lou to return. For this reason, Lou had disconnected the open-door warnings on the truck to pre-vent its battery from going dead. At the meeting, the dog bounded into Lou's lap, and it was then that Mike noticed that Rocco had a little leather-cord necklace around his neck—a necklace that exactly matched the one Lou wore around his own neck.

Lou's peculiar and disarming style meant that not only was it appro-priate to express sentiments and to employ manners of expression at his funeral that would have been inappropriate for others' formal remem-brances, but it was actually endearing, and even necessary. He would have worn jeans to a dockside funeral, too; he might've drunk a Bud Light; he definitely would've told jokes—or tried to, anyway.

"Some of our family," says Chelsea, "and some people not in the fish-ing community didn't appreciate, I don't think, the way we did things. They would have liked a more traditional casket." Lou's wife, Debbie, had his body cremated; she spread some of the ashes into the cove and the rest remain at their house. "I didn't even see my dad, you know—when they prepare a body, to say good-bye. I know the last memory I have of my dad . . . it's perfectly good and fine, and that's what I want to keep. I didn't want to see him in a coffin, and people kinda gave me shit about it. The boat, I understand, is bittersweet to a lot of people; a lot of people see it as the boat he died on. I know my grandfather has a hard time going down there. But on my dad's birthday, I had a place where I could go put a flower. It's not a graveyard; people are around."

The other services for Lou held just the same tenor. After the Decem-ber ceremony for his memorial, which has its own strange story (the story of the secret code), most of the crowd of a hundred or so headed over to Duffy's, an old and well-worn establishment. Duffy's had a dirt floor until the late 1960s—a fitting surface, given that the joint started life as a horse barn. Repurposed during Prohibition, Duffy's has slowly and steadily expanded from its original walls; it now has modern trappings—large windows, for example. It even welcomes women these days.

The Ricciarellis gave their guests a big feast in one of Duffy's newest rooms, one lined with windows rather than dark old wood plastered with faded five-by-seven photographs, which constitute much of the decor of the old part of the place. During the meal, Lou's friends, family, and colleagues rose to speak about him. About the fourth or fifth of them stood and said, "I got Lou's last joke."

An interesting way to put it. Everybody knew that Lou liked to tell jokes, and, of course, there must have been a last one, though it would be hard (or impossible) to determine which one it had actually been. Nonetheless, this fellow, Eddie Abraham, a childhood friend of Lou's, was offering an experience with Lou that no one there had had, except Eddie. He was turning an image of Lou that Lou had showed him toward people who had perhaps never seen that image before, or who would appreciate a novel reflection of it. "Now bear with me," he said. "I don't exactly know where the punch line was.

"Anyway, the son from prison calls his father at home and asks his father, 'How's everything?' And his father says, 'Well, we're not gonna be able to do the garden this year, because you always dig the backyard up for me, and you know, I don't have the stamina to do that anymore. It's too bad you're not here to do that.' So his son said, 'Well, Dad, don't worry about it; you don't wanna do that anyway, cuz that's where the bodies are buried.'"

This is an old Mafia joke, a joke about dead bodies and a son in jail. How could these elements form an appropriate—and funny—part of a eulogy for an Italian guy who had narrowly avoided a long prison term? There was a rumble of nervous laughter from a few people around the room, and a guy at the table next to mine surreptitiously asked: "This is a joke?"

Eddie continued: "So they finish the conversation, and next thing you know, the feds and the police all pull up, and they dig up the whole backyard, lookin' for bodies . . . and as a result the father was able to do his planting. The next conversation with his son was, 'You know, son, I'm not sure exactly what happened, but thank you for your help.' And the son basically said, 'Hey, I do what I can.' That was his last joke."

Not long after Lou's last joke, Jody King stood up and explained the secret code.

Jody had been vice president of the Shellfishermen's Association for the previous eight years, and friends with Lou for twelve. He had handled a great deal of the logistics involved in putting together Lou's memorial, and had even come up with the text for the stone. Jody had taken this work upon himself for complicated reasons, some of which became apparent immediately when he began his eulogy for Lou at Duffy's.

"As many of you know," he said, "I lost my brother Tracy and about a dozen other friends in the Station nightclub fire. I lost my dad about a year and four months after my brother, and what I've come to learn through these experiences is what we are doing here is more than just memorializing in their honor—we are celebrating Lou's life."

Note the grammatical disagreement: "their" and "Lou's." The Station Fire and his father's death weigh heavily on Jody. On February 20, 2003, one hundred people died and two hundred and thirty were injured when the Station burned down. That night, a small, almost ramshackle club in West Warwick had hosted Great White, a lousy, eighties hair-metal band. As they began their very first song, their tour manager set off four gerbs—cylindrical fireworks that shoot sparks. These sparks ignited the acoustical foam that lined the club's walls. Twenty minutes later, the fire was out.

Jody arrived at the Station at the end of that space of twenty minutes and spent hours trying to find his brother. At one point, Jody saw a fireman walk over to the mound of bodies near the ruined front doors of the club. The fireman bent down and pulled at something; then he walked over to the white tarps laid out for individual bodies and set down a pair of hands. He rose and walked back toward the doors. "I don't even like telling my enemies the shit that goes on in my head," says Jody.

Long after that night, he learned that Tracy, a bouncer at the Station, had been outside the building at least four times. "I know of four people he pulled out of the fire," says Jody. "Four different families came up to me within the first year of the fire to say thank you."

When the crowd at Duffy's started to break up, a guy went up to Jody and asked him about Tracy. Jody loosened his tie, unbuttoned a few buttons beneath his collar, and pulled his shirt aside to reveal a portrait tattoo of his brother above his heart.

Jody is fifty years old, a black man—rare among Rhode Island shell-fishermen. He grew up in Warwick, did a brief stint in the marines until discharged for injury, worked as a cook with his father for many years, and then took up bullraking about twenty years ago. For a time, after his father retired, the two of them worked together on Jody's boat, *Black Gold*. Once divorced, now remarried, Jody wakes up each morning before his four o'clock alarm goes off on his cell phone and sits in bed, staring at the thing, waiting for the moment, right before it sounds, when he can justify starting his day.

He grew up with the brothers who owned the Station, Jeffrey and Michael Derderian, both of whom received sentences for criminally neg-ligent manslaughter as a result of the fire. Michael, who served time in prison, was an especially close friend of Jody's.

But Michael hadn't been there that night, and Jeffrey had. Jody has worked with the two of them over the past several years on projects to establish both a memorial for the victims and an education fund for the victims' children, and, through this work, he and Jeffrey have bonded over their common trauma and their difficulties in assuaging the anger and repugnance for the Derderians still expressed by the friends and relatives of the people who died in that fire.

Confrontations with the consequences of death and dying have weighed heavily on Jody for seven years. When his father lay dying in the hospital, Jody slept by him on a cot for fifty-one nights. Death brings out obsessions in him. It certainly did when Lou died. Catharsis often takes unusual forms. The particulars of Jody's approach require understanding a bit about what went on about an hour before the dinner at Duffy's, at the memorial ceremony down at Gardner's Wharf.

The dedication of Lou's monument added another two eulogies to the litany. By quarter of eleven in the morning, a crowd of seventy or so had gathered and arranged themselves into an irregular crescent around the site. Beneath a maple tree stood a new, cast-iron bench facing the water and Lou's stone, an oval of granite, rough-hewn on its edges and flat and smooth on one side, facing back toward town. Chelsea held her six-month-old daughter; her brother Ross, done up in his National Guard fatigues, shook hands all around; their mother Debbie, short and white-haired, embraced her well-wishers.

Over by the parking lot on the fringes of the crowd, a guy they call Mudbelly, a bullraker active in the Association, wandered over. He was still a little fatigued from the Christmas party he'd thrown a couple of days before. "I made it to nine-thirty, I think," he said. All the way to 9:30 at night? "The college kids showed up, and they wanted to go," he explained. "They wanted to party." I'd had a little moonshine at the party, brought over by Mudbelly's good buddy, a guy they call Terminator, who actually had introduced Jody to shellfishing. "Did I tell you how he tests it?" he asked. "He pours a little out on the ground, lights it on fire, and if it burns blue: good stuff. If it burns red: no good."

Joey Amato came up about then, another bullraker, an old friend of my family's. Knots of people formed near the stone, and then a great crescent of them. There were about a hundred people in the audience when Bill Harsch, a lawyer, former head of DEM, and a friend to the Association, stepped up onto the curb at the edge of the site and began his speech to inaugurate the memorial.

"We're here to dedicate this site and to remember Lou Ricciarelli—here, where he kept his boat, where he worked and spent time with his friends and his colleagues. It shows how much those friends and colleagues really thought of Lou." Bill related a few comments he'd gleaned from his conversations with Lou's friends. He put special emphasis on what Bruce Eastman had said about Lou, which Bill quoted: "He was a shining example of a long line of commercial fishermen that this state has produced over the past several hundred years."

Bill then remarked on the stone itself: "I do have to say, when I came down the other day to look at it again, the memorial, that an awful lot of careful thought and planning went into it, a lot of contributions by most of you and by the aquaculture community and by the shellfishing community. Jody King did a great job pulling it all together. You're gonna have to ask Jody about the secret code that he decided to work into Lou's monument, and he might not tell you, just to see if you're bright enough to figure out how he did it. It's our own Da Vinci Code."

At about this point in the speech, which continued for several more minutes, a drunk guy wandered over and began to chat up those people whom he recognized. He really looked the part: He wore a scruffy brown ball cap; he had on baggy pants, an old army coat, and wire-frame glasses; and he had a good couple of days' worth of stubble on his cheeks. He held a beer can in his right hand, and it seemed that, by eleven on a Sunday morning, he had drunk enough beer to make him oblivious to the scene he was causing in the midst of a eulogy. An impressive feat of drinking.

"Hey, bro!" he exclaimed to a suddenly sheepish guy in dungarees and a jean jacket. "How y'dooin' man?! Nice t'see yoo! I haven't seen yoo in a coon's age!"—here he let loose the very archetype of the alcoholic fisherman's phlegmy laughter: "Hech-hech . . . huch-huch-huch!" While Bill spoke of Lou's family, the drunk man continued: "Yoo cut ya finger off on an electric saw, right? They grafted it back on? That's cool . . . hech-hech . . . How y'doin? How's Frank? . . . rrrrmmmm . . . hech-hech-hech . . . We're all friends!" Then the shushing started, so he roamed away, ending up behind Joey, Mudbelly, and me.

"S'up, brother? You know where I live, don'cha? Right across from the Mobil station." Bruce, standing just ahead of us, turned around, gave the drunk the stink-eye, and told him to quiet down. "Louie . . . he's my daughter-in-law's father, y'know. Louie befriended me when I came here . . ." This testimonial resulted in more shushing. "Hey, fuck off! . . . hech-hech-hech . . . rrrrmmmm . . . Yeah, I know: 'Be quiet' . . . Go fuck yerself! Hech-hech-hech . . . Goddamn, got a fuckin' stick up your ass . . . hech-hech . . . hech-hech."

"That was my father-in-law, Norman," Chelsea recalls later. "And he was not supposed to be there. That was a huge, huge embarrassment for my family. I went home and reamed him out . . . My husband was completely mortified, because he loved my dad. The funny thing, too, is that Norman's boat used to be right behind my dad's. When Sean and I started dating, we didn't even know for months that our dads were working side by side." She sighs. "My dad never judged people."

Eventually, Norman wandered off, way to the back of the crowd. Bill finished his speech, and Mike McGiveney introduced Lou's wife, who wanted to say a few words. As she began to speak Norman came back, but encountered heavier resistance this time. "Come on! Come on!" he pleaded, as a guy he apparently knew put a hand on his shoulder and whispered to him. "I know, I know . . . he was my friend too!"

"I know he'd be very angry at all of you for taking all this time and energy," said Debbie, eliciting laughter.

Norman said: "Louie, ya know, he . . . rrrrrmm . . . hech-hech . . . S'up? Th'hell with it! . . . Louie, Louie." One of the guys Norman kept trying to buddy up to walked him away from the crowd. A few minutes later, the eulogies came to an end, and most everyone headed over to Duffy's.

So what was the code? It began with the word *lease*. Lou's monument consists of a smooth-polished granite stone set on a pedestal about two feet high. The stone bears an inscribed image of Lou and his dog Rocco at the top, a poem beneath the portrait, and an oyster and a quahog carved to the left and the right of the poem, respectively. The poem is a version of the old Irish benediction that begins with some variation of the words, "May the road rise to meet you." Those of the punk-rock generation may know the version popularized by the band Public Image Limited, in the song "Rise." It's a good sentiment, and who could argue with a monument for a working man that recalls the second coming of Johnny Rotten? But even the formal, traditional text didn't quite fit the needs of a shellfisherman. The old lines confer an agricultural blessing; they use words of the land, not of the sea.

In fact, Lou's monument already constituted a departure from tradition. We New Englanders commemorate fishermen who die at work by adding their names to a wall or a plaque down by the water. They have one in Gloucester, Massachusetts, and Rhode Islanders have one in Galilee. Jody approached the community down at Point Judith to see if they would accept Lou's name on their register. They refused. Only fishermen who sail out of the port of Galilee qualify, and neither diggers nor divers of quahogs belong to that fleet.

This refusal proved serendipitous. It served as a kind of formal constraint, a rule that engendered creativity—and it justified breaking with tradition.

When he learned of Lou's death, Jody began to write poetry. He dug up a notebook and started writing verses. "I'm not a writer; I'm not an author," says Jody. He'd never tried his hand at writing before, but he wanted to think through what it meant to be a shellfisherman. And, when the need arose for a text for Lou's stone, he tried to write for Lou.

The words didn't come to him.

"I went to my brother-in-law's house one day," he says. "And he had this poem on his wall, and I sat and looked at the poem." Jody had entered some of his poetical efforts into his phone so that he could look at them when inspiration struck. He took it out and looked his stuff over, then looked back at the poem. "I said: Oh, pretty good . . . Somebody else figured out what I wanted to say!" He took a photo of his brother-in-law's wall hanging with his cell phone. "I brought it home and wrote it out on a big piece of paper, so I could sit and look at it, cuz I'm visual," he says. "I told Chelsea about the poem. I said, 'You know, Chelsea, this is cool. I finally found a poem with the right verses. This is the poem, it's an Irish poem; go look it up.' And she went on the Internet, found it, and she goes, 'Oh cool, really cool.' I said, 'Well, it says it for me.' And she said, 'It says it for me, too. And I sent it to my mom, and she said she likes it.'"

Everything looked to be in place. Something still didn't sit quite right with Jody, however. "A day later, I'm looking at the poem on a big piece of paper, and I went, 'Wow . . . 'field.'"

The fourth line of the blessing goes as follows: "May rains fall soft upon your field"—a farming benediction. "Lou didn't have a field," says Jody. "He had an oyster lease. They both had E's in them, which was the funny part. And I whited-out the word 'field' and put the word 'lease,' and no sooner did I put the word 'lease,' it was like the letters appeared throughout the entire poem. I mean, Da Vinci Code. I never thought of it like that until Bill Harsch said it, but all the letters popped out when I changed the word from 'field' to 'lease': 'Ricciarelli,' right from top line to bottom. I'm gettin' chills again," says Jody as he holds his right hand just above his left arm.

"I called up Chelsea and said, 'Chelsea! You can't believe what just happened! I changed one word and your dad's name, your last name popped right out.'"

Chelsea remembers the moment: "I was actually driving when he was telling me, so I was trying to drive and picture this. I was like, 'I gotta go home and look at it, cuz I'm kinda confused right now. I'm a visual person, so I gotta look at it.'"

Jody understood. He said, "I'm gonna have to write it on a piece of paper, and I'll highlight the letters for you with a marker, and I'll send it to you."

He did just that. He wrote out the whole poem again, incorporating his change, then took a highlighter to the letters R-I-C-C-I-A-R-E-L-L-I, as each letter appeared in sequence in this or that word in the body of the poem. Again, he took a picture of it with his phone and sent the image to Chelsea.

Thus, on Lou's stone, certain of the letters carved into the granite are carved in bold. Following them in order spells out Ricciarelli, and that is the secret code.

That's what Jody explained to everybody at Duffy's, eliciting a few puzzled looks, just as Eddie's telling of Lou's joke had done, but very much satisfying the curiosity of a good portion of the crowd. Lou Ricciarelli's eulogies could have been nothing else but what they were, not only because of his character, but because of the character of his family and friends, and the character of quahogging itself.

This uncertainty explains all kinds of behavior. Really, nobody had any more of an idea what to do than Norman did. Norman had shown up drunk to Lou's memorial ceremony—but it's not as if there had been any protocol to cover the situation. It had never happened before. Nobody memorialized quahoggers. They die out on the water sometimes, but it's rare. Quahogging isn't as dangerous as working a trawler. That's why, at first, the guys had to cast about for a way to do something for Lou. It just happened that an active shellfisherman, a well-known and well-liked guy, a board member of the Association, had died on the job, and that the right people, the right family and friends, were around to do the things that befitted him, things that were a little odd, a little excessive.

Excesses can hurt, of course. Norman's did—though his carried a certain fisherman's joie de vivre. Another excess of a similar kind hurt Chelsea at the dinner for her father. Toward the end of the gathering, Jody came up to Chelsea to thank her and to congratulate her.

"What for?" she said. Jody was congratulating her on the sale of her father's oyster lease. He asked her what she was going to do now.

"What?" she said.

This is how Chelsea learned that Ross had sold the lease out from under her. Chelsea doesn't really know what happened to Ross, why he did this. He'd had troubles with drugs before, but nobody knew what his troubles were now. Her brother forged her name on the bill of sale, took all the money, and split. Nobody's seen him since. Just like that, the oysters were gone.

A week after Lou's memorial ceremony, my father came home from the hospital. He couldn't walk. He had nerve damage in his spine that left his right thigh paralyzed—a very specific and very disabling injury. Plus, he was severely deconditioned after ten months in the hospital. We'd had a wheelchair ramp put in at the house, but it was at the back door, and we hadn't been able to get the ground paved yet. That day, the day after Christmas, my mother pulled and I pushed his wheelchair through the snow. We got him back into the house.

It is just a fact: You have to deal with the harm a quahogging father tends to bring on himself. Much of my father's physical troubles go back to his work as a bullraker, just as Lou's diving occasioned his death. Norman's drinking probably has strong roots in his work. Friends and family and neighbors can try to mitigate these hardships, but they must also accept that the quahogging life precipitates them. And this is a lesson not only for those around quahoggers, but for the guys themselves, especially those in the early parts of their careers.

CHAPTER SEVEN

Young Guys

This is why fishermen are not wealthy, despite the fact that the fishery resources of the sea are the richest and most indestructible of those available to man. By and large, the only fisherman who becomes rich is one who makes a lucky catch or one who participates in a fishery that is put under a form of social control that turns the open resource into property rights.

—H. SCOTT GORDON, *THE ECONOMIC THEORY OF A COMMON-PROPERTY RESOURCE: THE FISHERY*

A FEW YEARS BACK, A COUPLE OF DAYS AFTER A FULL MOON, AROUND midnight, by a rocky beach, Jeff Grant loaded his pickup with a staggering catch of horseshoe crabs. Jeff's a quahogger, but he goes after other fishes, too. The horseshoe crab is one of them.

These heavily armored creatures have hardly changed at all over the past four or five hundred million years. Where they have changed, they have done so cautiously. The species particular to the East Coast, *Limulus polyphemus,* settled its mutations a youthful twenty million years ago. The *polyphemi* resemble a two-foot-long cross between a trilobite, a flea, and a skate. About a third of their length consists of a poignard-shaped tail; the other two-thirds consist of a U-shaped shell in two parts, fringed at the back with stubby spines. Its carapace resembles a cross between a *kabuto,* a samurai helmet, and a World War II–era German helmet, the *stahlhelm.* In heavily nitrate-polluted coves, barnacles overfed by algae blooms encrust the crabs' wicked-looking shells. Worse, even on the clean, sleek, barnacle-free individuals, there are several big bumps in the shell—actually, seven eyes.

A wading beachgoer and a scuttling horseshoe crab sometimes cross paths in the shallows—a coincidence that may result in pricked feet, mutual or unrequited repulsion, or a nauseating investigation of the crab's underside. It's easy to render the poor thing helpless: You just pick it up by the rim of its shell, where the rim runs smooth. Flip it over, and there you have ten furry, waggling legs, and nothing else. The horseshoe crab is a cluster of legs with a cap on it. Unless you look closer and see that, in the middle of those ten legs, there gapes a fringed, jawless mouth. Somewhere above the mouth there lies another pair of eyes. This old beast is a disturbing assemblage of arachnid parts, but man can make use of it. Even such a grotesque instance of, and testimonial to, the horrors of evolution has its utility.

The State permits harvesting of horseshoe crabs for two purposes: for bait, and for medical testing. Fishermen chop up the crabs for bait, mainly for tautog (blackfish). Laboratory technicians draw blood from the crabs for medical testing purposes, about 10 percent of each one's total supply. It's a whitish blood, a strange ichor that turns blue upon contact with air and consists of a single type of cell that releases a coagulant in the presence of bacterial endotoxins. It sounds alchemical, but it's true; hospitals and pharmaceutical companies use an agent made from the crab's blood to test drugs and equipment for pathogens. After its bleeding, the crab gets to return to the sea.

The law opens a very narrow window through which fishermen may catch these crabs: one night a month, maybe two, a few days after each full moon. Horseshoe crabs mate on beaches under the full moon during the high tide. Find the right beach at the right time, and you'll see a crawling horde of the vile things mounting each other in the sandy shallows. It is the females that can grow to two feet in length. The males, not even half their size, clamber over them clumsily. The State disallows harvesting them at the apex of their orgies. By placing the peak of the coital period off-limits, the State handicaps fishermen; nonetheless, they still manage to haul up vast quantities of the beasts within the quota determined by the State.

Jeff's big night came when the crabs turned up a few days after their normal mating time. "They were confused, and it was awesome," he says. He's in his mid-twenties, a slender blond guy, tall, with bright eyes, a raggedy blond beard, and a guileless demeanor. As he says the word *awesome*, with a slight drawl on the first syllable, you can see him glorying in the memory of the catch. Jeff usually drives his truck down to beaches he thinks the crabs will deem fertile ground, then wades in the water, towing a pram behind him. He uses a hook to yank the crabs out of the surf and toss them into the pram. Then, he transfers the crabs from the pram into sturdy, plastic fish totes, which he hauls up to his truck.

This one time, however, the sand proved too soft for his two-ton pickup. Jeff had to park way up the shore. Under this arrangement, he and his brother, Brian, with whom he often fishes, would have had to drag totes overflowing with live crabs across yards and yards of sand in order to drive them off to their destiny with either cleaver or needle. Fortunately, the beach in question was a popular rod-and-reel site; lots of recreational fishermen were hanging out and watching their lines, which weren't seeing much action. Jeff quickly drove over to a liquor store, filled a cooler with a thirty-pack, came back to the beach, and strolled up to the fishermen.

"If you want, guys," said Jeff to the languishing rod-and-reelers, "you can help me drag all these crabs up and put 'em in the truck, and then you can help yourself to beers." Beer, the sure and traditional palliative for fishermen's melancholy, did the trick. In short order, Jeff had a work team enthusiastically unloading his prams and hauling his totes up to the truck. "That was one of our better nights," he says.

"There's not a lot of people catchin' 'em, the horseshoe crabs," says Jeff. "There's a few guys that catch a few of them, but the reason the quota closed is mandatory reporting requirements. You gotta send in a piece of paper saying how many you caught. Well, they did this with lobster about five years ago; they said, 'Oh, just report in what you caught, and we'll decide what to do.' Well, what they did was, they went back in everyone's logs and said, 'Oh, well, you didn't catch any lobsters, well, then, you can't catch any lobsters anymore; you caught a hundred pounds, you can only fish ten lobster traps.' So they shut everyone out of it, based on the reporting that people handed in. So what happened? The year after that, everyone was reporting they landed horseshoe crabs, even though they didn't. I talked to the biologist in charge, and he's like, 'Yeah, you know, we get these slips in, and this guy here, every month, he lands a thousand crabs or six hundred crabs, every month; it's an even number for every month, no matter what.' Guys are just turning 'em in so they have landings, so they don't screw 'em like they did with lobster . . . but it hurts the people that actually do it."

There are very few young men in the quahogging game in Rhode Island, but the youngest guys tend to have an impact on the bay that is inordinate to their numbers: They benefit from the ecological perspective that has come to dominate the culture of fisheries management over the past twenty years. Some of them have studied the topic formally. Jeff is one of these. He graduated at the top of his class from the University of Rhode Island—naturally, one of the best schools in the world for the discipline. A few of Jeff's former professors say Jeff is not only one of the best students ever to come through the fisheries management program, but also one of the best students to have come through the university, period. (A remarkable coincidence: two of URI's greatest alumni, brought together in a single book.) His education puts Jeff at a distinct advantage when it comes to questions of managing quahogs in Narragansett Bay, and when it comes to confronting the state's fisheries management agents over these questions, often to the chagrin of said agents.

Jeff grew up in an environment that prepared him to think flexibly about managing the bay, and he grew up quahogging. He got started bull-raking commercially at the age of twelve. His father, a former digger himself, now a taxidermist, got Jeff started picking over quahogs a little after infancy, and Jeff—the lucky dog—knew right away that he wanted to fish for a living. He and his father went down to see David Drew, who sold the young, blond kid his first gear and made him promise to go to college. Jeff kept his word. He used to dig in the afternoons while he was in high school, and he used to dig in the morning before his classes at URI. To an industry clotted with old blood, Jeff brought a welcome vitality—or, rather, a vitality that should have been welcome.

"It's funny," he says. "You get a new kid comin' in, and it's funny how the different age groups react—at least when I came in. There were people I was friends with, that my dad was friends with, that I could always go to, like, if I was lookin' for a spot. They were an exception to the rule . . . A new kid, comin' in, tryin' to start out, gets resentment from the middle-aged people—the people that have been doin' it for a while, but not the older generation. The older generation likes to see it. There's none o' that kinda competition. They're relaxed enough in their ways that they're okay with it. Some of the middle-aged guys, oh, they hated me—guys in their thirties, forties, fifties—but then you get the older guys, and they're just like, 'C'mon over!' It doesn't matter to them."

This doesn't mean that the old-timers went completely easy on young Jeff. They'd welcome him on the water, and they'd even take it upon themselves to show him a thing or two—but they taught him the hard way, by imposing example.

"One name that comes up in quahogging is Old Man Cole," says Jeff. "He's a guy from Apponaug. He was probably one of the best quahoggers there ever was—ever! Skinny! Skinny, skinny guy; nothin' to him, never had a hauler, even when they were legal. He was just finishin' up when I was startin'. I mean, this old guy could smoke me somethin' fierce; he could catch quahogs like none other, and I just know him as Old Man Cole. I don't even know his first name."

After a while, the older of the older guys moved on, and the younger older guys got past their snobbery—maybe because once Jeff got out of college, they were able to think of him as a true full-timer, another one of themselves, rather than an interloper. It was about this time, when he was gaining acceptance among the wider bullraking community, that Jeff began to get more serious about working in other fisheries. Horseshoe crabs, lobsters, snails, scup, stripers, tautog, steamers—even oysters when the bay got a natural set of them. Jeff had always dabbled in them, but it's difficult to make a living on these fishes.

For one thing, catch limits on fin fish render them unattractive to the commercial fisherman. If the State sets the daily limit for tautog at ten per license, then catching ten to sell at a few dollars a pound makes a profit-earning job into a money-losing hobby. This is just what the State means to do. Rhode Island's fishermen worked the tautog into commercial extinction, as they have done to a whole litany of fishes. The commercial guys had their turn, and now the State has made the tautog a recreational fish. Jeff, who likes both having fun and making money, would like to see different management of the tautog and other fin fish—weekly limits, perhaps. Give Jeff the choice of catching his week's limit of tautog or striper or what-have-you, and he'll catch it in a day. He'll trade a day of quahogging for a day of fin fishing and not lose out financially. In other words, the day of quahogging is the standard by which he measures his participation in all other fisheries. He'd like to mix things up throughout the week or the season, but he has to weigh his desire for new challenges against the earnings of bullraking.

And why shouldn't the State help him out? Rhode Islanders would get more fresh fish right from their very own bay, and Jeff would take great satisfaction in his work. He knows the counterarguments, however: Guys would catch their weekly limit every day. Not Jeff, but some guys would take advantage of the system, and that would quickly put a wrap on the whole thing.

Then there's always the idea of implementing an ITQ system—Individual Transferable Quotas—a program in which fishermen can trade their quotas among themselves, a system of renting rights. Iceland uses this management scheme, and investing the profits from it into the financial sector did wonders for the Icelandic, Dutch, and British economies. Jeff views the idea with ambivalence: "I see a lot of it going towards private sectors and ITQs; it works well once it's implemented, but implementing it's a bitch. You have to tell people how many pounds they can catch. So, say this guy hasn't fished for cod in three years, but he did it for ten years before that, and you gotta tell him, 'No, you can't fish for cod anymore.' And then the people that really slammed the fish the hardest, when populations were the lowest, are the people that get rewarded; you're rewarding people that are harvesting fish at high levels when the stocks are at low levels—that's what ITQ does."

Management of fin fishing is hard, but, Jesus, so is the work, and in ways different from quahogging. "When I was just offshore fishin'," says Jeff, "I'm not even talkin', like, trip fishin'—just goin' to Block Island striper fishin', scuppin', whatever I was doin' at the time—and, again, I don't do this much, I just got dabblin' into it a little bit. I mean, I find it interesting, and I plan on continuing it, but I was wakin' up at two o'clock in the mornin', and I was squeaking in at night. I had to run home so I could sell out my fish at six o'clock, then I gotta go back to clean up the boat for the next day—we're talkin' long, long-ass days—and it's just a different mentality. You can't have that 'I want to go out for three hours and make a day's pay' mentality—it's just not gonna happen. And a lot of quahoggers, especially—or clammers, or whatever they do—they have that mentality of 'Oh, I can go out for four hours and make a pay.' I had it, when I was just quahoggin'. I'd think, 'I have three hours before school; I'm gonna go make a pay.'"

Over the years, Jeff developed the mental habits that enabled him to strike out after other prey. Switching fisheries requires flexibility of attitude, because few fishermen other than quahoggers work alone. He went halibut fishing up in Alaska, in order to go musseling back in Narragansett Bay. He went out on a trawler and caught the massive halibut, a giant, pink-orange monstrosity, six feet long. Several weeks on a boat in the North Pacific in March brought him enough money to buy the *Icy Straits*, his thirty-one-footer, the big beast of a boat he dredges mussels with. The Alaskan work by itself would set him apart from the main body of quahoggers: Jeff leaves the bay to do it; he works with several guys on the boat; he takes orders from its captain. Not every quahogger has the flexibility of mind to switch industries in this way.

But Jeff's captain in Alaska, Tim Mosher, had done the same. Tim used to work as a quahogger, out of Greenwich Cove, and he was very, very good at it. He saved his money and headed up north to go fin fishing. Things went well enough for him that after some years, he was able to hire Jeff to work his boat, to help another young quahogger to maybe follow in his wake. But not everything went right. Tim's father had grown up one street over from mine, and his grandmother and grandfather continued to live there long after he left. They used to sell vegetables from their garden; my mémé used to take my sister and me down there to pick string beans. When Tim's grandmother died, Old Man Mosher got depressed.

One day, my parents were turning on to our street from Moshers' when they saw two police cruisers blocking the road. A few cops held them up at the corner. The elder Mosher had gone missing, and the police suspected suicide. "If he doesn't wanna be found, you ain't gonna find him," my father told one of the cops. Mosher was a woodsman, a hunter, and he could choose whether the police would or would not find his body. He chose to let them find him. He killed himself in a small pond that lay just past the point where his street meets with ours.

Tim named his trawler *Patience*, for Patience Island in Narragansett Bay. When Jeff bought his thirty-one-footer, he named it *Icy Straits*, for a forty-mile stretch of Alaskan water that proved to be excellent fishing grounds on his first time trawling. Tim, in Alaska, has a boat named for a place in Rhode Island; Jeff, in Rhode Island, has a boat named for a place in Alaska. Nice, classical, onomastic symmetry. It's superstitious to think that rightness in nomenclature augurs well, but it's pragmatic to give oneself the feeling that the taking of a new tack has been well handled. Calming the mind with a sense of justness or appropriateness helps one to focus—even if the satisfaction has an irrational basis.

A bit of Zen can be crucial out on the water—not only because the environment is inherently dangerous, but also because the environment often tempts you into danger. Up in Alaska, huge sea otters surface and attack the hooked halibut. The fishermen have to drive the big mammals off. Talking about this problem, Jeff says that sometimes you "gotta" or "get to" shoot the otters. There's nothing to be gained and something to be lost in clarifying what he said. The ambiguity is more interesting than the disambiguation: It is the mystery of who the hunter is. There are many different kinds of hunters, and each different kind wants different things. They may want to track; they may want to kill; they may want to provide. But all of these motivations require a similar mind-set if they are to be pursued successfully. You must be in the moment, but with self-mastery; even a bloodthirsty barbarian of a hunter, eager to drain the heat from his prey with his own teeth, must keep silent when the hunt demands it, or he will fail. The fisherman who reluctantly shoots the otter and the fisherman who greatly desires to shoot the otter must for some moments share the same way of being in the world. Where fishermen diverge is in the techniques each one uses to arrive at that state of mind, and how each one reflects upon himself as a fisherman.

Jeff thinks of himself as a go-and-find-things kind of guy. Look at the GPS on the *Icy Straits* and you'll see what he does in Narragansett Bay. Jeff uses the little device to record the paths he takes to find a commercially viable set of mussels. He can display these records on the GPS charts. The thin black lines that represent his preliminary trawls loop over themselves, snarl together, and then ultimately run clear, parallel to the veins of blue-black shellfish beneath the boat.

Jeff spent dozens of hours and hundreds of dollars' worth of fuel to strike upon a viable site. And that is what he likes: the process of figuring out where the stuff is—which is risky, because he needs to haul up thousands of pounds of product to make a day's pay. He might not ever find a set of mussels thick enough for him to recoup his investment. What's more, the risk inheres not only in the possibility of losing his time and money, but also in the pleasure he takes in investing them. At some point, he has to give up on the fun of looking for mussels and settle into the task of harvesting them.

The joy of hunting is always a temptation. It's almost absurd with Jeff. Head into his house and you'd think he's got to be kidding: three fillets of white fish on a cutting board balanced on the sink ("I like my fish to taste like nothin'," he says. "I'm a straight American."); he has his television tuned to some kind of hunting channel, broadcasting a show in which camouflaged rifle-wielding, marsh-dwelling rednecks stalk alligators; piles of hunting books, hunting magazines, and three-ring binders of hunting regulations cover the floor of his living room.

Brian and Jeff Grant and their catch of mussels, 2010. ROBERT SUKRACHAND

"I meat-hunt," he says, as he loads fish totes into the *Icy Straits* in sheer darkness. Quarter of five in the morning is a late start for him and his brother. Dead in the middle of summer, and pure night. "Me, I couldn't care if it's got antlers; of our protein, over fifty percent, between the fish we catch, the deer we shoot—well over fifty percent is hunted."

As the sun rises, he draws up to his mussel ranges and slows the *Icy Straits*. "I love quahogging," he says, as he and Brian unfurl the dredges—repurposed scallop dredges, their bags formed of interlinked metal hoops. "For like eight years, that's all I did. Then I got a bigger boat, and there's other things to do. I still love quahogging, and I can tell you: I can make no money goin' quahogging now and still enjoy myself. I used to beat my head against the wall if I wasn't makin' good money; I'd go nuts. Now I can enjoy myself, cuz I'm still payin' my bills." They put the dredge over the side and guide it to the bottom. Jeff eases the boat forward. Down below, the mouth of the dredge billows open and begins to swallow layer after layer of mussels.

The brothers harvest two seams of mussels, one barnacled, one not. The barnacled catch will go for fish bait; the other for finer dining. Jeff could not tell you why one seam developed barnacles while the other didn't; something about the odd currents of Narragansett Bay. But he knows why he must separate crusted from uncrusted mussels: pure visual aesthetics. Mussels are the most elegantly beautiful of the shellfish. Quahogs are attractive in the way that coins are attractive: They have uniformity and individuality at the same time, yet there's a vulgarity to them. Steamers are ugly. Oysters are pleasing because of their lumpy asymmetry, in just the manner of the weathered, misshapen mug of an old fisherman. Mussels have a blue-black shell with a touch of iridescence. A specimen ready for the plate is about as long as a finger and curves slightly, like a finger at rest. There is something of Constantin Brancusi's first *Bird in Space* in *Mytilus edulis,* the blue mussel—the most favored one for eating—except that the mussel has a slight raggedness to it. It secures itself to a good feeding site by its byssal threads, hair-like fibers that root their etymology in a Hebrew word signifying the finest, whitest linen.

To prepare the mussel as food, the cook rips out these threads (colloquially known as the beard) from between the mussel's valves and throws them away, as if sculpting the shell into further elegance. The barnacled mussels' free riders don't affect their taste, but they do look disgusting. Who could love a fine Brancusi if it were covered in verdigris or had lesser works braised onto it? Only an art lover with a rarefied sensibility. Why ask more from the average restaurant patron?

Driving the boat, one hand on the wheel, the other hooked in his rubber apron, Jeff watches the dredge line as it runs through the pulleys hung from the davit, the long steel arm extending out over the water.

"Maine mussels have a name," Jeff says. "Prince Edward Island mussels have a name . . . Rhode Island mussels—that's your economy mussel, for buying in high volumes at low prices." But Rhode Island mussels are secretly good. They have multicolored meats—orange, pink, and pearl, all nearly pastel. Mussels are simple to serve, too. There's really just one way: You scrub them, tear out their beards, and toss them into the pan or the pot, shells and all. You cook them in a sauce until they gape wide and then pick out the meats. It's always the same, whether lofty PEIs or lowly Rhode Islands—lofty or lowly only in the excellence of their marketing, of course, but when has Rhode Island ever excelled in that department? Especially with regard to shellfish and shellfishermen. In the pool of advertising, the shellfish of Narragansett Bay settle to the bottom.

"We had a program to sell quahogs to the consumers in Rhode Island," says Jeff. He's now vice president of the Rhode Island Shellfishermen's Association and sits on the State Marine Fisheries Council, too. A few years back, Governor Carcieri encouraged the Association to adopt a marketing strategy, something to get the Rhode Island name out there. The guys took some of the Association funds and paid a local cartoonist, Don Bousquet—who has made a career out of alternately spoofing and ennobling the bullraker—several thousand dollars to draw a logo for them. The logo went on bags. "Clam bags," says Jeff. "But we kinda messed up . . . We had a very good program; it was the same as Rhody Fresh Milk. We had Don Bousquet sketch up an emblem and stuff, but the problem was that because of the size of the bag, they never made it to the consumer. They went to the restaurant, to the supermarket, and they opened the bag and dumped 'em out, and the bag just got lost."

The buying and selling of quahogs is complicated, mainly because of the long shelf life of quahogs in general, and of Rhode Island quahogs in particular. Rhode Islands last for quite a long time, and so have earned a place with shellfish middlemen, and even restaurateurs. Rhode Island quahogs also have a reputation for excellent taste—but this is a much smaller one. That is the perception among those who serve quahogs, anyway: American palates have become too deadened to discern the superiority of Rhode Islands. In years gone by, the average barman could tell the terroir of a clam; now, very few are alive to such tastes. In short, it's not even clear what reputation a Rhode Island logo would capitalize upon.

Certainly there's no reason to blow any money on Rhode Island mussel bags. Jeff is actually lucky that he has a buyer for them at all. "I sell to Mar Seafood," he says. "They're a very big company on the East Coast. For decades, they bought mussels from one person: Wilcox, out of Wickford. They had a big boat that musseled, and that's what they did. He stopped doin' it, so right now, I'm the only one."

It was Don Wilcox who got the Rhode Island mussel market going in the first place—not the son, Don Jr., who told how Tommy Cole used to work, but Don Sr. The father died a long time ago. He and his son did a lot of fin fishing and trawler work, and together, with help from some of their friends and family, like Bunky Bennett, they built a huge fishing boat in Don Jr.'s backyard. Don Jr. made his living on that boat for many years. Now, he's retired from fin fishing and simply quahogs. He hasn't musseled in decades, but in his day, and in his father's day, he musseled on an almost unimaginable scale.

"My father was the mussel king; seriously, it was in the paper," says Don. "He caught more mussels in one friggin' year than Jeff Grant'll catch in his entire life. They used to catch two to four hundred bushels a day. He started the business; nobody could sell 'em before my father. He went to New York and drove to marketplaces, cuz there was no mussels for sale in Rhode Island. He used to truck his own mussels to New York, and the Mob was involved and everything else. If you wanted to go musseling, they'd put you outta business.

"My father, back in the fifties, paid fifty cents a bushel to the Mob, and it had to be paid in cash to unload. If you wanted to sell a mussel in New York, you had to be in the good graces of the Mob. He talked to somebody, and they said, 'We can handle it, but you gotta pay,' so they shook hands and made a pact. They put him on probation for a bit. When my father got goin', there was other boats, from other parts o' the country—Maine and that—bringin' stuff in, but a fella up in Maine, if their huntin' season came or if it was blowin' too hard, they'd say, 'Ah, we'll get 'em next time.'

"But when my father got control, his word was so good, if they would call his house and say what they wanted—a hundred bushel t'morra, fifty bushel, different dealers—it was like goin' to the grocery store with my father. You'd have fifty bushels t'morra."

Jeff has not had to make a pact with the Mob; neither has he had to truck his mussels to New York. But he is filling a niche that the Wilcoxes used to fill. Perhaps a smaller niche, though it seems incredible, when Jeff fills the *Icy Straits,* that he's harvested a mere portion of what the Wilcoxes used to get.

After a couple of hours, Jeff and Brian have the boat three feet deep in mussels, which is the only way anybody makes money on the things. The brothers will have to get them into shore discreetly; there are a couple other dealers who have their own musseling boats. "They haven't found where I've been working," says Jeff. "I've been going home weird ways." Then, keeping the two varieties of mussels apart, the barnacled from the bare, they'll bag them all up, load them on wheelbarrows, and wheel them up to Mar's waiting truck. The day's over by eleven.

He does mussels only in the summer, and only when he gets the call from Mar, maybe once or twice a week. In this respect, he works very much as Don Wilcox Sr. did: He gets a call the night before; the next morning he delivers the mussels. The product demands this kind of timing. Mussels go by quickly. Jeff puts himself on call, ensuring that his plans can be easily interrupted. A day of musseling pays out significantly better than a day of quahogging. What's more, musseling presents different challenges. Working a dredge is quite different from working a rake. Different things go wrong.

Not even an hour into the work, a rope slips from its pulley on the davit. That's a pain in the ass, but it's also an opportunity to take a break from driving the boat. Jeff gets to climb up on the roof, stand among the rigging, and thread his line through the pulley while the boat rocks in the water. It's tricky and an annoyance, but it's novel—at least for this week. Novelty is a big part of what Jeff's looking for.

All shellfishermen have a proclivity for change. The guys who stick to quahogging alone satisfy themselves with the changes they find in the details of quahogging. Jeff wants changes in the whole of his work. His tendencies have proved fortunate, as quahogging has hit upon rough times in Narragansett Bay. Guys aren't making the kind of money they used to—the kind of money they think they ought to be making working for themselves.

"People have left quahogging in the past couple years," Jeff says. "We were losing them steadily up until the recession, cuz people could go get jobs when they weren't makin' money. We did not lose 'em as quick during the recession; maybe some left and some came back. In the past, when there was a recession, everyone went quahoggin'. You would just buy a license and go. Well, now you can't get a license, and people who do have licenses might not want to work. It's not that lucrative anymore. I don't know if people are lazy or whatever, but it just doesn't happen," says Jeff as he carefully takes up a gaff, balancing on the roof of the boat. He starts to gently encourage the line into the pulley, as his brother, perched on the gunwale, waits for the rope to come through.

"Look at it like a chain with the weakest link," Jeff continues. "Right now, everything's been beefed up as far as environment's concerned, water quality; as far as market, it's weak at times, it's strong at times. I see this whole system as having a weak link, and it being the independent fisherman; there's not enough of us. If the number of fishermen could always bring in a high volume, things would stay more steady."

Because American palates have lost their sophistication when it comes to shellfish, quahogs have become a volume industry. The massive quahog farms in Virginia, the Carolinas, and Florida own the market now, with their huge quantities and inferior quality. When the farms came to prominence in the 1990s, Rhode Island needed to respond with its own big numbers, but it had closed itself down. Narragansett Bay's quahog landings have plummeted over the past twenty-five years for a few reasons: because so many guys have left the industry; because the industry and the State have made it difficult for new guys to get into quahogging; and, perhaps, because the bay hasn't seen good sets of quahogs. In a volume market, low landings mean low prices, which also drives guys away, leaving even fewer bullrakers to land the quahogs.

On top of this, Rhode Island's landings fluctuate. There's a boom in the summer, of course, but there's also a boom in the winter. Through an

Jeff and Brian Grant thread a davit pulley, 2010. ROBERT SUKRACHAND

accord with the Shellfishermen's Association, the State sets Greenwich Bay as off-limits in the summer and open for limited times during the winter. The transplant areas also come open in the winter months. On certain days, you can find four hundred bullrakers on Greenwich Bay in the middle of a snowstorm. This pattern is one of the reasons why full-time quahoggers get angry with part-timers. Denigrating the part-timer is a beloved pastime of the bullraker. The guy who works year-round, every day (as long as the weather's good), sees a big price drop when all these boats he doesn't know pop up on the water. He sees his earnings shrink because of them, and he blames them for his losses. But the problem might have a solution different from the one he first thinks of.

Jeff says, "Part of the reason we have a problem with dealers paying low prices for high volume is because it's in short bursts; they have their customers based on the number of clams they bring in over an average period of time, all summer. How many clams are you bringing in? Well, the more clams you bring in, the more customers you can have. Then, it's winter; maybe the demand isn't as high. All of the sudden, your product base triples; well, your consumer base didn't triple, so the price goes down. You gotta find consumers, markets, whatever. These price drops come from large change in volume, not necessarily the large volume, so if we had a bunch more quahoggers out there—if we had more full-timers who worked all the time, and Greenwich wasn't as good and didn't bring out as many people— we wouldn't have any problems. What I see is the number of licenses available is decreasing and the number of people doin' it is decreasing."

Really, what Jeff wants is for part-timers to become full-timers. All vicious cycles can become virtuous ones: An increase in fishermen, or even a better rotation of part-timers, would lead to Rhode Island's winning better market share, improving its name, and, eventually, someday way off, increasing the price for quahogs. This is precisely the sort of thing Jeff was trained at URI to figure out, and it's why guys want him representing the interests of shellfishermen before the State.

But first, he has to fix his hauler. Forty-five minutes or so after Jeff rethreaded the pulley, something goes wrong with the winch he uses to haul up the dredge. He and Brian have a good time looking for tools, taking the hauler apart, putting it back together. Fishermen tend to be worse mechanics than farmers are carpenters, but there's no one to save you out on the water. Jeff and Brian, with pliers and a screwdriver, work on the hauler. While watching Jeff ply the hauler's wheel, Brian's attention drifts, and he spots a spider crab on a nearby round of mussels. He executes it in a leisurely fashion. Jeff notices.

"At some point," says Jeff, "we need to deal with the predation control. The percentage of quahogs we take out compared to the biomass is very low, and it has been for a number of years, but the stock continues to decline. So even though we're basically catching no quahogs compared to previous years, stocks just keep goin' lower and lower."

Lots of quahoggers say this: The bay's not getting good sets. A set is a generation of quahogs. A good set is a boom generation. Some State agents say the same thing. Recorded landings have sunk like a stone since the mid-eighties, but the population of quahogs has also declined, say the guys. A lot of people think something's wrong out there, but nobody knows just what. As Arthur Drew put it, that day down the shanty: "We might be in a recession, but the goddamn quahogs are too!"

This doesn't mean it's time to panic. "It's not there yet," says Jeff. "But at a certain point, we gotta say, 'Okay, somethin's happenin' here, guys.' Is it the predators? How can we control the predators? Is it worth controllin' the predators? How expensive is it?

"All these questions—well, there's a lotta different factors, but I think it's predation. It could be other things, a lot of things, but I personally believe that predation is much higher than it has been in the past. There's really not a lot to eat—other than quahogs—in the winter."

Jeff waves his pliers at another spider crab creeping slowly over the mussels. "There's a niche of scavenging worms and dead things on the bottom, and you took away the winter flounder, and now the crabs are here, and now the winter flounder can't come back because of the crabs. They took up that niche, spider crabs in particular, cuz they were in the mud; a lotta crabs don't like mud, but spider crabs do, which is what the winter flounder like . . ."

Of course Jeff says this. What the fuck else would he say? He's arguing for an approach to resource management that calls for more fishing. Someone will have to catch the crabs. Who would that be? Who's going to figure out what kind of traps to use, and where and how to deploy them? Jeff says that certain varieties of Asian crabs have also become a problem. They are invasive species; unlike the spider crab, they came to Narragansett Bay in the bilge of cargo ships. It's not hard to imagine that Jeff would happily pit his skills and energy against the instincts and hardiness of both spider and Asian crabs. For a price.

It's a reasonable proposal. Overfishing wiped out the winter flounder; perhaps overfishing of competing species could help bring them back. Eliminating the quahog's predators to bring its numbers up should work even better, because the quahog is not overfished. Jeff is arguing a viewpoint that, if accepted by the commons, would work to his advantage—or, to put it more honestly, he's saying that the approach he is most familiar with—controlling effort—offers the best solution to the problem of declining stocks. What answer would a fisherman see other than fishing?

Everyone does this. The State Department of Environmental Management wants to impose a better management system. Environmental groups like Save the Bay want to see better regulation. A quasi-State agency like the Coastal Resource Management Center wants to execute shoreline projects that will improve water quality, such as sewer tie-ins. Contractors, for obvious reasons, want the same thing as CRMC. Scientists at the University of Rhode Island think some research could help.

Jeff understands all of these other positions, but, in the end, he's a fisherman: He wants to fish.

The debate is of the highest importance for the people who live around Narragansett Bay, especially insofar as they concern themselves with Jeff. The point where the problem of a low stock of quahogs meets Jeff Grant is the crux of the free and common fishery. The people who care for the bay, who establish it and keep it as a commons, must decide two things: Is there a problem with the quahogs? And, what do we want Jeff Grant to be?

The community around the bay first needs to decide if quahogs can even be a problem. Do they really care if all the quahogs disappear tomorrow? Another way to ask this question is: What do they want quahogs for? Rhode Islanders may want to eat Rhode Island quahogs, but, in order to get enough of them, they'll need a considerable amount of full-time quahoggers who will have to get paid well enough to do the work of providing quahogs. Or Rhode Islanders may want to have quahoggers—that could be a reason to have quahogs. They like to see the guys out on the water; they like to talk about how tough quahoggers are, and how hard they work, and how their cousin used to bullrake and how sometimes he still gets littlenecks for them. And so they care about the populations of quahogs in the bay, because the quahogs supply quahoggers. Or they could simply want to preserve the quahog for itself. The State takes something of this tack, especially in the orientation of its DEM.

Dennis Erkan, the principal marine biologist at DEM, responsible for overseeing much of the regulation of quahogging, has this view. "I don't think of management as supporting the industry," he says. "I think of it as supporting the resource—and the industry can fish it if they want to. It's not about piping plovers and endangered species; it's about the whole ecosystem."

It may seem peculiar to manage a resource as if it's not going to be exploited, but this approach has its argument: Establish the goal of a healthy ecosystem and, by reaching that goal, you'll necessarily arrive at a healthy exploitation of that ecosystem. "That's where everything's goin' in fisheries management," says Jeff. "Instead of species management, it's goin' towards ecosystem management, which is very difficult." It's difficult because ecosystems are extraordinarily complex, which makes their management complex, but, even more, the perspective of ecosystem management causes problems because it is an affront to human dignity.

Look at the combined sewer overflow system to see the complexity. Rhode Island built a gigantic storm-sewer system, finally, after years of pressure from people concerned about the bay, to deal with the overwhelming of sewage lines by high precipitation. In other words, to prevent shit from flooding into the Upper Upper Bay every time it rained hard. The State took 350 million bucks and used it to dig huge—astoundingly huge—tunnels under Providence and out to the bay. They bored shafts three hundred feet down, then tunnels three miles long, doing much of the work with explosives.

Mike McGiveney got to tour one of the tunnels, as the State and the shellfishermen both expected the new system to dramatically reduce the number of days DEM has to close the bay due to rainfall. Before the system, a big rain—over half an inch—would shut down the bay for a week. Now, Joe Migliore, the biologist at DEM who makes closure calls, waits for a three-quarter-inch rainfall, and sometimes has closures of shorter duration than a week. Cleaner water means more days when quahoggers can dig.

It can also mean more places to dig. The Special Area Management Plans advanced by CRMC did bring towns on the water to tie houses relying on septic tanks into the sewers, which do a better job of preventing nitrate pollution. In Greenwich Bay, a big patch of water in front of Apponaug Cove opened up, because Joe Mig's sampling and the Department of Health's testing showed bacteria counts consistently lower than 14 per 100 milliliters, the shellfishing standard. The water had become clean. The State moved the closure line back, opening a bed of quahogs that had been untouched for fifteen years. There was a bonanza, and that's just what the guys want.

There are millions and millions of bushels of quahogs behind closure lines because of mistakes made by the entire community living around the bay. The subset of Rhode Islanders made up of shellfishermen is minuscule when compared to the total population of Rhode Island: several hundred next to a million. It's the million's fault that the bay suffers from pollution, and the million did the right thing by paying for more-sustainable systems.

Ecosystem management problematizes these achievements. By looking at the whole bay, not just the lines of closure—by looking at what pollution does in the bay—you can come to consider, and possibly concede, that reducing pollution, especially nitrate pollution, hurts the quahog population. Cleaning up the bay starves the algae. Reducing the algae population starves the quahogs. Reducing the quahog population starves the fishermen. It's just the sort of counterintuitive result scientists and economists get off on. There's no indication that the story is true, but ecosystemic thinking brings it to mind and suggests further investigation, which is difficult and costs money. That's the complexity of it.

Ecosystem management also, in its ostensible goal, devalues human purpose and human worth, and it does so while telling people what to do. "Fisheries management is generally just the way you harvest fish," says Jeff. "It's rules: no dredges; you can have this many licenses, this size bullrake, this long o' teeth; you can't have a hauler if the rake's so big; and on and on, tons of 'em." The thing with rules is that they need to be fair; they need to do what they are supposed to do, and they need to align with the desires of those who follow them. A quahogger has to abide by DEM regulations and listen to DEM agents give him all kinds of shit and pay fines if he fucks up. Why? What for? To preserve an ecosystem? Preserve it for what? What is anybody going to do with an ecosystem?

Jeff says, "Things should be managed so that you can get the most out of the resource. Sustainability, obviously, is a big part of that, but it should be used—used wisely, yes, but it should be used. I see the value in a species, but having a million deer in the woods isn't great, unless someone's shooting them—that's the way I see it. It's great that they're there, and I want them to continue to be there. As far as I'm concerned, the quahog is useless until it's in my rake. Literally, it means nothing to me. Maybe it filters this or that, it has some ecological value, but as long as there're some of them, it doesn't have a value to me until it's in my rake."

That's fisherman talk—and human talk: Man before Quahog. The bay can only be in service to Man, not the other way around. Furthermore, it's silly to suggest that Narragansett Bay is artificial now, where it was natural before. Maintaining the ecosystem means preserving the particular artificial situation Rhode Islanders like best. And, even without the works of Man to foul everything up and cause confusion, there would be no natural system to maintain. As Donatien Alphonse François, Marquis de Sade, observed: "Nature . . . it does not exist." There's no true natural state for a ten-thousand-year-old estuary. There's no natural state for a four-and-a-half-billion-year-old planet. There are no natural states whatsoever. There are temporary circumstances that people either like or do not like.

Again, it comes down to what Rhode Islanders want to do with the seminatural abundance of food that they find in Narragansett Bay. They could go all-out against the quahog, declare war on it, and add its name to the list of bay fishes now commercially extinct. Or they could manage it with a few hundred years of fishing in mind—with the recognition that sustainable practices lead to good circumstances for people now, environmentally, economically, and aesthetically. All of these purposes come implicit in ecosystem management, in that any management system necessarily serves some human purpose, but the implementation of the means of achieving its goals can alienate and even irritate the people whom it most affects.

Ultimately, Rhode Island is confused about its feelings for quahogs, which is hard enough, but it also has to deal with the bay, and with Jeff. Jeff is young. One of the great challenges of any society is how to direct the energies of its young men. Young male mammals are always a problem. They have too much energy, too much strength, and too much ambition. They must be controlled or exiled. With Jeff, specifically, the question becomes one of how to make the most of his ambitions. He wants to make a living catching all different kinds of fish. Or, really, he wants to do all different kinds of fishing. He has something of a rush mentality, however. A guy like Jeff looks at a quantity of product and says, Very well; there is the quantity we are going to catch. Let's go catch it today and do something else tomorrow. That's what he means when he advocates for weekly limits. Let him catch a week's limit in a day. What difference does it make how long it takes him to catch the limit, so long as he keeps within its bounds?

"This fall, I had to go and do the daily limits of fluke and stuff," says Jeff. "I still did it. I woulda loved to do weekly limits—I think it's a great idea. All it does is, you catch the same amount of fish and make a lot more profit. Or it could be shellfish, it doesn't matter; if Greenwich Bay opened up and it was gonna be open three days that week, with a three-bushel limit, and I could catch my nine bushels in one day, I'd go do that, and now you're gonna make more money that week. Some people want to go every day—make less pay, but get to go every day. I can only assume that they want to work, they need something to do; I don't know what it is. I don't know the reasoning behind it."

Actually, he does know the reasoning behind it. He knows that guys will rip off the system by catching weekly limits every day; he knows that weekly limits might cause swings in prices; and he knows that a lot of guys just want to go quahogging. They don't share his desire to try other fishes. Jeff also knows the code of the day's pay. It's a shellfisherman's apothegm of sorts: "Makin' a day's pay—that's what it's all about." Guys say this in order to exhibit modesty and to instill the code in other fishermen, to create a moral community, and a sustainable fishery. "A day's pay" means the same thing as "living wage": middle-class remuneration. It's a goal, but also a limit. Anyone who aims for—or worse, attains more than a day's pay—is suspect. He could be fucking things up for everyone, economically and environmentally. It's a conservative position. New technologies and new techniques could overturn the old order, which obviously works, or else it wouldn't be old.

It's a question of what to do about wealth. The food wealth of Narragansett Bay can be converted into other kinds of wealth. Very well; to what extent should Rhode Islanders make this conversion? Just as there's a decision to be made about the resource—what's the quahog for?—so there is a question about the man: What do Rhode Islanders want Jeff Grant to make money for?

That's where Bunky Bennett comes into the picture. Just about everybody who has earned a living fishing Narragansett Bay knows his name. One guy calls him "a real waterman." Another calls him "a real bayman." When I asked my father about him, he said, "Oh! He was a true fisherman!" Jeff has heard a little of him. "The only thing I do know is he used to eel and snail and lobster and quahog," says Jeff. "And he had dates when he'd do everything; you know, on this date, April whatever, you put the eel pots in, and you take 'em out on May whatever. It worked for him over the years."

Bunky worked out of Apponaug Cove; he was one of the fishing Bennetts, friendly rivals of the Wilcoxes, especially on the matter of scallops.

As Jeff said, Bunky did it all, and he did it with precision—and with reason. Bunky made a hell of a lot of money working the way he did. It's the combination of exquisite habits and great success that makes Bunky admirable in the eyes of other fishermen, but it's also clear that guys take a much greater interest in the man's quirks than in his dollars.

"He hits the cream wherever it is," says Tim Trim, Bunky's nephew, as he is everyone's nephew. "In the wintertime, the transplant's open, he hits the cream. Eelin's in the springtime, and May, when you catch horseshoe crabs, cuz they're comin' ashore, right? So that's when the eelin's good, and he'll mow 'em eelin', and . . . What is it? Bunk told me that June ninth, I think it is, is the day that lobsters start runnin' in the bay, so my uncle Bunky was lobsterin' in the bay—and the ocean—but he'd start in the bay and work his way out. So that's what he did."

Bunky had an outstanding work ethic, even aside from the rigors of his fishing. He was the kind of guy who washed his truck every single day after work, never mind just his boat. Discipline dominated the man. He saved his money, invested in property, brought the best equipment. Beyond all of this, he kept records. Careful notes about the conditions that prevailed on each day he worked, and the actions he took in those conditions.

"Every year he had a new book," says Tim, "and it told everything he did." Even better, he kept each year's book, filed it away. He had records covering decades of fishing, and he taught Don Wilcox how to do the same.

"Bunky taught me," says Don. "He's a legend." Don brings out one of his own books from the 1980s, and he reads from it: "Water temperature, wind, air temperature, June 24th, 180 traps, 330 pounds of lobster, every trawl numbered, fifteen traps to a trawl." He closes the book and rests it on his shawl-covered lap. "It was all wrote down in miles and minutes. When I first started lobsterin', back in 1972, we didn't have no radar, no loran. I had a compass and I had a flasher—gave the water depth. That's all Bunky had, the same thing, a flasher and a compass. And you had a clock on your wrist; you timed a certain rpm, like if you were in a fog: At 1,200 rpms, I ran twenty-four minutes on a south-southeast course, and that's where my gear was. I don't know how we ever did it, but it's amazin' what you can do if you have to.

"His books would say, 'I ran twenty minutes, or an hour and twenty minutes at so much rpms, and then at an hour and twenty minutes, I turned twenty degrees to port.' I mean, they're useless to anybody—unless you know what it meant. It's like readin' a foreign language. It's like, What the hell good's this gonna do me? But it meant somethin' to him."

Those books would mean something to a lot of people. Decades of measurements and records kept by one of the best fishermen ever on Narragansett Bay—scientists, historians, even certain journalists, would go bananas over those volumes. Decoding them would be half the fun. Whole dissertations could be done just by charting out Bunky's path for a particular year. Those books constitute one of the great encyclopedias of the bay, but they are all gone. All of Bunky's books are gone.

"After my uncle died," says Tim, "my aunt threw away his books— all of his books." The complete works of Bunky Bennett got thrown in the trash.

Bunky's widow burned through the money, too. She gambled; she and Tommy Cole, whom she took up with after Bunky died. She poured hundreds of thousands of dollars in savings down the drains of slot machines. Boats and houses all got liquidated and poured down a slot. Slots are the worst form of gambling, worse than roulette. There is no way to influence their outcome. You can't even bribe a croupier when you're pulling a handle. She lost that money in the exercise of sheer luck, which is exactly the opposite of how Bunky had made his money in the first place. All of Bunky's care and forethought, all of his routines, constituted a direct assault on luck. Bunky used the information in his books to decide how to fish, and where and when.

It's a canard among certain economists that fishermen cannot become wealthy because of the role luck plays in their harvest. Bunky obviously puts the lie to that little thought experiment, as does the mere fact that it's possible to overfish a species. Man can catch as much fish as he wants. So little does luck matter in the act of fishing that every society must actually handicap its fishermen to prevent them from catching up all of the fish. The greatness of Bunky Bennett lay in his ability to rise to the top, even from within the bounds the commons placed on him. Bunky played by the rules; he was neither a pirate nor a gambler. Perhaps that is why his wife gambled away all of this money: to balance karmic accounts.

When the people around the bay consider Bunky's story, they have to evaluate what contribution his work and wealth made to their society.

Bunky provided millions of meals. The tally of calories delivered to the world by Bunky Bennett would be astronomical. The other wealth he generated, aside from food—the money he made—went, without too long a delay, right back into the economy. Mrs. Bennett played the slots at Foxwoods Casino, in Connecticut, a casino owned by the Pequot Indians. Casino money gets spent. It does not get destroyed, as it does on Wall Street. In a sense, there is never any danger from the wealth of the fisherman, because his wealth very quickly becomes the community's wealth, even among the most prudent of fishermen.

The workday ended for Jeff and Brian at eleven in the morning. Once they sold out, they headed back toward Warwick Cove, but stopped near its mouth to scrub down the boat. They washed it with bay water pumped up from below and shot through a hose. When I told my father about the day, explaining everything they'd done and how they'd finished by eleven, he said, "Oh, that's great! Then you can go fishing!" Jesus Fucking Christ. That is the parable of the fisherman's heart, just like the story of Bunky Bennett. They're all like that. They don't look merely at a single day in this manner, but at the whole of their lives.

Bunky died in his early fifties, but what if he had lived to retire? What would he have done? Probably, he would have quit his usual fishing and gone tonging. The only way for Jeff's community to understand him and to help him to direct his energies properly is to think of him as part of that tradition. Jeff is an inheritor of wealth who deserves to inherit. He belongs to Bunky's line.

This doesn't mean that Rhode Islanders need to get Jeff a notebook—or to encourage him to have a gambling problem. There is no clear rule to distill from the realization that Jeff follows in the footsteps of guys like Bunky Bennett and Don Wilcox. The narrative simply provides a way to confront what it is that Jeff does as a fisherman. The rest is for the commons to figure out.

For me, I knew how to handle the wealth Jeff and Brian produced: I asked if I could have some mussels. Jeff's an immensely generous guy. He let me shovel up as many mussels as I wanted off the deck, once they'd bagged up the catch. I scavenged a good twenty pounds or so. At least three meals came out of it. I took the bag of extraneous mussels home and granted myself the pleasure of being very selective with my cull. I tossed away pounds of mussels that would have been acceptable under any other circumstance, right into the woods around my parents' home.

My father was still in the hospital then, and my mother didn't have the wherewithal to deal with mussels. I took the catch back up to Massachusetts. My wife and I held two dinner parties on consecutive nights for two different groups of friends. The first night we had a pile of mussels in white sauce; the next night, a mound in red sauce. We gave away enough to make a third meal of the same size. And then we realized that we simply couldn't bear plowing through the remaining couple of pounds, so we threw them in the driveway. That is the meaning of what Jeff does. Even the dregs of his work amount to a feast, but you can get to these dregs only out on the water. For most people, even for most Rhode Islanders, shellfish come from a market, and for there to be a market, there must be a dealer.

CHAPTER EIGHT

Food or Money

*We'll get that fuckin' million dollars back, if he hasn't spent it already
. . . a million fuckin' clams.*

—WALTER, *THE BIG LEBOWSKI*

SOME QUAHOGGERS IN GREENWICH COVE MOVE THEIR SKIFFS TO THE
yacht club for the winter. The club lies at the north end of the cove, where
ice rarely comes thick. In fact, these days, not even the cove's narrow,
southern half gets much troublesome ice. Years ago, guys would tack tin
flashing to their boats to prevent ice floes from cutting through the wood.
Now, with fiberglass hulls and pollution—not immediately dangerous
pollution, but chemical pollutants that change the freezing point of the
water—ice isn't as serious a concern as it once was. Still, caution pays.

In mid-December, by seven in the morning, bullrakers have lined up
their trucks in the yacht club parking lot and are preparing to head out
on the water. Some guys have already started loading their boats; others
remain in their cabs, enjoying their heaters. One guy's listening to hate
radio; another has Led Zeppelin on. They're both smoking cigarettes and
staring at the docks and the water. Apponaug's opening today, which means
a short, tightly controlled workday, carried out in the midst of a pack of
hundreds of boats. The yacht club's more crowded than usual for this reason.

I walk past the trucks and down a ramp, trying to spot Joey Amato
or his boat, *Justin Time,* a pun on his son's name. Joey's short and broad
shouldered and often wears wraparound mirrored sunglasses. His father,
Junie, an Italian-American diminutive for "Junior," is going out on the
boat with Joey today. They're working two limits. The State has limited
the harvesting of the freshly opened area in front of Apponaug Cove

to five bags per license. Joey and Junie together can catch ten. When I find them, Joey's stacking buckets and Junie's in the cabin; "A Holly Jolly Christmas" is on the radio, and it's starting to snow. "White flakes and rusty rakes!" shouts Joey.

The Amatos are family friends of mine. Junie worked on the water with my father; his wife, Pat, did our taxes; and Joey was my wrestling coach in high school. Joey's still the wrestling coach for East Greenwich, which makes for long days during the winter. "You get down to the boat by six-thirty, quarter of seven," he says. "By the time you get hooked up and get ready, then you got eight to twelve to work, but then when you're done working, you still have to sell 'em, clean your boat and all that, and go home, take a shower, and then be at the high school." He's always been this way. When he was a teenager, he traveled in the other direction: He got to school at seven, got out at two, then headed down the shore to bullrake. In fact, he did it even before his adolescence.

"When I was in the seventh grade, or sixth grade, my father had a skiff with no motor," Joey recalls. "He would tow me out there with the anchor, pair o' tongs; he'd go out to work and four hours later, he'd come back and pick me up." Joey has a hustling, high-energy manner. His raking style and his wrestling style are all the same. In wrestling, it's a common tactic to slap your opponent's knee to get him to draw his leg back. When he does, you shoot in on his other leg. When I was sixteen, Joey showed me how to tap a guy's leg, then instead of shooting on the opposite leg, grab the guy by the crook of the same knee I'd tapped and use his backstep to pull me into a shot. The move requires quick reflexes, not only in the act of grasping, but in relaxing enough to exploit the opponent's momentum, which confuses him. A guy has to be a coiled spring to pull off that kind of shit, and that's just how Joey seems.

A bullraker like my father or Howard Drew digs with tranquility; you hardly see them moving. Joey's savage; he tears at the quahogs. But, as is the case with wrestling, his savagery is constrained and directed by technique. Apponaug's paved with quahogs; just the spot for a bull, but even in such a prime location, you can't just toss the rake in, jerk it around, and expect to get results. "It's open; the tide runs harder there," says Joey. "The bottom's stickier. You can go over piles of quahogs and miss 'em if you don't have the stars and moon aligned."

DEM's agents are there in their boats, patrolling the crowd of hundreds of skiffs. This is highly unusual for the winter, but that's how good everyone expects Apponaug to be. It's worth calling in sick for; it's worth working face-first into the snowy wind coming off the shore. The starting gun will go off at eight, which leaves a good twenty minutes to kill. Joey turns off Perry Como's "Frosty the Snowman" and turns on the little VHF radio the guys use to holler at each other nowadays. The hot topic is all of the part-timers who have come out to take advantage of the new fishing grounds.

First guy: "Fuckin' some of these guys came out here at fuckin' quarter past seven, sit here and wait for forty-five minutes."

[white noise]

Second guy: "Everybody's gotta be a critic."

Joey finds his place at the northern end of the pack, near to the mouth of Apponaug Cove, but far enough away not to have to worry about the closure line. He tosses in two anchors, one off the bow, one off the stern. His boat's a twenty-five-footer, which he got for lobstering; it has considerable mass. The tide and the wind will have him drifting back faster than he likes without some countervailing drag, but a single mushroom anchor won't cut it.

"This is really soft mud," he says, "so they're fuckin' like plows." He'll have to monitor the anchors carefully to keep the boat drifting along the line he wants throughout the workday, which should last about thirty minutes. That's the appeal of Apponaug: a day's pay in half an hour. It's a rare thing to see so many guys and so many quahogs.

"It's not even a third of the guys that were out there fifteen years ago," says Joey—and that's just winter numbers. The same goes for the quahogs: "You would think with things having gone from three thousand guys to about two hundred working every day in the summer, there would be an abundance o' quahogs, but there isn't."

It's a taste of the old days with regard to the density of men, and clams, but other things are different. Joey and Junie work differently than they used to. The guys use haulers now. In the mid-nineties, the Shellfishermen's Association began lobbying the State to allow the use of haulers in bullraking. A hauler's just a winch, the same thing Jeff Grant uses to bring up his dredge, the same thing a lobsterman uses to haul his pots. Bullrakers use it to bring up bullrakes. They tie a rope—a down line—to the rake, run the line around the hauler's wheel, then hit a button to bring up their quahogs. In this way they avoid the wear on the thumb-web that plagued so many old-timers, along with a number of other detrimental effects that come with hauling in a rake by hand. Of course, new disadvantages have cropped up with the adoption of haulers, because they bring up the rake so quickly and with such unrelenting force. One guy knocked some of his teeth out on his handle, and one guy went over the side when his stale got caught in his raincoat—but, generally speaking, it has made things easier for the guys, especially the older ones. Virtually everyone uses haulers now, but lots of quahoggers still feel uneasy about them.

Anything that makes the job easier merits suspicion. For one thing, allowing the haulers meant indulging in juridical shenanigans. There's no mechanical harvest allowed by law, but what is harvesting, really? Is it not merely the act of raking the quahogs, not that of both raking them and bringing them into the boat? That is the argument: Hauling the captured quahogs off the bottom now no longer counts as harvesting, but rather as *transporting* a harvest, not altogether dissimilar from bringing them to shore in a boat powered by an outboard motor. Dicing semantics so finely will cause the industry problems in the long run, as might the hauler itself, if it works too well. Plus, it looks strange when it comes up. The field of bullrakers looks different now, because the stales don't pop up overhead as they used to. The hauler brings the stale up on an angle, not vertically. This means that Jocy has to take more care about the guy behind him, especially because the hauler will continue to pull the rake, even when it has hit something, or someone.

Other things look and work differently. Picking over has changed. This is mainly Junie's job. It's the old cycle of life routine: As a child, Joey picked over for Junie; as a man in his seventies, Junie picks for Joey. It is still not an easy job, but it is easier now, especially off Apponaug. Joey's a good digger and he has the hauler. He pours quickly, sometimes one catch on top of another, sometimes in a spare bucket with a little water in it. Junie has to work fast to make sure his son doesn't get ahead of him. He shuffles the pile of quahogs Joey has made on the culling rack. He doesn't sort through them too much; he mostly just agitates them. Undersized quahogs fall between the rack's bars. By his right side, Junie has a bag and bucket prepared. The white plastic five-gallon bucket has no bottom; it sits in the mouth of the red-plastic fifty-pound onion bag. Junie pours the quahogs sitting on the bars of the culling rack into the bucket, which funnels them into the bag. The flow of quahogs sounds like gravel coming off the back of a dump truck, which brings to mind the alien quality of the little creature. A quahog is a stone with a soft, pale, sweet, and salty meat inside. And there are so many of them.

"They all look the same after a while," says Junie, and he means this in a couple of ways. Yes, the individual quahog is hard to distinguish from its fellows, but Junie is also remarking on a change in the job of picking over. The quahogs seem all the same because he doesn't have to look at them with a discerning eye anymore. When Joey and I were young—when Junie and my father were in their prime—*picking over* meant getting rid of the bycatch and grading the quahogs by size. We had culling boards, not culling racks; we just sorted through a pile of quahogs and bycatch on a sheet of plywood. Today, there is only the bycatch and one grade to pay attention to: undersized. All the other sorting—and another round of scouring out the undersized—takes place at the shop, when the bullraker sells out.

This is a big change, and may be, in part, responsible for the reduction in quahog sets attested to by the quahoggers. When I was quite young, I

Junie picking over, 2012. MICHAEL CEVOLI

remember struggling to heft bags of littlenecks or bags of cherries or bags of big ones onto the huge, scoop-shaped pan of an industrial-size hanging scale at the shop, while daintily trying not to get mud all over my bare legs. That was when dealers bought by the pound. In 1985 or so, they switched over to count, which practice continues to this day. All of a sudden, Cap'n Bill had a roller, rather than a scale, on the *Beacon*—a device with two long cylinders that spun constantly, set parallel, an inch apart, and at an angle. At that point, the quahogs went into a tray at the top of the rollers, and the guys guided the pile through a funnel at the end of the tray, the aperture of which lets the quahogs through onto the rollers one at a time. As the catch progressed single-file down the rollers, the undersized fell, heartbreakingly, through the roller gap. The littlenecks that passed muster knocked a metal flap on their way off the rollers, each knock registering on the digital counter.

Guys didn't like the move from pound to count for a couple reasons. First, they couldn't screw Finn as easily. While there are no industry standards that determine the transition between sizes, both bullrakers and dealers knew when an ambiguity between a littleneck and a cherrystone was strained. Dump your catch on the scale and everyone can see if you've got some chunky stuff in there, but there was always some leeway. Warren Finn might root around in the quahogs, if he felt like busting a guy's chops—"Looks like you got chowders in there by mistake!"—that sort of thing. The diggers had an incentive to push the upper limit of the littleneck size of about a couple of inches across. They wanted to get the most weight while catching the fewest number of quahogs. The switch to count reversed that incentive: It became more profitable to catch as many littlenecks as possible while transporting the least amount of weight, which meant targeting quahogs at the lower limit of the littleneck size, which is to say, on the edge of being undersized. That's the second problem the guys have with the count standard: catching too many young quahogs. They know they have a bad incentive. There's profit in depleting populations of juvenile clams. This is especially troublesome for quahogs, because, as is the wont of strange creatures such as the molluscae, most quahogs switch genders throughout their life span, and in a pattern that results in quahogs of roughly the littleneck size being 90 percent male. The count system's a sort of plague on firstborn sons, as the quahoggers

Converting quahogs into money at Rhode Island Clam, 2012. MICHAEL CEVOLI

are wiping out huge numbers of male quahogs that should have become female, which bodes ill for both reproduction and biodiversity.

Yet there is money in it.

Joey and Junie high-graded a little in front of Apponaug for this reason. "Just take the big ones out and put 'em in another bucket—the big shit," said Joey, after pouring the first haul. "Throw 'em overboard after, the real chunky shit." He held up a fat chowder. "Shit like that."

Junie high-graded for a while, but they got sick of it eventually. It made little difference and it was too much trouble. It was fucking freezing, and the snow spattered on their faces in tiny, hard grains. "I hate these goddamned gloves," said Junie, as he shoved a tag into the mouth of a bag and got caught up in the folds of plastic weaving. Between bagging the catch and tagging the bags, he began to give less and less of a shit about high-grading, especially when they were so close to getting out of the miserable weather.

"Not too bad," said Joey. "Twenty past eight, almost got the limit."

Two limits, in fact; his and his father's—ten bags.

"I'll go home," he said. "My roommate will still be sleepin'."

They packed it in. Joey dismantled the bullrake, Junie broke down the culling rack. They hauled in the anchors and Joey drove the boat carefully and a little ostentatiously through the mass of men who were still working, back toward Greenwich Cove, to sell out. An early departure from the fishing grounds, a leading departure, meant something to him.

A few months later, I was talking with David Drew, and Joey's name came up. "Good quahogger," said David. "I was over at Apponaug and he was done in about twenty minutes." That's one of the things Joey gets out of his work: a guy speaking well of him behind his back. Pride's a real thing.

It was the same with wrestling. My first wrestling coach was a guy named Scotty Viera. He was a few years older than Joey and had been on the team with him in high school. One time, Scotty was talking inspiration to a kid who'd taken a tough loss. "Look at Joey Amato," he said. "He was a hundred-and-five-pound freshman, and every time he lost he'd come off the mat, cryin', pissed off. He lost a bunch of matches. He worked hard that summer, went to camp, came back, and never lost another dual meet match."

This is true: Joey's record still stands at East Greenwich High. Pride matters with him, and he is not an unusual quahogger in this regard. But there is also the matter of making as much money in as little time as possible. And so he pulled the boat up to Rhode Island Clam to sell his catch.

There are a couple of dozen shellfish dealers in Rhode Island. Most are quite small; a handful account for the greater part of the quahogs moved in and out of the state. Rhode Island Clam is the largest. It has a tiny footprint, however. The shop simply isn't very big, for all of the millions of quahogs that go through it every year. The Harbourside, the restaurant connected to it—which serves far fewer quahogs than the shop takes in—is considerably larger. At the docks, quahog skiffs bunch up; at the loading bay, trucks line up. Between the two, quahogs and money, clams and clams, come in and out of the little gray building.

Joey waited just a few minutes for his turn at the dock. Not many guys had made it in before him, and it's likely that all who did had hit only one limit, not two.

He and Junie loaded their ten bags into a couple of wheelbarrows, which Joey pushed up the ramps leading to the shop. Junie stopped to say hello to Porky, short for Porkasaurus, a quahogger with a wonderful round belly and face. When Porky had pushed his own catch far enough up the ramps that he was out of earshot, Junie said, "That's about the nicest guy you could ever meet."

There's a story about Porky beating up a guy, but the guys tell it in order to show that he's a really decent fellow as well as surprisingly tough. Somebody was showing off to his new girlfriend at a bar by picking on Porky, even going so far as to slap him in the face. Porky protested as gently as he could, then took the guy outside and, among other things, slammed him into the wall so hard that pictures inside the bar popped off their nails. The key to telling the story well is to adopt Porky's cheerful, friendly voice when speaking his parts. "Hey! You should stop doin' that! You better not hit me again!"—in a high pitch, with a singsong rhythm. It's a morality play, of course, but one with real and recent truth behind it, and it's important for bullrakers to tell, because the industry attracts more than its fair share of bullies.

Junie headed into the shop through the doorway at the top of the ramp; it has one of those rubbery plastic fringe screens on it, so common in warehouses, especially those that stock food. Inside, guys checked out each other's catches, bitched about the price, and watched quahogs sluice down the rollers. Junie opened a Bud can. Not even 9:00 a.m., but fuck it—the guy's over seventy, and he just earned a day's pay quahogging. Let him drink his early Budweiser.

Drinking early is a fine tradition in the business. A few hours later, next door, in the Harbourside, Mark Finn had a Bloody Mary with his lunch of quahog chowder. Mark's a little shorter than Joey, not as broad, about ten years older, and wears a mustache. He worked with his father and his grandfather, the Warrens Finn, when the shop was still Greenwich Bay Clam. The property and the restaurant remain his. When he says that the quahog chowder—clear, as properly it should be—is not hot enough, word gets back to the kitchen and the knob gets turned up on the stove. The chowder really was lukewarm that day, and Mark was right to say so. He seemed slightly abashed telling the bartender about it, however. There were a few niceties playing out: Mark was exercising a little power, which in a good guy is always embarrassing; he was complaining about food in a restaurant to the person who served it. He was showing concern for his product; he was doing all of this in front of me, perhaps even suspecting that I was looking askance at the breach of tradition evident in the Harbourside's chowder—transgressive bits of parsley and celery among the onion, quahog, and potato.

Mark Finn has many different emotions—all of them running deep—concerning the shellfish business, across several of its aspects. A bowl of chowder is complicated for him. He forms a part of a long history, after all, a history that weighs on him and delights him. Behind where he's sitting at the bar, a staircase leading to the second floor displays old photographs on its walls, scenes from the old days, when Warren Finn Sr. and Jr. were at work. The images are just like the ones Arthur Drew set down at the table with David and my father: old trucks, old buildings, huge middens of oyster shell, all in milky black-and-white, only the Harbourside's photos are larger, framed, and protected with glass. Mark leans back from his chowder and settles a cradling hand on his Bloody Mary.

"My grandfather used to drive around in a 1962 Dodge Dart—it might have been later than that, even a '65," he says. "It was a piece o' shit car, and he dressed like he didn't have two nickels to rub together. He was always tryin' to sell somethin' out of the back of his car—shoes, anything. He looked like a homeless guy." He laughs. Mark's grandfather, Warren Sr.—known as the Colonel—has a considerable mythology around him.

Every old-timer can tell a story about the Colonel; often it's the same story, the one in which he screwed over Campbell's Soup—and perhaps changed clam chowder forever.

"That was before they found surf clams, which is all that clam chowder is now. Campbell's Soup actually used to use quahogs, and he was probably the reason they switched. The Colonel had done business with 'em for twenty years. They didn't have tractor trailers in those days, but they had big trucks loaded up, and they'd send two or three trucks down—just quahogs—to 'em, into Jersey or wherever the headquarters were.

"So one day, Campbell's got a new quality-control guy. They called my grandfather up and said you need to come down to the head office. He went down and my grandfather said it was a skyscraper, a twenty-five-story-buildin'. He went in and they said, 'Mr. Finn, we've come to the realization that you've been selling us a three-bushel barrel and only puttin' two and a half bushel in it.' They figured he was gonna be squirmin' and sayin', 'Oh, I'm sorry, I'll make up for it.' Well, he didn't. He went around the room, shook their hands, said, 'Thank you, gentlemen; you've made me a very rich man. Been nice doin' business with you.' And he left—never sold them another quahog."

Warren Sr. might have killed the market for chowder quahogs that day, but, for one thing, Campbell's clam chowder is swill, and no quahog should have anything to do with it, and, for another, lots of shellfishermen love that story. The Colonel gets a pass for fucking things up because corporations deserve to be screwed over, and because his behavior toward Campbell's made guys feel better about screwing over the Finns. The relationship between the Colonel and the quahoggers was always one of mutual dependency, mutual distrust, and, frequently, mutual fraud—and with occasional openness about these mutualities.

Another story that goes around about the Colonel concerns the time he short-changed Tommy Cole. When the weighing was done, most dealers would round up the payout, if not to the dollar, then to the quarter. The Colonel would count it out to the penny—not just to save money, but to fuck with the guys. He'd push a pocketful of change over to them, which was bothersome and something of a breach of etiquette, in itself, but, sometimes, he'd cheat them out of pennies, just to see if he could get away with it. He did this to Tommy Cole. Tommy found his pay three cents short and went right back to the Colonel, who admitted to having shorted him on purpose, and then he laughed about it.

Don Wilcox was there: "He told Tommy Cole this. I was quahoggin', and Tommy'd gone in to sell, and the Colonel said to Tommy, he says, 'Y'know, Tom, I get more fun outta screwin' you out of a penny than you do makin' a dollar.' I was standin' right there!"

There's huge balls in that, and an indication of what wealth really meant to the Colonel. From the guys' side of things, he was in it for the games, which was both bad and good: good, because that meant he was kindred to them; bad, because they often ended up losing to him. Everybody seemed to lose to Warren Finn Sr., and nearly all the stories about him ascribe a rash duplicity to him. "He was involved," says one old-timer, down in Greenwich Cove. "Not the son, the Colonel was, during Prohibition . . . ha ha! He was rentin' his dock to unload booze to the rumrunners, for money, and then he was gettin' money from the government to turn 'em in."

Another old-timer says the Colonel did the same thing to the quahoggers. "He had several quahoggers—this was in my time; the father was still alive back then. They would work in the cove, y'know, piratin', and when they would get too fat, and wouldn't work—so he lost his product—he called the game wardens on 'em! He'd tell 'em when they were gonna work. They'd get 'em, then he'd tell the guys, 'Well, I'll loan you the money to get a lawyer, and we'll fight it in court, but you gotta work harder.' It's a wonder nobody killed him."

From Campbell's to Tommy Cole to bootlegging to pirating, all of the stories describe the same personality, the same complexity in his relationship with the quahoggers. The Colonel might have been a man so at home in chaos that he tried to stir it up wherever he could.

"He went to an auction one time," says Mark, "and they had a case o' bourbon out on the table. He thought he was buyin' either two or three cases of bourbon, that's what he thought he was biddin' on, and it was actually two or three pallets. He got it for real cheap, but he had to come back with it. They were also in the finance business, my grandmother and him. He came back and he had to tell my grandmother. 'You damn fool!' she said. 'What did you do?!' He said, 'Well, I bought a couple pallets o' bourbon, but I got a real good deal on it. My only worry is I hope I live long enough to drink it.' And he did. He was the wild guy and my grand-mother was sensible, money-minded."

The Colonel fomented disorder everywhere. It's not just a wonder that nobody killed him; it's also a wonder he ever made any money. It's possible, however, that all of his freewheeling helped to keep the Colonel in business. The chaotic environment facilitated the efforts of the qua-hoggers to wreak occasional vengeance on him. Whether quahoggers felt wronged by the fact that Finn had money and they didn't, or whether the Colonel had actually screwed them, scoring some revenge, however petty, helped them to continue to come back to Greenwich Bay Clam, even if they'd sworn never to sell there again.

The guys had a few recourses, and defaulting on a loan was one. Call-ing the State to report that Finn was buying undersized was another. The most fun was stovepiping bags of clams. I saw the latter a few times down the shore. The Colonel was long gone by then, but the tradition had continued against his son. Jake Murray—my uncle Jake, who was a cousin by marriage—was always in on it. This was back in the days of weight measure, when you could simply throw whole bags on a scale—when you didn't even have to pour out the quahogs.

Jake was a tall, stiff man; he had trouble bending over. I could see the strain in him as he held a burlap bag open while another guy—I can't remember who, it could've been almost anybody; it could've been Cap'n Bill, for all I know—poured quahogs into the bag, taking care not to get any into the stovepipe in the middle, a stovepipe filled to the brim with rocks. Once the core of rocks was disguised, they worked the stovepipe out, topped off the bag with a layer of quahogs, and cinched it up.

Another time, I remember them doing it with a plastic mesh bag that had a wide, unbroken label around its middle, an eight-inch-high strip. They filled the bag with littlenecks to the lower edge of the label, poured in chowders to the top of the label, then finished off the bag with necks. They couldn't have gained more than a dollar or two, but Finn—it was Warren Jr. at this time—had pissed them off somehow, and now they would get back at him. Some customer somewhere, probably a restaurant procurer, would find himself fucked over, and the complaint would even-tually work its way back to Finn.

Such gestures were ultimately futile. They weren't able to hurt Greenwich Bay Clam much, but they mattered for their pride—which is why the Colonel himself used to make such gestures from time to time. He'd go into the quahoggers' bars and drink 'til the money fell out of his pockets—literally. This is another of the popular stories about him: He'd get stumbling drunk and drop cash on the floor on his way out of the bar. Eventually, Warren Jr. had had enough, and he confronted his father about this embarrassing practice. His father said the guys needed to see him like that now and then; they also needed the money, and they needed to get it from him in a way that made him look bad. He was disguising his charity with his own shame. Or perhaps he hoped to expiate offenses that shamed him by way of this secret gift.

Mark doesn't know every story about his grandfather, nor do I, about mine. But we both know that these men—Warren Finn Sr., as a dealer of quahogs, and Ray Huling Sr. as a digger of them—took up work that dominated and continues to dominate the lives of their descendants. Even now, with the shellfish dealership long sold, Mark works in food; his company even sells sustainably harvested seafood from time to time. The Colonel's methods also played a role, perhaps pivotal, in the survival and expansion of the quahog industry.

"Finn was the best," says Zorro. "I don't give a shit. You'd have a load o' quahogs, and a lotta dealers wouldn't take 'em: 'We don't need 'em!' they'd say. Warren would always take your quahogs. He might be a penny cheaper, but I think he was the best." Zorro means both Warrens here, but it was the Colonel—especially in the early days of the Depression, which were also the last days of Prohibition—who established the core principle of the business, which persists to this day: Always buy quahogs.

During Prohibition and into the Depression, Warren Sr. could always move his product when other dealers couldn't, because he used quahogs to disguise barrels of booze. The Colonel's approach of rum-running kept quahoggers in work during lean times—diggers especially. One of the Finns' great rivals was the Blount family. The Blounts relied on dredgers for much of their business, the Finns on diggers. By keeping diggers working, through whatever means, Warren Sr. fostered the quahog boom times of the 1940s and '50s, which led to the repeal of the Oyster Act in 1952, the gradual elimination of dredging, and the primacy of bullraking.

Mark knows this, and he knows that his grandfather had a wildly self-destructive drive in him, a real taste for chaos, which he satisfied through commerce. There is something socially disruptive about a rich old man who spends his retirement selling junk out of his beat-up car. What the hell had he been up to, making all of that money all of those years? Why take all of those risks? It's confounding, irrational. It can be hard to live with a person who upends order like the Colonel—who was not actually a colonel—did, both because of the chaos you have to endure, and the taste you yourself eventually develop for chaos. Mark has this predilection to an extent, which is why he enjoys stories about his crazy grandfather so much.

In the late forties, when the three-way fight of the Quahog Wars was in its beginnings, the quahoggers union sabotaged a number of the Finns' shipments, because they were buying non-union clams. Mark hasn't heard the story before. Kerosene was the weapon of choice. One time, a few union guys hid on a railroad trestle, under which they knew the Greenwich Bay Clams open-air trucks would pass. When the trucks drove under the trestle, the union guys dumped gallons and gallons of kerosene on the quahogs. Mark laughs. "That's awesome."

It's similar with Mark's father, but not the same. Mark stiffens when he talks about Warren Jr., sits a little straighter. "He was a tough man; he was pretty much captain of the ship. He was so old-school that he couldn't enjoy himself, no matter how much money he had or didn't have—that had nothing to do with it. I don't mean goin' out drinkin', partyin'; I mean, just enjoyin' himself, whatever that is."

Warren Jr.—also known as Sonny, or Pig-Paw—remained inscrutable throughout his career, even with regard to his career. I remember him as taller than my father, slender, but rugged; he wore wire-rimmed glasses, had short dark hair, and preferred an old-fashioned flat cap. He was several years younger than my grandfather; I knew him when he was in his late fifties and early sixties. When I was setting fifty-pound bags of quahogs on the scale, so was he. Warren had plenty of dough, but there he was in the shop, counting clams, counting cash, getting muddy, and he kept doing it well into his seventies. He and Mark finally sold the business in the mid-2000s. Long before then, he bought a horse ranch down in Florida. Four hundred acres. He used to invite my father to come down and see it, an amicable falsehood on which he knew he'd never be called.

But then Warren himself didn't spend all that much time there, and when he did, he kept his feelings on the place to himself. The big difference between the Warrens Sr. and Jr. was not one of philosophy or method, but of temperament: Every account of Warren Sr. has him getting a kick out of his mischief. Warren Jr. had a severity to him—he wasn't humorless, just hard, which made discovering his motivations difficult.

"It's funny," says Mark. "It's like a lotta older people you talk to: If he was makin' a million dollars a day, business coulda been better. He was of the opinion—and a lotta people are—you never want to tell anyone when you're doin' well, because they'll try to take advantage of you, so you really couldn't tell if he liked it or didn't like it."

Whatever Warren's feelings, he clove to the business and adapted his father's techniques in accord with the vicissitudes of the times. From the mid-1940s to the mid-'90s, Warren Finn Jr.'s name appeared in the papers every few years in accounts of his getting busted for smuggling undersized quahogs. The cases would stretch over years before being dismissed. "My father said he never lost a case and never won a dime," says Mark.

The first one came in 1946, before Warren's twenty-first birthday: 331 quarts of undersized, a new record for the State Division of Fish and Game. Finn's lawyer crafted some priceless legal sophistries to get his young client off the hook, the brightest of which was the argument that, because the statute on undersized was "designed to protect the shellfish in Rhode Island waters, the State, to be successful, must prove that the quahogs in question came from Rhode Island waters." Finn himself offered up sterling bullshit on the stand. One of the game wardens had testified that Finn had said, "If I'm too fussy, they'll sell them somewhere else"—testimony to which Finn objected and countered with his own recollection of the conversation: "We talked about pigeons."

Yet, the warden's account rings true. Warren used to justify his trafficking in undersized to Mark in just the same way. "My father had an affinity," says Mark. "Someone would come in and have undersized, so he'd buy the undersized from 'im. I was never an advocate of it. I'd say, 'Why're you doin' that? Why're you buyin' the undersized?' He'd say, 'Oh, we're helpin' 'im out; just go and take 'em.' And it was actually my responsibility not to get caught after he'd buy the undersized—and you know what? It wasn't like it was a major thing. When I was young, before I got into the business, my father got caught with whole truckloads—that was a major thing."

Both Finns had their illicit means of keeping guys working and trying to stay on their good side, without actually raising prices. Warren Jr.'s approach was to mix things up with undersized—or so he said. Certainly, he had an argument. Quahog landings took a big dip in the late 1940s, then ramped up to all-time highs in the mid-1950s, only to come down less steeply, but quite steadily, through the 1960s and early '70s, to reach a nadir in '75. Then came the swift, steady climb to the mid-1980s. The ups and downs had to do with changes in general employment and the elimination of dredging. For a few decades, changes in quahog landings tracked well with changes in employment and income inequality. Things unhooked in the 1990s, because limitations on licensing kept guys from entering the industry, and because the advent of quahog aquaculture caused prices to fall. At its peak, Rhode Island accounted for a quarter of national landings. Today, it provides about 8 percent.

Throughout all of this volatility, Warren needed the quahogs to flow. He needed guys to keep working: He traded in volume; he needed the guys to bring in lots of quahogs, which meant the guys had to be able to make a living. But he didn't want to pay a premium price. Lots of quahoggers remember Finn saying to them, "I do well when it's my cart and your horse"—or the other way around (though it's a confusion of the idiom in any order).

Whatever the case, it's true that a sale of undersized could keep a guy going, especially because the money came off of the books. There's an argument to be made that Sonny's smuggling of undersized worked in a fashion similar to his father's smuggline of rum: He made money on it, as one can always make money on loosely enforced prohibitions, and the industry benefited from it in the short term.

Finn used to make gestures of appreciation, too. He gave the guys a bottle of whiskey on Christmas. "Some rotgut, I don't know," is how my father characterized it. "He did that every year. He gave out turkeys for Thanksgiving for a while, then he gave out gift certificates." The guys found some amusement in these gestures, but they also perceived them to be mere gestures. "If he really wanted to help people out," said my father, "he coulda raised the price."

This is true. But Warren could always plead the pressures of the market when it came to price, and thus make his purchasing of undersized seem like an act of munificence. Still, his characterization of his trafficking in prohibited clams as part of a strategy for engendering loyalty doesn't quite fit, especially because it could facilitate the plots of those men who had become disloyal.

"Dean Lees was a warden," says Mark. "He hated my father, hated him." Lees was a well-known DEM enforcement agent whom the guys called "Redhair," because he had red hair. "He was so happy one day; he thought he had us dead to rights. He comes in with a warrant—he had a warrant! We had like five or six pounds of undersized hidden. I'm sure some digger sold 'em to my father and was pissed at him and called DEM up, cuz they don't find anything out on their own.

"So he gets a warrant and he says, 'No one leaves this building; there's other officers coming; we're gonna search this place.' Well, we had a Pepsi machine in between the bathrooms in the shop. We had the key to the Pepsi machine, cuz we used to load it, but he didn't know that. So we hid the undersized in the Pepsi machine. He searched the whole place and couldn't find any undersized. He said, 'I want to get into this machine—where's the key?' And we're like, 'You gotta call Pepsi.' He gave up."

All of that commotion for about five dollars of product. What was the point? It's possible Finn just didn't like being told what to do. He wanted to decide for himself whether harvesting undersized was right or wrong—or, really, he did decide: He decided it was fine to catch undersized and damn the consequences if the law disagreed with him. It's possible he bought undersized quahogs out of sheer recalcitrance, which is still admirable, even though he was actually in the wrong—even outside of the law.

As all markets do, Finn's shop involved everybody who participated in it in a snarl of conflicting moralities. Not even a kid could avoid the implications. Ol' Pig-Paw used to buy me sodas out of that larceny-abetting Pepsi machine. A little treat to maybe help draw in the next generation. I always asked for anything except Pepsi—an orange soda, lemon-lime, grape. I remember clearly drinking a Mug-brand root beer Finn had bought me while I watched Uncle Jake stovepipe a bag of quahogs.

The market for quahogs has lost much of the illicit practices that helped it to flourish. There's little trade in undersized anymore; hardly anybody pirates uncertified waters; and guys can't pad their catches with stones. There remain a few crimes, however, enough to engage moral interest.

A few months after I went out on the boat with Joey, a guy down the shore told me about how he saw a dealer screw over both him and a customer. The quahogger had sold out and was hanging around for a bit, bullshitting. A customer came in off of the street. Most of the dealers will sell to individuals as well as to food companies and restaurants. This particular customer wanted twenty pounds of cherrystones. The quahogger watched as the dealer—and it was an owner, not an employee—reached into the catch the quahogger had just sold, took out twenty pounds of chowders, and sold them to the customer for the cherrystone price. "I mean, I know he's gonna screw me over," said the quahogger. "But did he have to do it right in front of me?" There's some double-edged fraud for the law-school casuists to deliberate over.

On the other side of it, the quahoggers, without the old methods of illegally supplementing their income, have turned to what they call "private sales" in order to keep themselves afloat. The term's a misnomer in a way, as sales to dealers are technically private. But the guys mean both that the sales are not approved by the government, and that they are discreet. It is illegal for individuals to buy quahogs from one another. Only dealers can legally buy or sell quahogs, and to be a dealer, you have to establish a dealership, have premises and so on. As with so much else in the industry, this law goes toward establishing the trust on which the whole business depends, and rewards those who invest the most capital. Because of the bacterial paranoia fixated on the eating of raw shellfish, and because so much of the trade in quahogs crosses state lines, a complicated institutional framework regulates the living shit out of the industry. This framework is essential for the existence of the market as it stands, but it privileges the dealer over the digger, which is why the Finns got rich while the quahoggers made themselves a day's pay.

Quahoggers have never accepted the disparity between themselves and the dealers, and, over the years, they have resorted to various measures, from strikes to economic planning to pirating and smuggling, to win better prices for themselves. From time to time, the guys have even attempted cooperatives, in order to seize for themselves precisely the profits that dealers make, but such attempts have always gone under, usually beneath flurries of corruption and cocaine. The collapse in price brought about by quahog aquaculture has widened the divide between digger and dealer. In 1985, my father could sometimes get a quarter a piece for little-necks. Today, it's a big deal when the price goes over eighteen cents. Considering inflation, the difference between then and now is considerable, and a serious problem for everyone, though especially for quahoggers.

Lots of shellfishermen have quit the business because of the collapsed price; other guys never get into it for the same reason. Private sales, which are off the books and go for a few cents more than the dealer is willing to pay, have helped to maintain the number of guys on the water, but the dealers—who cannot make money from this kind of smuggling as they did with pirated quahogs, rum-running, and undersized—hate it, as does the State. You need two out of the three big players, at least, to be on board for a particular practice to support the market for long, but, for the moment, the diggers, on this matter, are going it alone.

It is important not to view private sales as a free market, operating in competition with the legal trade in quahogs and offering a more efficient model of it. When a quahogger sells his stuff to a bar on the sly, he makes a trade with neither regulation or taxes on it, and it's caveat emptor for the bar and, thus, the bar's patrons. But this trade does not actually take place outside of the regular market. It supplements the regular market, just as did the Colonel's rum-running and Sonny's smuggling of under-sized. There is not—and cannot be—enough trade in private sales to support even a few full-time professional quahoggers, under present demand, even if Rhode Island stopped buying quahogs from out of state. Private sales keep the guys on the water only by eking out the income they earn from legal trade. There is no other market.

In fact, it is vitally important to understand what the word market really means here, as the remarkable polysemy of that word has led to confusion and immensely destructive practices of late. Mainstream economics has developed a meaning for the word market that has no referent in the real world, but serves only to advance the interests of those who want to shape markets to benefit a certain class of people. Unfortunately, the economist's notion of the market has captured the minds of enough people that staggering amounts of energy and resources now go wasted, in order to satisfy the needs of an abstract principle. It is crucial to keep the economist's model of a market separate from an investigation of any actual existing market, because the model will obscure the reality of what the quahoggers are doing. This separation is always difficult to make, and especially so where fish markets are concerned, because of the role fish markets played in the development of the model.

In the late nineteenth century, when Alfred Marshall abstracted the discipline of economics from that of political economy, one of his core examples was the abstraction of the neoclassical economic idea of the market from the actual institution of the fish market:

We might as reasonably dispute whether it is the upper or the under blade of a pair of scissors that cuts a piece of paper, as whether value is governed by utility or cost of production. It is true that when one blade is held still, and the cutting is effected by moving the other, we may say with careless brevity that the cutting is done by the second; but the statement is not strictly accurate, and is to be excused only so long as it claims to be merely a popular and not a strictly scientific account of what happens.

In the same way, when a thing already made has to be sold, the price which people will be willing to pay for it will be governed by their desire to have it, together with the amount they can afford to spend on it. Their desire to have it depends partly on the chance that, if they do not buy it, they will be able to get another thing like it at as low a price: this depends on the causes that govern the supply of it, and this again upon cost of production. But it may so happen that the stock to be sold is practically fixed. This, for instance, is the case with a fish market, in which the value of fish for the day is governed almost exclusively by the stock on the slabs in relation to the demand: and if a person chooses to take the stock for granted, and say that the price is governed by demand, his brevity may perhaps be excused so long as he does not claim strict accuracy. So again it may be pardonable, but it is not strictly accurate to say that the varying prices which the same rare book fetches, when sold and resold at Christie's auction room, are governed exclusively by demand.

Supply and demand. You can see the curves move with startling regularity in the transactions of a fish market. Thus, on the day after a big catch comes in—after Greenwich Bay opens, or the transplant, for example— prices drop a lot. Sometimes the price-drop happens the day of—either from the start of the day, or, in the case of at least one infamous dealer, right in the middle of it. Guys have found themselves fucked by a price-drop while in line to sell out—meaning the guy in front of you could make twice your pay selling the same catch you have. There's a classical beauty to the motion of quahog prices, but the mapping of their curves has seduced economists into believing that these sinuous lines are the fish market itself, the reality of it, rather than an abstraction of an abstraction of one aspect of it. Further, as the economists drew out these curves with new idealizations—rational actors, utility maximization, omniscience, and so on, all necessary to make supply and demand work in their models as they say the law ought to work—they developed forms of even more grace, which they used to seduce the public in the service of capital. The unattainability of such an ideal beauty only made it more attractive, which phenomenon tells why so many people harm themselves seeking it out.

That is the thing to avoid. Then, there is the fish-stink reality of actual markets to embrace. When I demand a meal of quahogs, I have many sup-plies of it to draw from. Rhode Island state law entitles each resident to har-vest two pecks of quahogs a day—a half-bushel, roughly a couple hundred littlenecks. Because Rhode Island also guarantees rights of the shorelines, I have legal access to every inch of the bay's shoreline below the high-water mark. Or I could walk into Rhode Island Clam—which exists, and can only exist, at the pleasure of the state and federal governments—and buy my littlenecks there, using the special knowledge of the industry I have to prevent the shop from ripping me off. Or I could go down the shore and buy quahogs off of the guy they call Cap'n Solo, because he makes so much of his money through private sales—smuggling, that is. Or I could go to Whole Foods and buy some quahogs advertised as "Local! Wellfleet, MA!" or Stop & Shop, where they advertise "USA quahogs!" Or I could have something else for dinner. The upshot is that the market consists of all of these options, legal and illegal, and the market relies on the condi-tions established by American food policy, which have resulted in a massive oversupply of food. I don't need to eat quahogs, but, if I want to, I have a cornucopia of ways of getting them. Fish markets have always operated under at least these many competitive pressures, and with at least as much support and subsidy from the community, which is the only reason why the forces of supply and demand appear so clearly in their operation. In other words, fish markets work only in communities of well-fed fishermen.

In this regard, fish markets aren't even markets, according to mainstream economics. The poor guy who got stuck with chowders instead of the cherrystones he paid for demonstrates this. In the naive view of markets, in the layman's understanding of the concept as economics has defined it, the customer who got screwed over would never again buy quahogs from the dealer who screwed him over. In the mainstream economist's view, such things not only do not happen, but cannot happen. They assume that every person in every position in the market has perfect information and, therefore, can never be defrauded or fooled. The problem is that the naif who believes what the neoclassical economist says about markets doesn't know that the economist makes assumptions that are not only wrong, but also totally insane. For markets to work as the economist says they do, then the guy who got duped must not have been duped. Just the same, markets that work with perfect efficiency, as the economist's model demands they must (although they don't), would increase wealth without making anyone rich—that is, the Finns cannot make more money on the quahog business than the diggers. The whole rhetoric of markets disguises economic analysis and economic policies that benefit certain groups of people over others. The current position of Rhode Island's shellfishing industry illustrates this clearly, right there on the shop floor of Rhode Island Clam, and on the bar at the Harbourside.

When a quahogger sells a littleneck at Rhode Island Clam, he gets maybe fifteen cents for it. Rhode Island Clam gets thirty or forty cents when it sells the same littleneck to a restaurant. At the Harbourside, a littleneck on the half shell goes for over a dollar. There's work added to the quahog each time it changes hands, but, mainly, the increase in price rewards the seller in proportion to the capital he has invested. Thus, you get nearly a tenfold increase in price by moving the quahog fifty feet, opening it up, and serving it.

The proper understanding of the word *market* is absolutely vital to the good management of the quahog shellfishery in Rhode Island. When the people around the bay think of the market as an institution they shape in order to achieve certain results, namely, a healthy supply of both quahogs and quahoggers, then the shellfishery and the bay and the people do well. When they think of the market as the earthly imperfection of some kind of ideal market, then everybody suffers, except, for a time, the man with capital. When Rhode Islanders care for the bay as a commons, they think of fish markets as fishing people always have: a system of exchange meant to serve the community as a whole. Without this perspective, the shell-fishing industry would have dredged itself into oblivion by the late 1960s. Wholesale ignorance of mainstream economics has kept quahoggers on the water. But Americans have become fascinated by the economist's fantasy of the market, which, in the end, as a discursive enterprise, is rather like a bit of avant-garde poetry, an ode to nihilism written out in mathematical formulae. As a bit of rhetoric, as an idea that has led people to martyr themselves en masse, the market is one for the record books, right up there with Jesus H. Christ.

All of this doesn't mean to say that Rhode Islanders have always gotten things right when it comes to managing their quahog shellfishery. The State did the right thing by raising objections to permitting large-scale, commercial quahog aquaculture in the bay, but it failed to recognize its duty to then establish a market that achieved the State's desired ends within the new context created by the rise of quahog farming elsewhere.

In the early eighties, Rhode Island quahoggers, a good number of them from Greenwich Cove, used to winter down South. They skipped the whole business of working in the freezing-ass cold. They would caravan down to the eastern shore of Florida, about halfway down the peninsula. They traded one estuary for another, Narragansett Bay for the Indian River, the main waterway of the Indian River Lagoon system, which is loaded with marine life, from manatees to tarpon to sea turtles to quahogs.

The guys slept in tents, cooked on campstoves, and bullraked the river for three months or so, making much easier money than they would have during a Rhode Island winter. None of the locals seemed to mind, as they didn't have much of a shellfishing industry, and the northern quahoggers spent money in town. In about 1984 or '85, however, the Rhode Island bullraking caravan pulled up to the banks of the Indian River to find PRIVATE PROPERTY and NO FISHING signs staking the place off. The signage extended the full length of the fishing grounds they'd been working the past few years, which they'd traveled fifteen hundred miles to reach. The men went to see the sheriff, and he told them it was true: The river was now closed to wild harvest. Someone was putting in a quahog farm there. Southern quahog farming would begin to put the bite on the market ten years later. Now that twenty-five years have passed, farmed quahogs dominate the market.

This is Smitty's problem, the one he has to guide his business through. Bob Smith bought the shellfish dealership from the Finns several years ago. He's a small, dark man, bearded, with a little gray. He's the one who paid Joey that day. He sat in a little booth, scribbled down the numbers his guys running the rollers yelled out to him on a slip, then counted out the cash (not to the penny). Smitty has run the show there for several years, though he has worked in Rhode Island for a couple of decades, and in shellfishing for thirty years. His office in the shop borders on full analog: The screen of the lone computer is shingled with Post-its. There are a couple of filing cabinets, photographs pinned to the walls, a couple of auto-parts posters, a small wooden model of a quahogging skiff. Smitty works in here in the same way he did inside the booth, scribbling on paper and talking to people.

"I grew up on the South Shore of Long Island," he says, "in the Oakdale-Sayville area, where the Blue Point Oyster Company was originated. Growing up there, I used to see all the trucks come in from all over the country to go to the little ol' Blue Point Oyster Company, and I would say, 'They're comin' in here for these clams that we dig, and they're goin' all over the world. Do people really like this stuff that far away?' So that's how I got interested." Smitty's a dealer, and dealers are different from diggers, but he has some of the latter's mentality. Although Smitty has employees and works in a hierarchy, he still retains something of the digger's casual disdain for office work.

"I was workin' for myself," he says. "It was kind of a creative business; there really wasn't this structure, a pecking structure, like in corporate, where you work to move up the ladder and get promotions. You were only as good as you are." Smitty offers this satisfying indictment of meritocracy in the corporate world without so much as a shrug to mitigate it. His abilities as a dealer concern him, which, perhaps, further distinguishes him from corporate boys. There's a special challenge in this work, one which Mark Finn expressed succinctly: "It's the only business that you're in—as far as a dealer is concerned—that you buy product that you don't have sold and you have a week to sell it, and if you don't buy it, then you piss off the diggers and you don't have the supply when you need it. But really, you're buyin' like a time bomb you gotta move in a week." Mark and Warren handed the time bombs off to Smitty, which is just what Smitty wanted. He's no less prideful than Joey or anybody else, and the situation that gives him the opportunity to earn his pride is the competition with aquaculture.

He thinks Rhode Island mishandled the advent of aquaculture. Internally, for the State, it's always been an issue. Hopeful investors started lobbying for the leasing of quahog beds by 1923, at the latest. Oyster farming had already begun its decline by then, no longer yielding, according to a letter to the editor of the *Providence Journal*, "a direct return of consequence to the State." The context provided by W. V. P., the author of the letter, in his argument for clam farms, is startling: ". . . it is due to lack of interest in their conservation and cultivation that the Rhode Island clam [*sic*], as a commercial proposition, has practically died out . . . [O]f course, there would be objections. The professional clammers, largely extinct, would perhaps object."

Good figures for quahog landings in the earliest part of the twentieth century do not exist, but the numbers would begin a steady climb in the mid-1920s, not long after the publishing of W. V. P.'s letter. The argument assumes a dearth of professionals and an oversupply of amateurs— the weekenders, says W. V. P., tear up the clam beds, which, he implies, quahog farmers, in their gentleness, would not do. That's an absurd implication, but he really gives away the game by asserting how easy it would be to cultivate the clam: "[A]ll that is needed to obtain a large crop is to leave them alone." This is true. The quahogs are simply there; you don't have to bring in transplants, as the oyster barons were doing with oysters at the time. The State could lease beds to quahog farmers who wouldn't have to do anything but harvest the quahogs. In other words, a man with capital could simply buy up ranges, pricing less-well-funded diggers out of their jobs, though he might hire some of them for harvest-time—or he could rent time on his grounds to them.

Fifteen years later, the editors of the *Journal* themselves would argue for quahog aquaculture in a specious and sleazy piece titled, "Who Owns the Clam?" The Hurricane of 1938 had devastated the Northeast and wiped out the oyster industry in Rhode Island a couple of months earlier. Now, it was time for a new kind of shellfish farming. The editors appealed to property rights, the plea of the rentier, who makes money not by producing things, but by owning. There's a disingenuous, eristic quality to the way the *Journal* editors argue, using the oyster industry as an example, stating that, because the bay and its treasures constitute a commons, individuals should be able to rent pieces of it; otherwise, the people's ownership of the commons would be in doubt. "The people, owning these resources, charge a rental for their use, for the dual purpose of asserting ownership rights and encouraging aquatic farming ..." It's almost vicious. Yes; the oyster barons cannot turn up on the bay, dump their oyster seed, and claim a right to State protection over their property without paying a fee. But extraction of rent is only one way to assert ownership. Another way is to refuse to provide the barons with protection, or even to prevent them from seeding the bay.

The editorial then raises the point that undermines its argument: "Until we approach and solve this problem intelligently, we shall fail to make the most of a valuable natural resource." Yet, the model they have in mind is the oyster industry, which is an unnatural resource in Narragansett Bay. The real problem is that the clams are already there. The State went through the same arguments in the 1990s, only this time, the discussions made their way into the legislature. The Finns and the Shellfishermen's Association fell on the same side, against aquaculture, and they testified to their views at the State House. It was all the same problem: The quahogs are already there. There's no work to do farming them; there is, in a Rhode Island quahog farm, only rent to extract.

In other words, the problem is abundance. Too many quahogs. The bay is loaded with them, and the people who live around the bay have to contend with this fact. Whom should they privilege? Who gets to benefit from the superabundance of quahogs? So far, Rhode Island has privileged the diggers over everyone else—over dredgers, and over rentiers. Had the State chosen dredgers way back when, then they would have wiped out the quahog as a commercial fish in the bay—which, ironically, would have lent strength to the position of the would-be quahog farmer, as he would no longer be benefiting from what Warren Jr. used to call the "natural gift of the quahog." Scrape the grounds bare, then seed them—which is, actually, the essence of all farming. The diggers and the Finns won out, and the shellfishing industry remained wild and sustainable.

But all of this was internal. Other states privileged other groups, and, in so doing, they did what all capitalists absolutely require their states to do for them: They created a market. While Rhode Island did the right thing in preventing quahog aquaculture in Narragansett Bay, the State did the wrong thing by denying the diggers what the capitalists would have received: state investment and subsidy in the form of a market.

Market conditions had changed by the time the shellfishermen beat aquaculture at the State House. What the quahoggers didn't recognize was that they should not have argued to keep their industry the way it was; they should have argued to change their industry in the right way. This is what Smitty sees now. "The people that are invested in the local supply and the local harvesting—primarily the fishermen and some dealers—would say, 'Hey, this aquaculture thing is no good; it's gonna manage the industry. It's gonna manage us out, and we don't want to participate in it. It's control; it's a few having control of a lotta volume. We don't want that," says Smitty. "It's a free and common fishing industry, and we want it to be accessible and open to the public."

All of that was right and good, but it didn't go far enough. Southern aquaculture product had already started to flood the market. What threw off the Rhode Islanders was the shittiness of their competition. Down South, in warmer waters, the quahogs grow too fast; they develop a balance of enzymes that make their taste all wrong; they don't take well to refrigeration. They don't keep as long as Rhode Islands, and they don't taste as good, and everybody in the State thought that everybody else knew these things and that they cared. Everybody did not.

"I think people kinda thought the Rhode Island name was so strong, and that people were so aware of the quality that the quality would speak for itself," says Smitty. "They think it's like a commodity that's traded in the gold market, that mental management has now managed them out of the box, because now the aquaculture and the states that don't manage like we do have taken front position. Even though we want to buy American, and we want to buy native and we want to buy quality, the bottom line is, we can't afford it. Most people come in here and say, Well, you know this Rhode Island clam thing, we need to market this better; we need it to have its own identity. We're really missin' the boat. We wanna start this 'grown in Rhode Island' thing. I would laugh them out the front door. We will literally price ourselves off the menu. I was on the Rhode Island seafood council board—I was president of it for a short time—and the State really did not get behind the Rhode Island industry. Other states—Louisiana, Maine—you could go to the Boston seafood show and you would see the Maine seafood council."

It was a supply-and-demand problem: Rhode Island discovered that, for quite some time, it had not been meeting demand for superior product, but rather, for lots of product. People in Ohio wanted lots of quahogs, not good ones—or, even worse, they couldn't tell the difference between good and bad clams. The demand was for mere supply. That's what no one knew, and when they did come to know it, they didn't know which choice to make: whether to create a market by building the Rhode Island name for quality, or by managing the fishery to create a steady and large supply of quahogs. The guys tried to do the former; they tried to grow the brand, which is not something a bunch of quahoggers should do.

As Smitty pointed out, however, Rhode Island had little interest in marketing its seafood in general, never mind its quahogs in particular. Governor Carcieri advised the Shellfishermen's Association to do some kind of marketing initiative, and they did: the Don Bousquet bags, which went nowhere—or, rather, which went into the wholesaler's trash. But the quality angle constrains the thinking of much of the Association's membership, which is quite the opposite of Smitty's. "We have been very inconsistent on consistent production," he says. "That has been part of our struggle with market share. If we had consistent production with consistent good quality, we would have consistent high revenue."

Jeff Grant says the same thing: It's the variance that kills the price, not the quantity. This is where the law of supply and demand seems to break down, unless you recognize that steady supply is what is demanded. If customers preferred Rhode Island quality, then inconsistent supply would raise the price. Instead, a large influx of quahogs from Narragansett Bay would lower the price initially, but as it remains steady, it should eventually raise the price, as Rhode Island establishes itself as a reliable supplier of volume. In order to arrive at that position, the State would have to reduce pollution in the bay—because rain closures make supply inconsistent—and increase the number of fishermen on the bay—because small numbers of fishermen produce small numbers of quahogs, compared with aquaculture. The State, with some prompting from the Shellfishermen's Association, has made some changes to help push the industry in the direction of volume, but not enough to establish a market for Rhode Island quahogs that is competitive with Southern quahog farms.

This puts Smitty in a bind. "The Upper Bay would open and the fishermen would come in and they'd be angry because the price dropped, and I'd say, 'Well, you're gonna catch four times more today than what you caught yesterday, regardless o' whether or not I can sell it.' Doesn't matter if milk is on sale, you're not gonna buy more of it, unless you just got a lot of cats, so that puts the onus on the dealer of being either educated or having good contacts to sell the product.

"I have twice in my career set up two complete distribution routes in the State of Pennsylvania, and after the second time, after re-setting it up and solidifying it and making all the contacts and making the delivery schedules and supplying the customers consistently, we had massive declines in production," Smitty says. "So after the second time, after I set up a complete route, I trashed it. I've disintegrated my own goodwill twice, and we're at the point now where we say there isn't anybody in Pennsylvania that would even answer the phone.

"Some of these customers would say, all right, I'm gonna need a hundred bushels for Thursday, and then we'd get these huge rainstorms, and then the Upper Bay would close. So after the customer got burned two or three times, he said, 'You know, quite frankly, I don't care where these things come from; I've got customers that are gonna come buy 'em whether they're from New Jersey or from Rhode Island, but I gotta have 'em, and you guys screwed me last week, where I lost X number of dollars because I didn't even have the product, because you promised 'em to me. You told me the weather looked good—as long as it didn't rain, I'd get them—and then you had a freak thunderstorm on Wednesday night, so all the bay closed on Thursday, and you didn't even deliver 'em to me on Friday, so I can't put my eggs in your basket anymore.' With the swing of the production cycles and the rain and the no-show, they were forced to look elsewhere, and some of the states they looked into, they decided that they were gonna try this aquaculture product. What they found was, yeah, the product was nowhere near as good, taste-wise, but it was certainly more affordable cuz there was controlled costs."

Rhode Island quahogs do fill a niche, even now, because of their quality. They have become a sort of quahog insurance. "The customer base chose to manage in a different way," says Smitty. "They would analyze their weekly and monthly needs; they would see where their peaks in sales were, and they would do things like, 'Okay, I'm gonna need a hundred bushels of clams this week. I sold eighty last week, and I think this'll be a better week. I'm gonna buy eighty outta Virginia, and I'll buy them Wednesday through Friday, and then on Friday or Saturday morning, I'll buy twenty Rhode Islands. I'll pay more money for them, and I'll keep them for my anticipated higher usage. If for some reason I don't reach that higher usage, I know the shelf life on the Rhode Islands is so good, I can keep 'em 'til next week.'

"So the following week," Smitty continues, "they don't buy eighty Floridas or Virginias, because the weekend was rainy and they didn't use any of the twenty that they anticipated, but they were so confident that the quality of the shelf life of the product was gonna carry them through the next week, so they adjusted their needs on the opposite end. We became the fill-in state, and it annoyed us, because we were getting the fill-in business and the customer base expected us to survive and to distribute and to be able to continue to keep our employees and our businesses thriving with being the fill-in guy."

For Smitty, it comes down to controlling effort, but here, he thinks a good part of the problem lies with the fisherman himself, not with the system of management.

"Years ago, in the fifties and sixties," he says, "it was frowned upon when the woman worked. The woman's place was in the home, raisin' the kids, so for the most part, you didn't have dual-income earning like you do in this modern day and age—primarily because no one can live on one income anymore. That fisherman was being leaned on as the sole provider for the family. Fast-forward, you have a dual-income-earning need. Back then, the expenses weren't there, the tradition wasn't there—but when you had a situation where you had inclement weather, guys pretty much worked. We used to kid people and say, 'On a good day, now, we produce what we used to produce on a bad day years ago.'

"To be understanding and not to be just a blockhead—to say, Well, I want those guys to fish, regardless of how dangerous it is—I have to be realistic and say they gotta make money doin' it too. The problem is—and this is the problem for the dealers—is that we have gotta be here as a service to the fishermen, and the fishermen can come and go as they please—to the point where, even if they choose not to sell that product to me once they harvest it, they can go elsewhere if they want to."

It's a situation similar to those the two Warren Finns faced throughout the years: how to keep a big group of guys on the water, and how to keep them working. Smitty can't adopt the Colonel's tactic of getting guys busted for pirating and then loaning them money for a lawyer, nor can he buy undersized from them. He has no rum to run. The lone practice that helps to keep guys going outside of the regular market—private sales—hurts Smitty. Ultimately, because he can neither force nor convince the guys to do what he wants, his problem comes down, not to individual effort, but to total effort—the total number of fishermen. But then he has another problem.

"The fishermen don't want more fishermen, because they'll have more product that they'll have to share with others, which means less money for them. The less fishermen that are out there means the better return on the fish for the limited amount of fishermen that there are. That's completely the opposite for me. If we have a recession—when I lived on Long Island in the early 1970s, we had a huge recession—most of the contractors, if you lived in the township and had proof of residency, you could go to the town hall or the city hall and get a shellfishing license. You could hang your hammer holster up, because you were unemployed, and go clamming. You can't do that in Rhode Island. So recessions, in some states, could produce more product. That puts the onus on the dealer, to see how good he was. Even though it was hard to sell with more volume of product, it forced you to sell, so you became a little better based on how good you were. You had the numbers, and the numbers rule this industry, good and bad. In Rhode Island, that's all strangulated and regulated, and we have a tendency to all start dropping down a notch. If the fishermen have less guys out there, which means less clams are landing, it means more money per clam."

And that's where the State and the Shellfishermen's Association remain bound by their own misperceptions. They are men who work in an anticapitalist industry that's trying to make its way in a capitalist world. They know that advertising works under capitalism, precisely because capitalist markets are not markets in the mainstream economic sense, and so they want to do an advertising campaign for their superior product. They know that the point of their industry is to produce food and well-paid fishermen for the conceivable future, but they don't know how many well-paid fishermen they want on the water. The trauma of 1985 persists, and the cruel joke is that Rhode Island's landings from that era would now constitute about a quarter of the national total. At the '85 level of production, Narragansett Bay would lord it over the market, so long as the quahogs remained in abundance.

Viewed this way, the task of creating a competitive market for Rhode Island quahogs would mean increasing both the number of fishermen and the number of quahogs available in certified waters. The former amounts largely to changing the policy on licenses. The State could just remove the cap and guys would strike in. But then the problem becomes one of increasing the resource simultaneously, either by moving back closure lines, as happened with Apponaug; reducing the amount of rain-closure days, as the combined sewer overflow project did; or transplanting quahogs from uncertified to certified waters, as the transplant program does.

All of these are considerations of supply, but there is also demand to create or instill or elicit, which should not be all that difficult to accomplish. There is, after all, very little that one can do with a quahog, other than eat it. Thus, advertising the quahog mainly amounts to making it appetizing. There are numerous ways to do this.

CHAPTER NINE

The Point of Quahogging

For all kinds of shellfish, use pepper, lovage, parsley, dry mint, a little more of cumin, honey, and broth; if you wish, add bay leaves and malobathron.
—APICIUS, *DE RE COQUINARIA* (CIRCA 450 CE)

SOMETIMES, A QUAHOGGER FORGETS HIS LUNCH. OUT ON THE WATER, HE looks for his lunch pail, but can't find it. *Son of a bitch!* He realizes he has left it on the seat of his truck. Oh, well. His lunchlessness occasions no disaster. He's on the bay, after all. Maybe he'll make a short workday out of it, head in early for lunch. Or he'll just eat late.

Or, as hunters sometimes do, he may dip into his catch. He'll lay open a few big ones, a few chowders—the cheapest and quickest way to satisfy his hunger. Two or three pounds of the largest quahogs would bring him twenty-five cents or so at the dealers. By eating them instead, he gets lunch for a quarter. On the other hand, he may opt for a treat: a dozen littlenecks. Lunch for a couple of bucks. Why, he might even go for some undersized— the rarest treat of all. Worthless clams or the most expensive ones, depending on the quahoggers' proclivities, but always the tenderest and most succulent.

Whatever his choice, it's a cheap lunch and one of the highest quality—the freshest possible clams, with the finest ambience, as he eats them on their own terroir. He has their home water on his fingers. Who but the quahog's marine predators enjoys more favorable dining circumstances? Indeed, only the extravagant act of actually eating them underwater could take him closer to perfection. Only the crab and the starfish dine better than the forgetful quahogger.

As well, he might even open them nearly as primitively as those bottom-feeders do. Why bring a clam knife on a quahog skiff? Unless he has already learned a lesson or two about forgetting one's lunch. No; he might have to smash his quahogs open, perhaps on a cleat, perhaps with a hammer, a wrench, a short length of stale. He'll perform the smashing as delicately as he can, because he wants to afford himself the most dignified manners possible, given his circumstances. Spilling the meat all out of the shell and onto his rough and dirty hands, pinching the soft, beige flesh between a hard finger and thumb, dangling it into his maw—such graceless ministrations would not do. He must sever the quahog's muscles, then elegantly gobble the poor thing out of its shell, and so, to preserve his own dignity, he sacrifices the dignity of the clam.

He serves himself the inner body of the quahog on a platter made of its own outward bones. A cautious smashing of one valve, then a meticulous picking of the broken shell from the whole one, which is soon to become a serving dish. Perhaps he might even dunk the exposed quahog into the water, in order to clear away any resilient grit—and also in order to give the meal a dash of bay seasoning, Narragansett sauce, quahog gravy. A quahog is very little more than the concentration of estuarine waters into animal form. To cover this little beast with some drops of the water from which it drew its body amounts to a basting of the quahog in its own constituent juices. One might even say that the quahog doesn't filter the sea, but rather intensifies it, purifies it into a substance fit for us to eat. You could say the same about humanity itself, of course. Consumption of the quahog brings man as close as possible to his own primal being.

Eating a quahog on the half shell always has a ritualistic, even sacrificial aspect to it. This is so because, to be honest and accurate, one does not eat a quahog raw. Certainly, it can be served uncooked—it is raw on the half shell in that sense, but it is also something more. A cut of uncooked tuna's cheek served on a tightly tucked roll of rice is raw and merely raw. The quahog raw on the half shell is alive.

This fact goes a long way toward explaining the high cost of raw shellfish at restaurants. All of the care taken in the harvesting, shipping, and preparation of the quahog keeps it alive. Thus, the reason you sometimes find a cook or barman struggling to work the little bastards open: They don't want to die. But what animal has ever withstood the palatal desires of man? Their shells parted with a specialized tool, muscles severed, cradled carefully on a plate or platter of ice or salt, and delivered—mortally wounded, doomed to die, but alive—to their ultimate predators, who may then douse them with acids tabacco, lemon juice, horseradish—before swallowing them whole. One may as well serve up the quahog on an altar atop a ziggurat, with a superfluity of kris-wielding priests in attendance. The whole ceremony is excessive, but nutritious and spiritually satisfying, and it is this method of consuming the quahog that sets the standard for the industry.

Such was not always the case. The quahog on the half shell came into commercial prominence in the late nineteenth century as a substitute for the oyster during spring and summer, when that more-exalted shellfish had exhausted its meat with spawning. Prior to then, the quahog enjoyed immense success as a base for chowder. For a while, the two purposes of the quahog complemented each other quite well and made a diversity of quahog sizes valuable, but, as the quahog became more and more elevated as a luxury food, it became less favored as a staple. No clear story accounts for that change.

Certainly, quahogs on the half shell never pushed chowder out of the home. The quahog-as-living-victim became all the rage as a restaurant or barroom dish, and remained so, even as homemade chowder disappeared from kitchen tables. We never ate raw quahogs in our house while I was growing up, and I know of very few people who did. My father offered a salient explanation when I asked him about the phenomenon: "I dunno . . . maybe cuz women and kids don' like 'em," he suggested. It's a hypothesis, but it doesn't explain why quahog chowder lost its popularity. To get at the question another way: Why did my family make so much chowder, while other families didn't? And I do mean *so much;* where Louis-Ferdinand Céline ate washtubs of noodles as a child, I ate bathtubs of chowder. I had that stuff for breakfast. The obvious reason why is that my father was a quahogger—but what about his being a quahogger? Chowder quahogs were cheap at the supermarket when I was a kid, and they still are now. Our slightly cheaper supply was never that big of an advantage.

It may have been the opening of the quahogs that dissuaded people, the one task that makes quahog chowder difficult. Rhode Island quahog chowder is simple. Take a stockpot, three- or four-gallon capacity. Slice up some salt pork, not too thick. Cover the bottom of the pot with the slices. Cut up an onion and layer the pieces on top of the salt pork. Heat until the onion and the pork fat are translucent. Cut up a potato and throw it in. Cover the potato with water. Cook until the potato's halfway done. Add lots of ground-up quahogs and their liquor. Cook.

Sometimes, we made this chowder—pure, simple, Rhode Island chowder—with ingredients we produced entirely ourselves. My father dug the quahogs or we gathered them as a family, together, in the shallows, by the boat. We also grew vegetables and occasionally kept pigs. The quahogs, the onions, the potatoes, the salt pork—all ours. Even the water came from our well. Only the sourcing of these few ingredients distinguished us from other households, however. We didn't prepare our chowder in a cauldron hung from a brandreth. Other families had similar, if slightly inferior, foodstuffs readily and cheaply available to them. Even better, they didn't have to dig up the potatoes and onions or slaughter their pigs—but they did still have to open their quahogs, if they had bought them live.

It's not easy to convince a quahog to quit this life. I can recall my father standing at the sink, huffing and puffing while he pried them open. I often have a hard time with it. The traditional method is to take the quahog in your off hand, positioning the hinge near the heel of the palm, with the little bump or knob at the back, called the umbo, pointing toward your thumb. Perhaps you offer thanks to the Quahog Spirit for the bounty it has provided (though I tend to think that such an entity would seem as pleasant as William Blake's *The Ghost of a Flea*). You slip the edge of the clam knife between the lips of the shell with your dominant hand, then curl the fingers of the other hand around the spine of the blade, nearer to the bolster than the tip. Then it's squeezing time. You have to squeeze like a bastard, but carefully, so as not to chip the shell, because chipping may both introduce grit into your chowder and also make the quahog harder to open. Once the knife sinks into the shell, you slice the posterior and anterior adductor muscles, which lie at either end of the hinge. Then you scrape the poor guy into a bowl.

Once we had plenty of meat, we ran it through an antique, cast-iron grinder, manual, heavy, and black. The process was relatively elaborate— relative to cooking processed or prepared foods. From this angle, it is possible to think that quahog chowder lost ground as a staple, because of the time and effort required to prepare it. Within the context of the new food system, chowder too became a luxury. Even resorting to the old chef's trick of heating the quahogs in their shells in a skillet until they pop open—which we didn't use, because it tends to toughen the meat—still leaves a lot of work to do, including shucking from a hot shell.

On top of all of that, the work is messy and odiferous. Quahog liquor is a potent substance, even compared to other seafood. When dealt with in quantity, it requires real care. Greenwich Bay Clam used to sell the stuff.

"Clam juice, quahog juice," says Mark Finn. "Once you spill it, it's the nastiest substance known to man. There's nothing else in the world like it. This kid comes into the shop one hot summer day. He was driving a brand-new convertible BMW, with the top up. He said, 'I need a gallon of clam juice.' So the guy I had workin' for me was hung over to the hilt. He gets the clam juice—it was real quahog juice—and he put the wrong lid on. So the kid pays his three bucks or whatever and drives off. I say 'kid'—he was probably twenty-five. He comes back ten minutes later and says, 'Can I get another gallon of clam juice?' I said, 'You mean you were makin' a chowder, and it wasn't enough?' 'Oh no,' he said, 'Someone cut me off and I slammed on the brakes and the lid came off on the front seat. What should I do?'"

At this point in his tale, Mark adopts an expression of horror. You can imagine all of the guys in Finn's shop with just that look on their faces, glancing sidewise at each other. "One of the guys workin' for me said, 'Sell that fuckin' car as fast as you can.'"

That was back in the days when dealers used to have people shucking quahogs and shellfish right there in the shop. Shucking was big business when the oyster barons reigned, when Scalloptown was booming. Women and young men, especially, found work rendering oysters and scallops into mounds of shells and barrels of meat and liquor. Not only did my grandfather do it, but so did his mother. But the time came when shuckhouses needed to bring themselves up to new codes—hairnets and gloves and standards of general shop hygiene that far exceeded those already in place. It was too much for most shops to deal with. People wanted the market to favor big processing plants. The great middens, bigger than the shops themselves, shrank to nothing more than a thin layer of broken shell paving the ground.

The regulators did have a point when it came to quality control, however. My grandfather remembered how the dealers used to eke out their oyster liquor with cove water. When a barrel of oyster juice needed filling and they'd run low on oysters, or they just wanted to get the damn thing on a truck, tout de suite, they'd dip a bucket into the cove to get the ullage.

So, it's harder to get quahog liquor and shucked quahogs these days, but it isn't impossible. What's the problem, then? Why not chowder? It may have something to do with snobbery—or, rather, a lack of it.

There's a tribalism to clam chowder: taking a pose of snobbishness about the stuff and then setting out the precise ingredients that snobbishness dictates sketches an identity, places the poseur in a clan. Food's a choice medium for delimiting *tribe*, because there is and always has been so much of it to dispose of. That's the reason for food taboos: too much food. One does not identify as vegan for lack of meat. And there are advantages to such rejections: Constraining ingredients can spur experimentation in cookery, actually expanding the tribal menu, much like writing a novel without using the letter "e." The Levitical injunction against shellfish (11:12: Whatsoever hath no fins nor scales in the waters, that *shall be* an abomination to you), along with all of the other biblical food taboos, has guided the development of other varieties of chowder. Artificial, arbitrary restrictions on food sharpen both the tribal palate and the borders of the tribe. Also, it feels good to denigrate other peoples for the gross things they eat.

When the stars are right, all of these elements come together in clam chowder. The most well-known debate centers on the broth: white or red? Milk or cream? Or tomato juice? It's a Boston versus New York contretemps, and, every now and again, in the media of the Northeast, you'll find some joker affecting to prefer one or the other, to claim one or the other for this or that tradition, in order to needle his rivals in the other town, or to act contrarian toward his fellow residents. Of course, neither city ever acknowledges the truth—that the best clam chowder doesn't resort to either kind of broth, but is, in fact, clear. Moreover, real chowder, Rhode Island chowder, Narragansett chowder, isn't clam chowder at all. It is quahog chowder.

Quahogs are not actually clams. Quahogs are quahogs. The nomenclature matters, as does the pronunciation of the word. Both are ways of securing an identity. Lots of old-timers insist on the distinction between quahogs and clams, even when used to form derivative words. "If you called me a clam-digger," says Ray Wyss, "I'da knocked you down. I was a bullraker, a quahogger." For a hundred years, at least, local newspapers have remarked upon the insistence of Rhode Island shellfishermen that the quahog is not a clam. This nicety continues to this day. A quahogger will refer to a quahog as a clam, but only when his meaning remains unambiguous. When a quahogger comes in to the dock with his day's catch, his buddy might ask him, "How'd y'do?" "Ah, the clams weren't bitin'"—and both know he means quahogs.

To say "clam" over the phone, however—"I made out pretty good on clams today"—would suggest that the quahogger had worked steamer clams that day. The gerund and the participle, clamming, never have this trouble; they always put steamers in mind. When Tim Trim says he had a good summer, because he "did some lobsterin', some quahoggin', some clammin'," he's not being redundant.

The distinction is also important, because it has caused some confusion over the etymology of the word *quahog*. Dr. Robert Beard, a linguist, notes a peculiarity in the word *quahog*—at least when spelled "quahog," which is far more common than the formal "quahaug."

"Folk etymology changed the *haug* in this word to the similar English word *hog*. We still haven't decided what to do with the *qua*, but its likelihood of survival is very low." Beard posits thereby that "quahog" finds itself "halfway through folk etymology." True, so far as some quahoggers are concerned. A few of them have said that they've heard that the word *quahog* comes from the practice of using pigs to find them on the shore. Pigs set to rooting for quahogs in Rhode Island as they do for truffles in France? It never happened. Yet, there is a pig connection, and one which further clarifies the distinctiveness of *quahog* from *clam*.

Sickissuog is what the Narragansett Indians called the soft-shelled clam, which Rhode Islanders colloquially call the steamer. Roger Williams, in his *A Key into the Language of America*, a presentation of his learning of the Narragansett dialect, remarks that the *sickissuog* is the favorite shellfish of that tribe, eaten itself and also used for seasoning soups and breads. Women gather them. And then he tells us this: ". . . the English swine [he means "pigs" here, not Englishmen] dig and root these clams wheresoever they come, and watch the low water (as the Indian women do); therefore of all the English cattell, the Swine (as also because of their filthy disposition) are most hatefull to the Natives & they call them filthy cut-throats . . ." Spelling the word "quahog" puts the hog on the wrong clam.

Williams continues with a definition of *poquauhock*. He gives the Narragansett word in full, though common usage reduced it and Anglicized it through apheresis, the dropping of a sound from the beginning of the word, and lenition, the softening of a consonant, to "quahog."

"This the English call Hens," Williams writes, and already things have gotten confused. Today, a hen clam is a surf clam. How this change happened, no one knows, but Williams's description makes clear that "hen" used to refer to quahogs: "a little thick shellfish which the Indians wade deepe and dive for and after they have eaten their meal there (in those which are good), they breake out of the shell about halfe an inch of a black part of it, of which they make their Suckauhock or blackmoney, which is to them pretious."

The quahog holds the purple wampum; the surf clam holds no wampum at all. According to Dawn Dove, a teacher of the Narragansett language, *poquauhock* means "drilled shell," again a reference to its use as wampum, though wampum never served as money. Linnaeus himself had this use and misunderstanding in mind when he classified the quahog as *Mercenaria mercenaria*, suggesting that the quahog had to do with wages or money. He let the misunderstanding of it as a kind of specie determine its species.

The true etymology of the word may well direct the movement to eliminate the "qua" half of "quahog," as Dr. Beard suggests might happen. Certainly, something is going on with that portion of the word. There are five competing pronunciations of quahog, with two frontrunners:

	Ō (OH)	Ô (AW)
K	kō-hôg	kô-hôg
KW	kwō-hôg	kwô-hôg

Sometimes, speakers drop the "w" and leave the "k," which is syncope; sometimes, they alter the initial vowel to make it no longer the same as the final vowel, which is dissimilation. The fifth pronunciation also comes from syncope: kwôg. My grandfather used to say it this way, as did Cap'n

Bill. My father remembers a guy selling out on the *Beacon* saying, "Bill! 'Quahog' is two syllables!"—which drew a confused look. Though all five of these possibilities are used, only the traditional "kwaw-hawg" and the upstart "ko-hawg" hold much territory. Jeff Grant uses "kaw-hawg," and my father switches from "kwaw-" to "kaw-" when he says quahogger. The whole goddamned state of Massachusetts, however, holds obnoxiously to the newer way of saying it, kō-hôg. This is wrong, of course. No less an authority than Roger Williams says so.

I remember hearing Ella Secatau, formidable, imposing medicine woman of the Narragansett, champion the "kwaw-" pronunciation and vilify the "ko-." "It's 'kwa-hawg'!" she said, during a lecture on the history of the Narragansett. "Not 'ko-hawg'! It makes me crazy when I hear that." But the accepted pronunciation may be headed in the non-native direction. It would not surprise me if, in a hundred years, people referred to the hard-shelled clam as "coin-hog."

There is a habit, even a mission, among Massachusetts writers, especially those from Cape Cod, to prescribe the "ko-" pronunciation. They actually tell their readers to prefer it, incredible as it may seem. That's tribalism; they're trying to distinguish themselves from the people of Narragansett Bay—and the very same motivation colors their approach to talking about chowder.

Take one extreme example. Sometime in the 1960s, a Cape Codsman—or a group of Cape Codsmen—put together a book titled *Clam Shack Cookery*. There are billions of clam-shack cookbooks out there, but this one stands apart because of its peculiar style, its homespun illustrations, and the way it captures the arrogance and parochialism of a certain subset of Cape Codders in their most egregious instances—to wit, when it has to do with quahogs. The book teaches a master class in the tribalism of food, nowhere more didactically than in the chapter on chowder, wherein Cap'n Phil Schwind, the pen name of the book's author (or authors), tells a story of "Cape Cod Girls," in order to privilege his recipe.

The conceit of the story is that a Captain Ron Nickerson, fisherman and farmer, buys an ad for a new wife. He wants to wed a true Cape Cod girl, and he will put all applicants to a quahog cooking test to determine their fitness for his marriage bed. The first girl to apply has webbed feet and seaweed in her dark hair. She takes up some quahogs of all sizes and makes a paella of them. He eats the food and rejects the girl.

The second one is a redhead. She takes the largest quahogs and makes stuffies—a quahog stuffing cooked and served in quahog shells. The old man gobbles them up and literally tosses her out of his house, along with the shells he has emptied.

The last girl is blonde. She immediately identifies the Nauset Marsh origin of the quahogs he sets before her, and she even derides them as being of an inferior terroir. First, she lays open the smallest necks and serves them to him on the half shell. Then, she whips up the quahog chowder recipe that Schwind will soon present. Last, she serves the chowder to the old prick and goes back into the kitchen to comb her hair with a codfish bone. He marries this one.

What a Masshole—for several reasons. To start with, this is a paragon of WASPish ethnic repulsivity. Dark hair and paella? Stuffies and a red-head? Sounds like a Portuguese and an Irish—both were intolerable for their cooking failures to the Codsman, but, on account of their ethnicities, did they ever really have a chance? Then, he complains that he bit into the quahog shells when he ate the Portagee's stew, which called for cooking the quahogs in their shell, as a mess with rice, tomatoes, and seasoning. He couldn't handle parting cooked quahogs from their shell? What a rhubarb. After this, and aside from his misogyny, he says, when he sees the redhead using shells for dishes: "You could have used the best china if you'd been a mind to." He doesn't say the same thing when the blonde serves him littlenecks on the half shell, however.

His worst error comes last, and with the chowder recipe. To praise the blonde's chowder, he declares, ". . . when she cooks quahogs, I eat quahogs." Does he? Not according to his recipe: "All these ingredients she put together: the quahogs and their juice, the potatoes cooked in milk, the salt pork scraps, and the onions in their salt pork fat. She gently stirred them until they were hot and blended, then she slowly stirred in a dollop of heavy cream."

Milk? Cream? Why not just pour in some ketchup, if he wants so badly to disguise the flavor of the quahogs? The actual recipe does noth-ing to exculpate the Cape Codder: "One quart of milk. One generous dollop of heavy cream, stirred in at the last moment."

Schwind's prescriptions and his absurd justifications for them should ring as discordantly as the sound "ko-haug."The whole episode's bizarre. Why denigrate unfamiliar ways of preparing the quahog? The point of the story is to place the recipe in a context. The authors want to color their own preferences as authentic compared with the cuisine of more-recent immigrants. The only gustatory argument made in the story—that a quahog recipe should showcase its primary ingredient, not disguise it—fails, because, by implication and extension, it should prefer clear to creamy chowder, Rhode Island over Cape Cod. No; the real intent is to offer creamy clam chowder as a way to make believe that you are experiencing something of Cape Cod by eating what Cape Codders eat. It's a silly exercise, but you can imagine its effectiveness on certain kinds of people.

Quahog chowder may need just this kind of thing to bring it into prominence. It has become a luxury food, anyway; it may need a luxury branding. In fact, it may take on such a brand whether anyone wants it to or not. Shucking quahogs is labor-intensive; it takes time and considerable effort; it makes a mess, which takes more time to clean up. Even once you've got everything clean, the scent of quahog lingers, especially on the hands, because you've just killed and butchered a live animal. For all of these reasons, the contemporary person cooking at home might disdain quahog chowder as the meal of a fishwife and reach instead for a can of Campbell's New England Clam Chowder, which is, invariably and reprehensibly, creamy and made from hens.

The local food movement as a whole faces just this problem: It's hard to get prepared local foods. Mainly, the movement looks to provide ingredients for cooking from scratch—and that kind of cooking is either luxury or drudgery. The ready availability of processed and prepared foods relieved households from the long labors of home cooking. They got a reduction of work in exchange for shitty, malnourishing food produced unsustainably—probably a fair bargain in the short term. To reject such shortcuts in food preparation is to announce to the world that you have the luxury of time and good nutrition; it's aristocratic.

Quahog chowder could appeal to those who want to luxuriate in the aristocratic diversion of preparing peasant dishes. There's even space for shades of snobbery that would obscure me: "Quahogs," said Cap'n Schwind, "should be chopped fine in a mixing bowl, not ground to mush in a modern gadget." The captain looks down his no doubt straight and well-proportioned nose at my family's manual meat grinder.

Perhaps it is too bad that food forms a locus of conflict between snobberies and tribalism, but it does. This doesn't mean to say that the appreciation of authentic cuisine always divides people. It can bring them together, even despite themselves. In 1985, certain ladies of East Greenwich, many of them from old families—old enough for their names to appear in my genealogy, from time to time—published *A Legacy of Greenwich Recipes: From Generation to Generation,* a cookbook featuring the culinary rememberings of East Greenwich residents, as certified by the East Greenwich Preservation Society. It was a signal time for such a book, about a decade after White Flight began to hit the town hard. The ladies could have meant the book to separate the old from the new residents, or to indoctrinate the new in the ways of the old. Neither scheme could have possibly succeeded, but the book has tremendous value for those looking for luxurious recipes—although, as happens with Cap'n Schwind, quahog chowder proves controversial.

They try to grant authority to their recipe by placing it under the rubric "South County Chowdah." Rhode Island has many accents, and the one most familiar to the world is that of Providence—a sort of degraded New York accent with Bostonian notes. The state has many other ways of speaking, however. "Chowdah" is not universal. Further, Rhode Island has no South County. The ladies are playing colloquial in a couple of ways; in addition to transcribing dialect, they are using the informal name of "South County" to refer to the official "Washington County." They very much want to signify the authenticity of their recipe. But not all Rhode Islanders drop their final "r"s—and Washington County is home to many who actually deepen them. You find North Kingstown in that county, and, in North Kingstown, you find the locality of Swamptown, whence comes—many believe—the appellation "Swamp Yankee," which refers to a sort of New England hillbilly. The Swamp Yankees are my people, and a good number of them, such as my grandfather, transform the alveolar palatal approximant "r" into a retroflex one, the "r" of a very deep *grrrr.* To this day, I have to be careful when I introduce myself, because people often mistake the way I pronounce "Ray" for "Gray" or "Greg." All of which should attest to the authenticity of my own view of chowder. What is more, the ladies' recipe suggests the viability of substituting bacon for salt pork, which is nuts. The smoke of the bacon would clash with the flavor of the quahog. What is worse, they call for milk (which I pronounce "melk"). To put it squarely: The recipe and the pronunciation they offer both come from Cape Cod.

This is what food is all about: identity.

Although sustainable food has good, rational arguments in support of it—like providing health benefits, and helping to ensure the continued existence of American civilization—good consequences alone will not be enough to sway public opinion.

Appeals to identity may make forward progress, however. The recipes proferred by Cap'n Schwind and the *grandes dames* of East Greenwich may get things all wrong, but they are not misguided; they try to curry favor by appealing to petty prejudices. No small number of restaurants and food companies do just the same thing by advertising their products as bad for the people who eat them. They appeal to the thrill of doing something wrong, or taboo. Take heart-attack burgers, for example—hamburgers specifically designed to contravene recommendations for healthy eating. Such treats aren't meant merely to taste good; they also serve as a medium through which to express an identity. Eating these foods shows scorn for people whom the eater doesn't like, people who, the eater believes, want to control him, people who show weakness by caring about the health of their bodies and their society. You could call it the *psychology of gustatory resentment*—a real mind-set in the American world, and something the sustainable food movement must deal with.

An obvious tactic would be to attach sustainable food to a wild, self-destructive, independent activity—especially if said activity itself produced the sustainable food. This could prove to be a tricky prospect, particularly when it comes to the question of whether to enlist the sustainable farmer or fisherman to advocate for the food he produces. For when it comes to the eating of quahogs, not even all quahoggers are on board.

CHAPTER TEN

The Man Who Doesn't Eat Quahogs

A rising tide lifts all boats.

—NEW ENGLAND SAYING

SOMETIMES THEY CALL HIM MUDBELLY. HE USUALLY WEARS A RUBBER apron at work, a sheet of rubber, really, trimmed here and there, pierced in four places to make eyelets for the clothesline he secures it with. The apron extends from his collarbones to his knees. On transplant days in spring, he comports himself this way, and, after a couple of hours of hauling up muddy messes of cove-bottom stuff, which he doesn't rinse too well, after bagging up the product and loading the bags onto the dump boat, his aproned belly bears heavy streaks of mud—more mud than the average guy—and so his buddies yell out to him, *"Mudbelly!"*

Confraternities take notorious delight in nicknaming their members, and the community of quahoggers is a prime example. They bestow sobriquets upon each other for fun, of course, but also to create a sense of belonging—and even to provide cover for themselves when they engage in or talk about illicit activities. The origin of most of these names is often quite obvious. They come from physical attributes: Pumpkin, Haystack, Terminator, Hercules, Big John, Big Bird, Little Jesus, Peanut, Tiny (who was tall), Too-Tall, Henry Weak-Eyes, Jumbo, Pig-Paw, Porkasaurus, Short Boy, Black Beauty (for his luxurious, black hair), Brawny (because he was short), Redbeard, Cabbagehead (my grandfather, whose head was large). They also come from habits, or even individual incidents: Auntie, Banzai (went to Japan), Cookie Man (used to sell cookies), White Shoes, Harpo (for chasing women), Wacky Jacky, Donald Duck (fell overboard with hip waders on), Captain Hate, Asshole, The Professor, Silent

Al, Mudbelly. Then there are names that have obscure meanings: Osie Padosie, Pep, Slingfoot, Old Man (wasn't old), Pa (wasn't old), Hackey, Bo-Peep, Burt (real name, George), Bay Fox, Little Jo (real name, Theodore), Beebe, Hub, Teeley, and, my favorite, Cherry Pie.

The nickname game can result in confusion. Just as you might know a guy only by his boat rather than by his own appearance, you might know him only by his moniker. When Zorro went through a hospital stay, he received several cards addressed not to Matthew, but to Zorro. This ambiguity can help when somebody's telling a story about a guy over the radio, and the story has to do with smoking dope, beating somebody up, driving drunk, sinking a boat, burning a boat, stealing something, dirty digging, illegal sales, sleeping with somebody's girlfriend, and so on. Usually, guys are happy with this usage, but nicknames can cause bad feelings, too. Brawny hated his nickname. My uncle Jake gave it to him, after the brand of paper towels that features a giant as its icon, and, when Jake saw that the name got under Brawny's skin, he started teasing him further, by doing things like leaving a child-size stepladder in front of the door to his truck, or placing a tiny, plastic cowboy hat in the cabin of his boat.

Jake did better by me. When I was ten, Jake began calling me Rambo, sometimes Ramby, because I had long, curly hair, and I thought Rambo was awesome. He persisted in calling me this name for as long as he lived. This was okay with me, but I very nearly lost the name when I was eleven or twelve or so. I was down the shore with my father, and Jake pulled up and cried "Rambo!" One of the older guys—Cap'n Bill or Arthur or Howard—had never heard of Rambo, so he said, "Rainbow? What'ya callin' 'im that for?"—which was an excellent example of the kind of folk etymology called an "eggcorn." "Rainbow" didn't stick, but it would've been cool if it had. That's how Queequeg got the nickname Quahog, after all.

All in all, nicknames are a useful thing to have when talking about quahoggers, particularly when it comes to behaviors that fall slightly out of line with community standards.

Mudbelly is one of the better-known guys on the bay, because of his humors, both good and bad, and because of his active involvement in the industry. What's more, he's picturesque, photogenic, and a good speaker on quahogging—not because he always has his information right, but because he can cut out the swearing and still maintain an authentic bull-raker's voice. Also, he throws good parties.

He does three parties a year: Christmas, Halloween, and St. Patrick's Day. In back of his house, he has a simple T-shaped outbuilding, consisting of a wide hall crossed at one end by a narrow workshop. The hull or shed has a dirt floor and is quite large; the workshop has a cement floor, wooden workbenches, and loads of machinery and tools. Mudbelly makes bullrakes now and again, and has been working on a new boat for himself for several years. There are good reasons for the cramping heaps of stuff in the back.

The big shed also lends itself to Christmas parties, especially because Owen has insulated it with tautly stretched shrink wrap. It's still a little cold when things have only just gotten going around six o'clock. Mudbelly and his wife have cleaned out the shed, making a sort of dining hall out of it, with long benches along the sides and a couple of cafeteria tables near the entrance. They've set out a big spread, mainly of meats and meat-pastries, with some calzones and pizza strips and lots of soda and a little booze. Mudbelly put a keg of some brand of light beer outside of the workshop door earlier in the day, and stuck a small, undecorated spruce tree at the end of the hall, near the inside entrance to the workshop. Then he put on his Santa suit—and it is in this costume that Mudbelly shows his gift for leveraging his fisherman's qualities.

He has a gray beard and gray hair, both a bit wild and both of which he lets grow rather long in the winter. By late December, he's sporting a mane around his chin. He doesn't wear a mustache, either; the fringe of hair sprouting from under the trim of his toque wraps around his cheeks and blends into his beard, forming a cone of gray that amplifies his tanned face. He's weathered and bright-eyed; he's loud; he speaks with a thick Warwick accent. Over the past several years he has even developed what he calls his "Pop-Tart Pouch," a big round belly, which, he says, has relieved him of the need to stuff his Santa suit so much. With his suit and his toque on, he sets a cardboard box filled with coal in front of the tree, a flourish that somehow results in long streaks of coal dust running up and down the back of his Santa jacket. In the end, he's a dive-bar Santa; though he's short and—today, at least—quite jolly, you can imagine children cowering from him.

Guys start showing up, a few of them with their wives. They fill beer cups, load plates; a couple of the guys dig into their food with a plastic fork between thumb and forefinger and a cigarette between forefinger and middle finger. After a while, enough people have come in to warm the place up a little, but, by then, the air's gotten bitter with smoke. They don't seem to mind the infusion of cigarette smoke in their food. The calzones and pizza strips get wiped out quickly. A few guys bring dishes of their own. One sets down his famous apple pie; another, a tray of his famous stuffies. The stuffies are gone in an instant—not just because they're so prized, but because they're still hot. You set the hot shell in your palm to eat it, which is pleasant in itself. Some of the guys bring booze. Mudbelly's good friend, Terminator, pops open a bottle of moonshine. He doesn't make the stuff, he just buys it—and pours it out generously. In his thoughtful way, Terminator has mixed the clear liquor with a sludgy lemon syrup, to disguise its horrid taste. "It's Limoncello," he says.

"That's not Limoncello," says Mudbelly's wife, who is drinking Limoncello from a tall shot glass. She made most of the spread: lasagna, meatballs, cookies, and a pile of especially good chicken wings. But no chowder, no steamers, not even any fin fish. The stuffies, already gone, constituted the sole presence of the kind of food from which virtually everyone in the room makes his living. It's all Mudbelly's fault. "He doesn't like seafood," she says. "We used to eat scallops once in a while, but not anymore." She draws from her cigarette. "He doesn't care for it."

They've been together for almost thirty years, married for fifteen. "He can never remember our anniversary," she says. "Because he proposed to me on Valentine's Day—that's the day when he stepped in it, he says—so that's what he remembers. It's even in our wedding rings; mine has our anniversary written inside of it, and his says 'hook, line, and sinker.'" She waves her hand toward the workshop. "He keeps his in the back."

"They're smokin' me up!" cries Mudbelly from the workshop. He and five other guys lean on the cluttered workbenches and pass a joint; the marijuana smoke, soft and complex, is a welcome cover for the boorish, acerbic fume of tobacco. "I haven't smoked in four years! They're gettin' me!" A very short, white-bearded, and curly-haired guy in his sixties, a guy they call Ho-Ho, is telling dirty jokes, while the others circulate through the joint. One of the guys puffs out his smoke, leans over, and says, "Ho-Ho, one time, he showed me movies of guys with animals, you know, like with a chicken, like this." He holds his hands in front of his crotch, spreads them chicken-wide, moves them back and forth at moderate fucking speed. He turns to Ho-Ho. "Ho-Ho!" he says. "Remember those movies with the guy and the chicken?! Jesus Christ!" Ho-ho, just starting another joke, interrupts himself to explain: "I'm French!"

Mudbelly and a few of the guys wander off once the joint is all roached out. Ho-Ho and Carl, a tall, stout black man in his late sixties, begin to share their experiences with various techniques and equipment for recovering and maintaining erections after prostate surgery. Then Ho-Ho tells another joke.

"A girl wants to borrow the car. Her girlfriends call her up and say, 'Let's go out!' She says, 'I'll have to ask for the car.' Her friends really want to go out, so she goes downstairs to ask her father if she can borrow the car. Her father's in his chair in front of the TV, and he's all fat and a slob, stinking, eating junk food, greasy, and the girl asks him, 'Can I borrow the car?'

" 'Blow me!' he says.

" 'What? What are you talkin' about?!' she says. 'Why don't you let me borrow the car?'

" 'Blow me!' he says. She runs upstairs crying, and she calls her friends. 'I can't get the car! My father's crazy!' She's crying, but her friends really want to go out. 'We're gonna have a good time—you gotta get the car!' So she says, 'All right.' She goes back downstairs.

" 'Dad, can I have the car?'

" 'Blow me!'

So she gets down and starts doin' it"—Ho-Ho curls the fingers of one hand and makes a stroking motion in front of his mouth—"then she stops and says, 'Aw, you taste like shit!' And the father sits up and says, 'Oh yeah! I already let your mother borrow the car!' "

"That's terrible," says Carl, furrowing his brow. "Oh, man . . . terrible."

And yet, not enough for Ho-Ho. After a while, he finds 'Belly outside, near the keg of Miller Lite, complaining about the weather with another set of guys. Ho-Ho tells the joke again and elicits the sought-for reaction: "Whoa! Ho-Ho! What's the matter with you, brother?!"

"I'm French!"

Mudbelly swings around and lumbers over to the back of the shed, just a few feet from a tall, gray wooden fence, hoists the puffy trim of his jacket, and begins to piss.

"I got a picture of him pissing!" says Ho-Ho. "I took it last year. He was right where he is now, and I had my camera, and"—he holds an imaginary camera up to his face. "I gotta get it blown up and give it to him. I should give it to him framed!"

Mudbelly readjusts his suit, pats it down, and steps up to the shed door. Leaning back with his hand on the door handle, he says, "I'm gonna go ask Carl if I can borrow the car!"

After a while, a bunch more guys show up. They start bitching about the price, the state, bad sets, bad weather. Mudbelly, beer cup in hand, arms folded, holds forth on the management of the bay. He hates aquaculture— at least insofar as private aquaculture is concerned—but there is the problem of low numbers of quahogs.

"There's not a great deal o' money to be made out there right now, cuz the shellfish ain't there," he says. "We started off just walkin' in the water with a rake"—he's referring to himself and Terminator, who has just tried, unsuccessfully, to get another guy to try some moonshine Limoncello. "That's when there was pleny o' clams available—we could go anywhere and get clams. You can't do that now. I was nineteen or twenty when I started, just got outta jail. I did a couple o' B 'n' E's, and I got in trouble."

Mudbelly speaks softly about his wrongdoing, but he doesn't sound ashamed; he sounds puzzled. He made bad choices early, and was able to make good choices later, only because, thirty years before he took up the rake, a whole host of diggers had fought to make nonmechanical harvest the only legal means for commercial harvesting of the quahog. He got his second chance, because the Rhode Island constitution keeps the bay a commons and enshrines the privileges of the shore, and because the quahog is superabundant in Narragansett Bay.

"It was easier back then," he says. Easier, because the price was better and the quahogs more plentiful, especially in the shallows, where he started, with his rake, his waders, and his basket buoyed by an inner tube. "You didn't need a boat," he says. "Just walkin' on the shore."

For Mudbelly, the big problems the industry faces are low prices and low landings, with the latter being in large part the cause of the former. On this point, he agrees with the dealers.

"A lotta this is aquaculture," he says. "In the eighties and nineties, we had most of the market. Rhode Island had the market cornered, we had so many clams comin' in; there was a lotta people diggin', a lotta clams comin' in, had the whole market cornered." Then, after aquaculture came in, the big southern quahog farms transformed the market; they made consistently huge landings a necessity. The phenomenon of low landings itself has two causes, he thinks: fewer fishermen and fewer quahogs. Mudbelly has a theory about the drop in quahog densities, which, even while drunk and high, he advances with admirable coherence.

"It all started when we started doin' the count, overfishin' the small stuff," he says. "Because of New York—all because of New York. That's what they want; all the restaurants wanted small-count stuff. They started buying by the piece, and the guys in New York that are buying by the piece, our stuff goes there. That's what ruined this business, goin' by the piece. The count system ruined this business. When the price was always by the pound, I made out better. Everybody thought they were going to get rich by the piece, but come to find out, this was terrible."

The new standard of measure did more than lower the price, however. The count system hurt the quahog population and, thus, landings—just at the moment when high volume made overall landings so important.

"Most of the time," says Mudbelly, "when you went to work an area and you got all small ones, you would up and leave. 'I ain't diggin' that damn stuff: There ain't no weight to 'em.' A quahog that big," he says, making a circle of a diameter just over an inch by holding his thumb and forefinger against his beer cup. "When you got a quahog that big, when it was by the pound, you'd leave that area; you'd say, 'I'll wait for that stuff to get bigger,' and that stuff would just sit there and percolate, put off spawn and seed everywhere, you know.

"Now, when they went by the piece, everybody hunted the little guys. I was talkin' to Jeff Grant, and he said where if they're that big"—again with his fingers and his cup, he sizes the quahog, about an inch and a half—"they're all males. When they're that big"—he expands his fingers to a diameter of over two inches—"they turn into female, so everybody huntin' them little guys is takin' away the males, so when they spawn, what's happenin' is, they're lettin' a lotta sperm, and they're not lettin' a lotta eggs in there. So I think that over the years, it's progressively gotten worse because of that fact, because of huntin' the little guys. That's what my thought is on that."

But what to do about it? It would take a federal law to abolish the purchasing of quahogs by the count. For Rhode Island, the only way to jump up quahog landings is by increasing the number of fishermen and the number of quahogs available for harvest. As of right now, the dominant method of increasing landings is the privatization of public waters for quahog aquaculture. Mudbelly adamantly opposes all leasing of the bay—not just for quahog farming, but for oyster farming too. He votes against every oyster-lease application that comes down the pike, no matter what. The free and common fishery is what enabled him to turn himself around, after all.

"We don't wanna lose that," he says. "That's the one thing we don't wanna do. Once they come in and privatize that shit, we ain't gonna be able to do nothin'." This is true, but the quahoggers do need to do something to increase the volume of the product they deliver to the market, and, paradoxically, some of them have come up with quahog aquaculture as a potential solution.

Over in Greenwich Bay Marina in Warwick Cove, at Brewer's Wharf, the Shellfishermen's Association has put together a small quahog farm. They call it the "public-enhancement aquaculture project." The farm is almost invisible; unless you know what to look for, all you'll see at the wharf are docks and boats, but along one set of docks, running parallel to shore, are a few extraneous floats taking up positions boats ought to hold. Docking for small vessels rarely runs any wider than is necessary to allow two people, each carrying an armload of gear, to pass by each other comfortably. But the floats double the width of that one stretch of docks.

They're strange to the eye of the waterman, and, upon closer examination, even stranger, because they hum. They form an upweller system, a machine for growing quahogs from seed to field-plant size. The floats open outward from the center, like the valves of an old cellar bulkhead. Inside are quahogs suspended in vats. It's always a little disturbing to open the floats, just as it's disturbing to open a beehive. The interior clashes against itself, at once disorderly and ordered, organic and inorganic. In a typical float, the vats or silos sit in two rows of three, with a submerged motor in between them, draining water from the tops of the vats and pumping it out the ends of the float, which draws water up through the screened bottoms of the vats and through the piles of juvenile quahogs, tens of thousands of them now, each clam the size of a fingernail. The tiny animals look like grubs in cells, only more disgusting, because they are so chaotically sprawled all over each other.

Materially speaking, that's all there is to the public-enhancement aquaculture project. A few floats, a few motors, some vats, several million quahogs. But the upwellers must stay clean and the quahogs cannot get too crowded. The juvenile quahogs require caretakers. Principally, that job falls on a quahogger named Owen Kelly. Owen's in his mid-fifties, and, like Mudbelly, has a big gray beard. He doesn't like to eat quahogs, either; to Owen, they're "nasty little rubber bands." The project really began ten years ago, when Dale Leavitt, the shellfish aquaculture guru up at Roger Williams University, and my own instructor in oysters, helped to institute an aquaculture program for the state of Rhode Island. Owen was the first volunteer, and for a while he took care of the cleaning and the housing of the quahogs by himself. Now, several guys volunteer their time to care for the baby clams, and a couple of dozen participate in the annual planting party, when they sow the quahogs they have grown into the fishing grounds of the bay.

The shellfishermen plant when the farmers harvest, late October, early November. A few guys volunteer their boats for transporting the field-plant-size quahogs, big enough to have an excellent chance of survival. It's

Owen Kelly down the shore, 2012. MICHAEL CEVOLI

a remarkably fast operation, but any harvest always is, relative to the growing phase. The guys and, usually, a few students of Dale's, often women, pour the quahogs into fish totes, which go into the skiffs. Once in the totes, away from the cellular structure of the upwellers, the juvenile quahogs seem more familiar, although not perfectly so; they're too small and too clean. You almost never see quahogs that look the way they do—and certainly not in such abundance. The upwellers bathe the quahog seedlings with the plankton-rich water of the cove, shelter them from predators, and hold them several feet above the bottom. These quahogs have never touched mud. About the only way you ever see quahogs this small is when they come up in a rake clotted with bottom muck.

David Drew tells the story of a time when he was a teenager and, after a day of digging quahogs in muddy bottom, in a fit of whimsy common to adolescents, put his anchor on the bow, rather than in the boat, which left mud all over the place. After he tied up, one of the older guys—Cap'n Bill or Jake, someone like that—came over and pawed through the mud, saying, "Look at that." There were loads of juvenile quahogs hidden in the mire. "In a few years or so," the old-timer said, "that's gonna be a good spot."

The guys who volunteer for the project get a kick out of a couple of things. For one, it's neat to see quahogs as a bullraker rarely sees them—not only because they're so small, but also because they're *notata*, meaning, they have strange markings. Dale needs a way to gauge the impact of the vat-grown quahogs on the natural population, so the project uses only notata quahogs—quahogs with a heterozygous recessive gene that gives their shells a red zigzag. This notatum appears at a rate of about 1 percent in the natural population, but, in one area where Dale and some of the guys took samples, a couple of years after seeding, they found notata at a rate of about 30 percent. The guys see the fruits of their labor coming out small and strange-looking, and that's rewarding for them. They also get to be generous, which is the second thing they get a kick out of.

Generosity's an important virtue among all fishermen, not just quahoggers. It accounts for much of the fisherman's profligacy. One of the dangers of getting paid in cash every day—among the dangers of strippers, cocaine, dope, and new fishing gear—is, of course, booze—especially booze in bars. Not for oneself, because it's hard to run through lots of cash getting drunk alone, but for friends, acquaintances, strangers, and even enemies. My uncle Jake had a habit of carrying around several hundred dollars in his pocket expressly for this purpose. He could always recoup a good portion of his spending the next day, after buying drinks for everybody in the Fireman's Hall. When Cap'n Ron talks about what makes quahogging better than other jobs, he stresses generosity as one of the principal benefits of having money.

"It's really great. You're not havin' to go to work every week and get that one paycheck, and if you take one day off you can never catch up again. And you don't even want no company cuz you can't even buy a six-pack. Bullshit! One day I'm rich, next day I'm poor; go right back the next day, I got money in my pocket. Go out and stay out there if I wanna make fifty dollars or a hundred dollars, that's what I do." These are social men, afraid of the embarrassment of not being able to afford hospitality. For men like these, it's a thrill to throw quahogs overboard, knowing that neither they, nor anyone, will ever catch most of them.

Out on the water, a couple of the volunteers jump into one boat with a few hundred thousand quahogs. One's Don Goebel, short and curly-haired. The other's Bo Christensen, one of the most recognizable guys on the bay, for his long, white hair fanning out from under his ball cap, his long white beard, and the dark goggles that hide his eyes. They pull up a ways off of Sally Rock, dip their hands into the totes, and scoop out the quahogs, which they toss over the stern. The operation's over in a few minutes, but those few minutes come after months of labor.

They first put the seed into the upwellers in May; Dale's the technical advisor to the project. He showed the guys how to put together and maintain the floats; he and Mike McGiveney led the process of securing grant money; Dale procures the seed each year; and he oversees the installing of the seed, which looks like very thick oatmeal when it comes in. Then the guys—Owen, Bo, Don, and others—take over.

"I think they had six or eight guys that were spending a couple hours a week there through the summer," Dale says. "They have to go in and pull all of the silos out; they have to rinse everything down with freshwater; and, once every week, or every two weeks, they have to pull the silos and pressure-wash them to get the fouling organisms off." It's not a lot of time every week, but the work requires agricultural consistency. Husbandry is not the bailiwick of the fisherman. But, over several months, they did it. Then, in

November, before five minutes have passed in Bo's boat, Bo and Don have cleaned the totes and even carefully picked up all of the straggling baby quahogs that had earlier slipped out of their hands, flicking them over the stern.

Bo gestures to the fading wake, which leads back to where the water splits by Sally Rock, falling to Goddard Park on one side and Greenwich on the other. "If they send out some seed, the tide'll take it either way." That's it. Chris Hermanowski pulls up; he's a good friend of Owen's, and a well-known and excellent quahogger. He's just gotten done with a few hundred thousand quahogs of his own. Somebody comes out with a six-pack of light beer. Chris passes over a pint of Jaeger, which is gross, but preferable to Miller or Coors or Bud Lite. The guys talk a bit, then head back to Brewer's Marina, where other volunteers have set up a couple of grills.

The after-party is an odd sort of Thanksgiving: The quahoggers and Dale and the students reward themselves with a minor feast, but they eat none of the food they spent months growing and just got done harvesting. As a practical matter, quahogs of field-plant size are inedible. Plus, they just came out of uncertified waters. Perversely, it is just these qualities of inedibility and unattractiveness that have led to contention between the public-enhancement project and the State. Rhode Island DEM and the State Department of Health have regulated the project capriciously. The state agencies argue that it's unsafe to take quahogs from closed waters—cove waters, where the upwellers are—and put them in open waters. This reasoning goes to explain in part why areas that receive quahogs from the transplant program remain off limits for six months. But the quahoggers argue that the tiny quahogs from the public-enhancement project are different from transplant quahogs, extremely difficult to catch and nearly impossible to eat. The shellfishermen and Dale had the right side of the argument: The field-plant quahogs constitute a public-health threat only in a scenario in which they are eaten. What is that scenario?

There is none. But the State, to remain the State, must exert its will. For the first few years of the project, the State confined the sowing of quahogs to closed waters, mainly in Greene's River. Then, it discovered that it had never actually legally closed the river. An agent who had retired a few years earlier had made an illegitimate closure, which meant that the public-enhancement product had been growing out in open waters the whole time. At that point, the State chose to review the argument made by the project's volunteers, and found it more pervasive. The current regime remains subject to the whim of State authorities, however.

This is not to say that the guys themselves don't fuck up now and again. Last year, when it came time to harvest the project's quahogs, the volunteers opened up the floats and found a number of cultch bags hung inside of one—plastic mesh bags holding shells on which oyster larvae had set. One of the students had installed them for some experiment or other, and everyone had forgotten about them. The oysters had grown fat and long from enjoying the nourishing bath of the upwellers, and nearly as much protection as that provided by the vats. This was a problem. The State views oysters as an attractive nuisance—literally, that is the term. The average yokel will much more readily pop open and gobble down an oyster discovered in forbidden waters than he will a quahog, the State reasons. Therefore, it is best to have few oysters in the bay. The two bushels or so of oysters fed on cove water would piss off the State to no end. The guys set to work; they scared up knives and gloves; they started tearing into the bags and smashing apart the clusters of oysters. There arose the music of the quahogger: "Cocksucker! Son of a bitch! Why ain't you helpin'?"

Owen wandered over to the site of the great oyster smash, leaned against a shore-power turret, which provides electricity to the docks, and sipped from a bottle of beer.

"You know it ain't getting done when you're standin' around lookin' at 'em!" said Hermanowski, who was using a box cutter to slice the mesh of a bag nearly riven already by bulges of oysters.

"I ain't got no gloves," said Owen. Oysters can indeed be quite sharp, which is the real reason why oyster-shucking is a respected art. "I ain't gettin' cut up with no gloves."

"You got no gloves?! I'll give you mine!"

Owen shrugged off the tower and spread his hands. "I'm burnt out."

"Well, we all know that!"

"Hold on," said Owen, "I'll go get us a beer." He strolled off. A few minutes later, he came back with an armload of Bud Light. He was burnt out—and why not? He'd been years at the project, coming in from digging and setting himself to work farming. Aquaculture always looms over the aquaculturist, in a way that digging quahogs does not cloud the mind of the quahogger. At the upwellers, you cannot put things off for long. When the project started off, if Owen went through a period of exhaustion (which happens—a guy can find himself dead tired at the end of the day for weeks at a time; the work just catches up with him), during which he wanted only to get off the water, go home, and sack out on the couch, he still had to open up those floats and haul out the silos and clean them down.

"I give them high regards," he said, tipping his beer toward the guys who were hacking at the oysters. "When you get ten, fifteen guys, it ain't that hard. When I first started on this seeding project, I was the only one doing it; it adds to your days, but if you want a better price, there's your solution."

The quahoggers of Narragansett Bay take just over twenty million quahogs out of the water each year, which is, historically, extremely low. At its best, the public-enhancement project puts five million quahogs back in—some of which will not survive, many of which will successfully spawn, few of which will ever be caught. To get back to a 25 percent share of the market, Rhode Island would need to deliver something like 75 million quahogs a year, which is still considerably less than it produced in the mid 1980s. Owen's labors may contribute to increasing the population of quahogs in the bay, but he will never see the gain in price without a concomitant increase in fishermen. Even then, it might not happen for him. Owen's fifty-five, and he's been quahogging for more than thirty years. He may follow Cap'n Ron's example—at least with respect to staying out on the water, if not with regard to continuing to raise hell—and continue digging for another twenty-five years. But that's an outside chance. He's trying to wind down a bit.

But the returns to himself don't matter to Owen—and that's the particular grand danger presented by the public-enhancement project to Rhode Islanders. The Shellfishermen's Association has tried to get local, municipal support for expanding the project. They want to put upwellers in coves all over the state, starting in Warwick.

"Me, McGiveney, and Jody King, we met with the mayor himself; we made up a little CD about growin' the clams. We took it to 'im and said, 'How'd you like to have clams?' Myself, personally, I think you get better results if you sit down and talk face-to-face. We said, 'If you go back in the day, everybody came to Oakland Beach to dig clams. We could have that again: ten thousand dollars for a million clams. Think of the trickle-down effect of all those folks comin' down to dig at the seawall.'"

What a phrase for a guy like Owen to use: "trickle-down." It's the slogan of the tax policy of supply-side economics, a wholly discredited doctrine and one inimical to the interests of median income earners like Owen. Yet, there is a tenuous connection between Owen's thinking and that of the saps who sincerely believe the lies of supply-siders: Owen does see himself as increasing the supply of quahogs, which would then have trickle-down effects in the local economy, as people come in to harvest that supply. He wants to convince the Town of Warwick to invest a quite small portion of its budget in an enterprise that will produce big returns in the future.

Owen has a lot of ideas like this—putting windmills all along the shoreline, for example, which would mean seizing property for the purpose of producing clean energy. He even argues for better guard labor: He wants DEM to do a better job of policing bullrakers; he wants DEM to enforce daily catch limits more assiduously. Owen thinks in terms of protecting and nourishing supply, and so he takes up the jargon of voodoo economics, but understanding the difference between the trickle Owen thinks of, and the trickle supply-siders think of, is crucial to understanding the public-enhancement project.

Where supply-side economics ostensibly wants to increase private capital in the hands of the wealthiest—based on the argument that the wealthy invest their capital wisely, and so increase prosperity for everyone—Owen wants to increase a natural resource. Where Reaganomics is about the hoarding of raw cash, Owen's way of allocating abundance (you could call this way "Owenomics," except Owen is not an arrogant prick and so would find the term an embarrassment) is about freely distributing food. The tax policies of supply-side economics always lead—always—to increased private consumption of wealth that does next to nothing to benefit society. Public-enhancement aquaculture immediately increases the public resource.

Owen's way correctly applies the old New England saying, "A rising tide lifts all boats," which supply-side economics has appropriated and perverted. The metaphor refers to a rising of wealth from below, from the poorest to the richest. The tide comes up; it does not trickle down. By increasing wealth from below, starting with the poorest and slowly moving upward, all boats, from skiffs to yachts, will rise; people of all incomes will do better.

The supply-side co-option of the saying holds that any increase in the total production of the whole society makes everyone better off. On the view of this little bit of sophistry, if everyone in a community sees his earnings drop—except for one guy, who sees his earnings go up enough to increase gross product, even in the face of all of those losses—then, somehow, everyone has benefited.

Really, they are not two interpretations of the same metaphor. They are two different metaphors, only the supply-siders are bad poets who confuse their terms—or, at least, want to appropriate someone else's work, in order to hide behind it. In the expression "the land between high and low tide," the intertidal zone represents the wealth of the different classes. As the tide comes in, new water, new wealth, reaches the low land first, the poor; then, the water reaches higher, the middle class; finally, at high tide, the water reaches the wealthy. Throughout the whole process, all of the boats in the water rise. Indeed, even if the tide doesn't reach the high-water mark, all of the boats rise. The wealthy do better, even if their incomes don't go up, while the incomes of the poor do. That is the heart and soul of the saying.

The correct metaphor for supply-siders is the bathtub. This scenario is about displacement. Water is still wealth, but it doesn't actually increase. As the one big yacht in the tub—a yacht amid many smaller boats—grows bigger and bigger, it displaces more and more water. The level of water in the tub rises, and all of the boats do, too. But there isn't any more water in the tub than there originally was, and the yacht is now crowding the little boats. In the end, there will be nothing in the tub but a yacht, all by itself, with barely any water. That is trickle-down theory, and it is just the opposite of what Owen means by the term. He has appropriated the metaphor of Reaganomics, just as the supply-siders appropriated the metaphor of the old New England saying. It seems to have worked out fair in the end.

Poetical exegesis aside, the two outcomes of the two interpretations of the phrase "trickle-down" amount to no more or no less than two ways of destroying wealth. America is absurdly wealthy. Its biggest problem is figuring out what to do with its overwhelming riches. A supply-sider wants wealth to be destroyed in the private consumption of a very tiny minority of the population. Owen looks at the wealth he has—the wealth his community made it possible for him to earn—by giving him the opportunity to work hard for an actual, measurable reward, and he chooses to spend some of his wealth and some of his leisure time on a project he may never reap the benefits of. When Owen volunteers at the upwellers, he loses more than he gains, and his community benefits from his losses.

When Owen—or Bo or Don or Chris, or any of the guys—tosses those quahogs in the water, they may as well be throwing money in the streets. Forget harvesting for sale; Owen won't even eat the fucking quahogs. It's as if he were a teetotaler trying to outspend Jake Murray in a contest to see who can buy the most drinks for the Fireman's Hall. Even more—and this is Owen's big problem: The public-enhancement project is like that box of charcoal underneath Mudbelly's Christmas tree: It's almost an insulting gift—only the quahogs are more insulting than the coal, because the quahogs are in fact useful. That's the problem: When Owen suggests that other people take up shellfish farming for public benefit, he's asking that his neighbors be as willfully, pridefully profligate as he is. Willful, prideful, and also wise; Owen burns up wealth in a way that generates more wealth, and that's the flaw, the thing that makes his argument unpersuasive. His wisdom makes everybody else look foolish. To suggest to a man that he stop giving his wealth to the rich, that they might destroy it in their orgies, and instead spend his wealth in a way that benefits him and everyone he actually knows, is to suggest that this man has been a sucker all of his life. Especially if, as was the case for the mayor, he has to say he can't even afford to change his ways, because he's already given away his and his city's wealth in moves that actively undermine his community. Owen's whole way of being is antithetical to the values and self-image of greater American society, post-Reagan.

To put it another way: Owen ought to borrow Mudbelly's Santa suit to wear when he volunteers down at the upwellers. The two men, one with his parties, the other with his farmed quahogs, are doing much the same thing. Each improves the conditions of his industry by expending some of his excess wealth—Mudbelly, by raising the spirits of his friends and colleagues; Owen, by materially improving the bay. It's all the same kind of generosity, and cultivating this value is one of the keys to maintaining a commons.

CHAPTER ELEVEN

Of Unions and Associations

NO CONTRACT

NO QUAHAUGS

—QUAHOGGERS' UNION SIGN, 1946

THE CHARLESTOWN SEAFOOD FESTIVAL. THE CHAMBER OF COMMERCE
puts it on every year, and the Rhode Island Shellfishermen's Association,
alone among the dozens of food vendors, offers a raw bar. Charlestown
is in southern Rhode Island, a flat region with sandy beaches rather than
rocky ones, and lots of open space. The Festival has a typical layout: booths
of random content by the gate—raffles, some kind of military charity, a
honey stand with a display of live bees. Then comes a fork in the path—
food in one direction, vendors of assorted goods in the other; a concert
stage set back from the booths; a midway, separate from the long row of
food booths, loaded with rip-off games and throw-up rides.

The food isn't all that great clam-wise, largely because the vendors
trim the quahog content of their offerings—chowder, clam cakes, and
stuffies—down to almost nothing. Traditionally, the clam cake consists
of deep-fried dough with quahogs in it, but, at the Festival—and in most
venues in Rhode Island—it's merely dough flavored with clam liquor. In
the end, sadly, the only place where one can assure oneself of a good
apportionment of quahog meat is at the raw bar. The Association guys
serve steamers and mussels, too, laded with a secret dressing heavy with
garlic, herbs, and salt. The steamed shellfish are superb, but it's really the
raw stuff people line up for. The booth's a fund-raiser for the Association,
but the sales go through a dealer, Twin Shellfish, to comply with shellfish
vending law. The guys volunteer their labor. They stand for hours over vats

of ice, shucking quahogs and oysters, their hands dripping with quahog juice as they shuck and serve and occasionally reach for a plastic beer cup. You can find Joey and Owen and Chris Hermanowski there one day; Jeff and Brian another; on other days, Jody King, Bruce Eastman, and, of course, Mike McGiveney.

Mike seems tall, but he isn't. He has tall personality. Like Dale, he has coolness: long ponytail, shot with gray; a ratty visor cap; an earring; a short beard. He's bright-eyed and happily weathered. Down at the raw bar, the quahoggers mainly go in for sleeveless T-shirts, because they have the arms for it, though not in a conventional way. Mike's exemplary in this regard. He's in his mid-fifties, so he doesn't have a lot of definition; his skin's a touch loose, but you can see the deep solidity of his muscles as he works his clam knife, his biceps like smooth, round stones under leather. The bullrakers know they look different from bodybuilders, and they take a certain pleasure in flaunting this difference. It may be the case that some of the many folk who line up for the raw bar line up for this reason, as much as for the shellfish. Whatever the case, the customers do line up, and they guzzle quahogs and oysters by the plateful. The money, collected by a dry-fingered digger, goes into the Association's account, to pay for its operational costs, which are minimal, and occasional projects, such as Lou's memorial or the doomed Rhode Island Quahogs ad campaign.

The Shellfishermen's Association doesn't focus on initiatives, however; it functions mostly as a deliberative body that, as representative of the shellfishing industry, holds precatory power over the management regime for the transplant, Greenwich Bay, the upwellers, and the commons in general; they get to say what they would prefer to happen, but no one has to implement their decisions. The Association has eighty members or so; lots of the guys want nothing to do with it. The facile psychologism used to explain the bullraker's reluctance to work in concert with his fellows is that he is too independent-minded for such things. He is too self-reliant to work with anyone else, even guys just like him.

Mike likes to joke about this perception in a Rhode Island way. At the apex of the dome of the Rhode Island State House stands *The Independent Man*, a fourteen-foot-tall, faux Renaissance, bronze statue of a man holding a spear. The artist who rendered the figure intended him to represent Hope, the Rhode Island state motto, but no one calls him *The Hopeful Man*, perhaps because the iconography is so abstruse: Just what the fuck does a bronze guy in pseudoclassic dress with a spear in his hand have to do with hope? Especially the verb. Rhode Islanders refer to the statue as they do because during the deliberations over its design, some called for a depiction of state founder, Roger Williams, oft imagined to be "an independent man."The figure never held the form of Roger Williams, but the term and its sentiment stuck, which is typical of Rhode Island.

People looked at *The Independent Man,* an object of state art, and, impressed by the aesthetic exercise of state power, took a liking to him. No one considered that the statue—five hundred pounds of metal—soared nearly three hundred feet in the air on a platform composed of hundreds of tons of white Georgia marble shaped into the traditional form of a capital building. No one asked, *Why would an independent man need the State to hold him up?* Of course, making such a figure the symbolic embodiment—and the literal height—of State authority enables hucksters to cash in on the fantasy of a figure who stands apart from the community, independent from it. One of Rhode Island's hate-radio personalities—just the kind of asshole who mewls about the ill-gotten gains of State workers from a position that exists and can only exist because of the government's monopoly on the airwaves—refers to himself as The Independent Man. It's the posture of a useful idiot.

Mike plays on these sentiments, but, as president of the Shellfisher-men's Association, he relies on methods in accord with the reality of the Independent Man's position, not the fantasy of it.

"You know the *Independent Man,* on the State House?" he says. "He should have a bullrake in his hand!" That's his appeal to the romantic view of the statue and the quahogger. But, after shucking and joking for a while, he starts talking about what the Association has been up to. He expresses his excitement for a memorandum of understanding between the Shellfishermen's Association, DEM, and the Narragansett Bay Com-mission. The agreement establishes the institutional relationships that will keep the transplant program going for the next several years.

"I'm really proud of that," he says, gesturing with a clam knife in one hand and a dripping quahog in the other. "You have these different organizations all working together, committed both legally and, y'know, spiritually or whatever, on this program."

The quahogger, the Independent Man, stands on a foundation erected by a team of State and private actors. There are guys who never participate in the transplant, guys who think it's unnecessary, a waste of resources. They argue that the industry doesn't need the program. They may have a point. But's that tantamount to saying that the Independent Man doesn't need to stand on the State House. You could take the statue off of the dome and set him on the sidewalk, where he could stand on his own. Maybe. He is not on the ground now, however, and neither does the shell-fishing industry currently stand on its own without the transplant.

From Mike's perspective, it was always this way: The quahoggers have always acted collectively to ensure the sustainability of their industry. Throughout the modern history of the bay, they have worked together, so that each man may work apart.

"In the fifties, we were a unionized bay," he says, head down, hands in the ice, digging for a quahog. "My uncle Jimmy, Jimmy Rice, my grandmother's brother, was a union representative in the fifties, when the bay was unionized, and back then Old Man Finn, the Colonel, basically was tryin' to break the union. So what they did is, the union sent their goons down, these big Italian guys, in their Cadillac, and they'd pick up my uncle Jimmy and his bullrake at the house to drive him down the shore, in case there was any muscle problem."

He takes real pleasure in the stories of those days, when the guys worked together to overcome their troubles, though in a way quite different from his own. "If you know East Greenwich," he says, "this is a cool story. You know the big stone bridge where the jail is—over on King Street? Back in the day, Finn used to bring his clams to New York in open trucks—there was no refrigeration, this was the fifties. The guys hid up on the trestle with buckets of kerosene, and when the truck went under, they all poured the kerosene on the clams, so when they got to New York, they were all ruined!"

Telling the story, Mike doesn't know that word has it Jimmy Rice—whom the guys used to call Peanut, because he was short, and who was good friends with Howard Drew and my grandfather—was one of the guys up on that trestle. This is good: Mike enjoys his genetic connection to the guys who came before him, but his spiritual connection came first. He didn't even find out his uncle Jimmy had been a rep for the shellfishermen's union until well after he'd become president of the Association. He didn't need the bonds of family to convince him that those guys back in the day were doing the right thing. When he did learn of his family's role in the history of Rhode Island quahogging, the stories became something to laugh about and contemplate on a more-personal level, much as Arthur Drew thinks of his father's oyster poaching. Neither Mike nor Arthur do the sorts of things their relations did, but that's because circumstances are different for them.

Normally, this is where the standard American notion of inheritance would come into play—the idea of a tradition of progress. Things have gotten better over time, because Mike and Arthur don't have to struggle as the guys in the old days did. Americans, when they think of the past at all, burden their ancestors with the responsibility of making sacrifices so that future generations could have better lives. When quahoggers today look back on what the quahoggers of yesterday did, they see the old-timers making sacrifices—not to make things better, but to keep things the same. Conditions were different on the bay and in Rhode Island sixty years ago, but the responsibility to the future was the same then as it is now: to ensure that men can make a good living as diggers of quahogs, not that men can have easier lives, either by doing easier jobs or by harvesting quahogs more easily. Not better working lives, but working lives equally as good. This understanding of tradition—of the responsibility of one generation toward the next, which is the tradition most common in human history—runs counter to the American view. It is the tradition of sustainability; it is the proper mind-set for a society that wants to sustain itself indefinitely; and it is anathema to the American mythology of progress.

This ideological conflict explains why the struggles of the quahoggers of yesteryear—and of quahoggers today—seem so puzzling to Rhode Islanders. In the 1940s and '50s, the local papers referred to the disputes among the diggers, dealers, and dredgers as the Quahog Wars. The papers meant to be condescending. When the quahog conflicts really got under way, in 1946, the United States was still suffering the consequences of unprecedented naval warfare. The victory over the Japanese formed by far the greater part of America's participation in World War II. The people of the Ocean State knew the Pacific Theater intimately. While some men, such as my mother's father, served on the water, many others, such as my father's father, built ships. Rhode Islanders built and served on the largest vessels ever built, in the most terrible naval warfare ever known, in the biggest war in all of history. They had just gotten done with all of this. And then the quahoggers, on their little boats, in their little bay, started getting into disputes with each other. Worse, one faction spouted rhetoric that seemed bizarre at best, at least in the papers: The diggers were trying to sell the idea that they should be able to continue at their hard labor, in just the same way as they always had. They were against progress in the conventional sense.

One man said, "These power dredgers have it pretty soft, and if they had to drag a bullrake for a living, they'd know what it means to make a dollar." This was Alfred Turgeon, Cap'n Ron's grandfather, talking to a journalist.

Over the course of the 1930s and '40s, the practice of dredging quahogs with powerboats had become prevalent on the bay. The State had confined dredgers to certain areas, mainly deeper waters, which tongers and bullrakers, with their wooden-handled tools, couldn't reach. But, for one thing, the dredgers were pirating at night—mostly clean pirating:

Pickets of the quahoggers' union, 1946. HOWARD DREW

taking quahogs from areas made off-limits for management purposes, not because of pollution. For another, the dredgers had wiped out the quahog populations in the waters legally allotted to them. The dispute between dredgers and diggers arose mainly because the diggers were finding their fishing grounds had been obliterated by the dredgers under cover of darkness, and because the dredgers were lobbying the State to open more water to dredging.

Alfred Turgeon brusquely pointed out that dredging was easier than digging, and this was true. New technologies had enabled the new generations to work with less effort than their forebears had. Alfred was still working with tools developed in the nineteenth century. The obvious justifications for him and others like him to prefer digging over dredging were environmental and economic. Another digger, James Sisson, summed up the argument just right: "Figure it out. We get four to five bushels of quahogs a day, after six or eight hours of sweat and strain. We don't hurt the bottom. We are able, all fourteen hundred of us in Rhode Island, each with a family, to supply the market and make a day's pay. A power dredger comes in, runs a dredge six minutes, and pulls up as many bushels as we can get in a day. In an hour, he takes fifty bushels and he can easily load up to a hundred or a hundred and fifty bushels. One powerboat can put thirty of us out of work. We don't want any part of those fellows, and they'll know it if they start fooling around."

These arguments are exactly right, in terms of sustainability. Environmentally, it is better to maintain a resource than to wipe it out. Economically, it is better to have many earn a living wage than have a few become rich. Alfred spoke to more than just these two points, however. He looked unfavorably on dredging, because it was inherently weak. Outside of the economic and environmental damage it did, dredging also took away the opportunity to work hard—and some people need this opportunity.

His grandson speaks of quahogging in just the same way. "I like to see the young fellas out there," says Cap'n Ron. "Makes me feel good when I see the young fellas out there. It reminds me of the old days, you know. We did it, raised hell, it was good—a good, healthy job; good, strong job." He makes a fist with one gnarled hand, a hand that dug quahogs just a couple of hours earlier. "Teaches ya a lot, a lot ... to know about the water, to survive, cuz y'never know what's gonna happen out on that water."

Some people need this; they are happy when they reckon with hard work; they are miserable when they don't. It behooves a society to help its individual members find work that suits them. For men like Alfred Turgeon and Ron Turgeon and Mike McGiveney and lots of quahoggers, working a dredge would make them miserable. By restricting the harvesting of quahogs to hand tools, the people of Narragansett Bay meet environmental, economic, and—to go with Mike's flow—spiritual needs. Three out of three isn't bad.

But the argument wasn't advanced merely with courtly debate. As Sisson implied, violence would play a role in determining the course of quahogging in Rhode Island. It was a matter of territory, of lines not to be crossed, all the better because it was on the water, where lines cannot be seen. "Let the power dredgers stay out," said Frank Card, a digger. "If they come in, their boats should be sunk." The men attacked each other, on the water and off, usually to little effect, which was of great delight to journalists covering the story, because the pettiness of the violence only made the Quahog Wars funnier.

At one point, fifty or so dredgers, along with a couple of dealers who regularly bought product from dredgers, turned up at the State House to press the state director of agriculture and conservation to open more waters to dredging. Tongers and bullrakers heard about the meeting and a dozen or so went up to oppose any expansion of dredger territory. At most, there was a bit of punching. The director, Dr. Raymond Bressler, got the men to agree to send delegates to another meeting to be held a few days later. Down at Oakland Beach, a few nights after the donnybrook at the State House, a couple of hundred diggers gathered to select delegates and plan their attack. One guy told a reporter the quahoggers were ready to fight it out on the State House steps. In his excitement, the reporter's hands no doubt warped the pages of his notebook.

In the end, the dredgers lost the fight because they made their own arguments, rather than hire a lobbyist. They were not ready to handle the public eye. They were brazen about their pirating. Many of the dredge pirates had learned their craft by rum-running. These guys said, straightforwardly, in testimony delivered at the State House, that they had pirated and would continue to pirate, because they earned far more money than any fine would ever cost them. "I've never heard so many people admit an illegal act as the dredgers have today," said Herman Ferrara, a state representative. "And they do it with a smile."

The dredger side also argued that dredging actually improved the bottom. This argument included the presentation of alarming landing figures: 800 to 1,000 bushels of quahogs were coming out of the Sakonnet River, where dredging was allowed, every single day. The dredgers put forward these numbers to demonstrate that their work made the waters of the Sakonnet productive, which point naturally raised the question of why, then, they needed more grounds. One of the dredgers had the answer: ". . . that's all fished out at present." Between their brazenness and their shortsightedness, the dredgers left little room for the sympathy of the State, and so, gradually, but inexorably, the State squeezed them out, establishing nonmechanical harvest as the ultimate law of shellfishing in Rhode Island.

The dredgers had already done their damage, however. Ray Wyss is old enough to remember coming across patches of empty bay floor that the dredgers had left behind.

"It was a fight," he says. "Before I got there, they opened up from Providence Point over to Mill Gut and down to Poppasquash and over to the island—they gave it to the dredges . . . twenty days. I remember Lester tellin' me, in twenty days they had everything cleaned up and they were pushin' the lines, and the State finally had to cut 'em off. They wiped everything out, and it took years for anything to come back in that area. The only place we worked there was Deep Point and so forth; we'd get into hard bottom, where they didn't get into."

The diggers won. Or, at least, the dredgers lost. All of the advantages of tonging and bullraking—the economic, environmental, and spiritual gains—continued to pass through the generations, as they had for so many years before. This was not the only fight, however. The other front in the Quahog Wars concerned, not territory or technique, but straight cash. This was what got the union going—and what spurred slightly more serious violence.

"David Drew," says Mike. "His dad told me, the old man, where a guy'd be diggin', and a boat would pull up and a guy with a shotgun would tell him to go home, and the other guy would pull out his shotgun and say, 'I ain't goin' home.'"

Just this sort of thing really was going on. The union formed in response to a fifty-cents-per-bushel price drop by all of the dealers on the bay at the same time. There had always been something like the Shellfishermen's Association. There were a couple of protective associations prior to the formation of the union, and they functioned in much the same way that the Association does now—in an advisory capacity. These loose organizations had undertaken strikes before, but the guys felt the times required a more-formal stand. The diggers joined up with the United Mine Workers of America, AFL, Local No. 13,175, District 50, in order to combat the price drop arranged by the dealers. Thuggery soon ensued on all sides. As Mike said, bent-nose types from New York soon came up to provide a helping hand.

The most well-publicized incident concerned a tonger named Harold Bryden, who also worked as a special police officer. It happened that the union had declared a strike and brought to bear the usual tactics. The pickets came out and blocked deliveries to Finn Brothers. They turned supply trucks away from King Gorman's until he broke, and they then directed quahogs meant for Finn to Gorman's instead. The outgoing trucks they couldn't stop, they sabotaged with kerosene. In one case, they forced a Finn Brothers truck off the road in Connecticut. That was the work they did on the dealers.

They also went after diggers who refused to stop working. Four or five union guys would pile into a skiff and head out onto the water, looking for anybody working tongs or a rake. They'd drive up, brandish a weapon, and tell the digger to dump his catch. Most of this action took place over on the East Bay, because there was an east-west divide, with most of the union guys working out of Greenwich Bay. Bryden worked out of Warren, and the pickets caught up with him in Bristol Harbor. They made him toss four bushels over the side, a full day's work. The next day, Bryden went right back to work, tonged the same spot and everything, only this time, he'd brought his police revolver with him. The pickets pulled close, but when Bryden drew his pistol, they veered off, vowing to sink his boat. Word of the confrontation got around, and the journalists came down to fawn over Bryden.

The major media in Rhode Island are the same as any in America: They hate anyone who works for a living, and so they hate unions. "The waters are free," said Bryden. "No one's gonna chase me off the waters"—and the reporters swooned. Freedom! Plus, the whole silly scene gave them another chance to mock the squabbling of the quahoggers. What could make the Quahog Wars more risible than a firefight that didn't happen? Even better, Bryden could articulate powerful sentiments in opposition to the shellfishermen's union. "If we join," he said, "they are going to tell us when to work, how much we are going to dig, and whom we are going to sell our catch to." Certainly, Bryden should have known how unions operate: He was president of the Warren Oysterman's Union, and he complained that, had the union guys tried talking to him, he might have gone along with them.

For its part, the union was ill-prepared to deal with anything outside of direct confrontation and direct bargaining. They didn't understand the media at all—again, much to the delight of reporters. The incident with Bryden showcased the union's ineptitude in this regard. The union president was a digger named Robert Murray. He was an unfortunate choice. The day of the standoff with Bryden, he called the paper and decried Bryden's actions. Bryden had violated the civil liberties of union members by waving his gun at them, argued Murray. Furthermore, the union guys had never even spoken to the man. But the reporters wanted to know: Were these the same men who had dumped Bryden's catch the day before? "Yes," said Murray. Then, he realized what had just come out of his mouth. "No!" he said. "I don't know who they were. They might have been some dealer's men. They could have been hired by dealers to discredit the union." And so Murray's quotes got splashed under a wonderful photo of Bryden at the dock, a good-humored man leaning against a piling, cigarette in his hand, revolver shoved in his waistband, smiling a huge smile.

That's how it went with that front of the Quahog Wars: bad publicity for the union, but enough property damage and disruption to hurt those who didn't want to fall in line. "It got things straightened out there for a while," says Cap'n Ron, who was a very young man when the union heated things up. "We shut the bay right down so nobody could work and all that, so anybody who was working they took and broke their tongs, broke their rakes and everything else—guys that went out in the boat, even the little dealers and stuff, anybody they caught workin', they'd break all their gear. I picketed down at Finn's down there, cut the tires on his trucks. It worked out at the time; you had to stick together, if you wanted to get anything done."

The damage began to add up, and the dealers—who were just as dumb as the dredgers and the diggers when it came to the press—helped out the union by admitting to crimes in the paper. One anonymous dealer from East Greenwich explained the price drop that had started the whole thing off as follows: "The price on Narragansett Bay has been from fifty cents to a dollar too high for several years, because we've been squabbling among ourselves." Indeed, when the dealers stopped competing with each other and agreed to fix prices, they were, as a group, able to bring prices down to where the dealers thought they should be.

The union got the price back up, but the Quahog Wars continued well into the 1950s. Ultimately, the diggers won against the dealers, too—not so much because the strikes kept the price up, but because the diggers changed the standard measure of a catch. Back in those days, quahogs went by the bushel, and this measure gave the dealer the advantage both ways. To sell a bushel, a quahogger had to top the basket with a very high crown, which meant pouring the quahogs over the basket until they spilled over the rim. Then the dealer would take the bushel, swipe the crown off, and sell it to his customers. This is how the Colonel made so much money screwing over Campbell's Soup. The bushel measure became a point of bitter contention between diggers and dealers.

"My grandfather was one of the ones that started it at that time," says Cap'n Ron. "You had to go in and sell by the bushel, and they wanted you to run the bushel right over on the floor. He's the one that came through arguin' there, 'Why don't you weigh it?,' and then they started to weigh it up. That's what started all that off." The standard of measuring catch by weight gave an advantage to the quahogger, an advantage that lasted all the way until the mid-1980s, when the count method became dominant.

The diggers—whether they sided with the union or not—won the Quahog Wars, on all fronts. Their victory preserved their way of life, benefited Rhode Island's economy, and fostered the population of quahogs in Narragansett Bay. They did it in a picturesque way, too. Look at Jim Robinson in David Drew's old photo. Leaning on his picket, his short-sleeved, button-down shirt open at the neck and taut with muscle; he's having a grand time of it. The union guys knew they would win. The reporters covering the story, for all that they wanted the diggers to lose, couldn't resist the odd poetic phrase evocative of life down the shore. "Gathered in a small Scalloptown tavern," one of them wrote, as he covered a union meeting. Wording like that helped the diggers' cause. It evoked those romantic sentiments that could only favor the individual fisherman who worked with traditional tools. Scalloptown, with its sprawl of shanties and docks, skiffs and gear, busy with men dressed in hard-rubber boots, oiled-canvas overalls, shirts with rolled-up sleeves—men who put in the hardest of hard days and then came in together in the evening, at that small tavern, which was, in fact, the Bucket o' Blood, to stand together against the dealers, who had ganged up on them. All of those old-timers who are gone now were there then, in that old building across the street from Finn's and King Gorman's, where a parking lot is now. Jimmy Rice, Lester Arnold, Howard Drew, Jake Murray, all the rest. Even my grandfather—never a barroom man, who almost always worked alone and was almost wholly confined to his house in the woods—even he went down to the Bucket o' Blood to join with the union.

It was in these meetings that the men came to articulate their working wisdom in terms the wider public, who had perceived only a dim and distorted image of the quahoggers, could understand. Robert Murray expressed the idea of a day's pay and of the quahogger's willful, mindful commitment to his work with eloquence rare for him: "We used to be considered men with plenty of muscle and no brain. But we are better educated now, and better able to take care of ourselves. In the face of a rising cost of living, we must have a living wage." The quahoggers talked about these things at these meetings. They talked about what people thought of them and their place on the bay, and how they could secure a decent living for themselves by continuing to work as they had always done. In that moment, each man depended on all of the others in order to preserve his particular livelihood. They were Dependent Men. And they remained so, even after they'd won the war, even after the union had dissolved. They depended on their unity to create the conditions that allowed them to work independently.

This is just how the Shellfishermen's Association works today. It is a collective that fosters independence—which is the only way independence ever happens. But there is a price. The Association maintains circumstances that directly undermine collective action. It makes guys feel independent enough not to work with the organization—as do all of the institutional arrangements that make shellfishing a viable way to earn a living on Narragansett Bay. In this respect, all of the quahoggers' efforts over the years have succeeded in the task of giving the next generation the opportunity to work just as the previous one did.

Mike McGiveney has inherited this task. In the main, the circumstances he faces are quite different from those of the old days. For one thing, Mike works in peacetime. He does not have to concern himself with excusing the violence of quahoggers against their enemies. Along the same line, Mike has a voice. He's at ease with both reporters and lawmakers. He took up quahogging while earning a political science degree at the University of Rhode Island. Despite the hair and the beard, he is well groomed. Most important, he does not have clear groups of enemies. He has no need of kerosene. The two main forces he has to contend with are quahog aquaculture in other states and Rhode Island's management of the bay. Aquaculture changed the market entirely; bay management is dynamic, requiring new thought and new arguments every few years. Neither situation will settle into stability anytime soon.

But when Mike first got involved with guiding the industry, it was, in fact, on an issue that recapitulated the battles of the past. "What happened was we had the digger-diver clash," he says. In the late 1970s and early '80s, guys with diving gear realized that putting on a helmet or strapping on some tanks did not violate regulations prohibiting mechanical harvest of quahogs. Loads of new diggers—hand diggers—came in and dove on the bottom. They made a killing.

"I'd always been involved, since '82. I was in my twenties. I went to all the meetings and stuff, but it was really the digger-diver controversy that got me, cuz I saw what was goin' on. Jim Boyd was the vice president then; Phil Holmes had just taken over for Eddie Agin, and he was blamin' the divers for killin' everything—and the thing is, we were kickin' ass back then. I mean, I love Phil; he'd be complainin' we weren't makin' money, and we were doin' two thousand count. You're makin' two-hundred-forty a day, and this was back in '82! I'm twenty-three years old!

"I just saw the whole thing collapse. I was an experienced digger of four or five years back then; I was good, and I would catch four or five bags each day, let's say. These guys . . . I'm in line one day, and the guy's got eight bags—a diver—and I say, 'How ya doin'?' He says, 'Oh, good! Second time out!' He's got twice my catch, and it's his second day out—ever! There were some greedy friggin' pigs. Neil the Eel, he was just the cheapest, piggiest guy. He went over the line before they opened it up, and he put out all these tires and filled 'em with clams, so when it opened up and everyone tried to dig and couldn't get 'em, he'd dive in there and pull 'em out. There was another guy, Rollin' Thunder; he had this huge Mako, this hundred-thousand-dollar boat; he sold out in front of me in Warwick Cove one day, and I had five bags, y'know, I was good. He cut me in line; he had twelve bags, not one culled; there was shells, undersized . . . He was a fuckin' douchebag."

Mike moves easily between polished and unpolished quahogger talk. He can put a bow tie on his rake when he needs to, but few guys take such pleasure in the liberties of quahogging as Mike McGiveney. When he calls someone a douchebag, he does it with a twinkle in his eye.

The quahoggers would lose to the divers. Mike sees the outcome as a collapse of the bullrakers' argument. The bullrakers wanted the divers pulled right out of the water. Divers hurt the price; they used dirty tricks; they didn't respect the principle of a day's pay. Safety regulations gave divers cover. The law said bullrakers had to give a diver's boat a wide berth—a fifty-foot radius. Some divers would park off of a group of guys whom they knew to be working a hot spot. They would then pull their boats from under the water into the midst of the bullrakers and tell them to back off. It is, of course, a mistake to try to pull this kind of shit on bullrakers. Out came the cherry bombs. Guys would look for a diver's bubbles and then toss over M-80s by the handful. Some bullrakers didn't have the heart for that kind of warfare and so merely threw big stones at the bubbles. It was a battle similar to the one between the dredgers and the diggers, but divers neither harmed the bottom, nor brought in anywhere near the volume of quahogs dredgers did. They worked respectably hard and didn't threaten the resource. A real bummer for the bullrakers, who actually thought they would win.

"The thing was, we had everybody on our side," says Mike. "We had the *Journal* supporting us, in editorials; we had the Marine Fishery Council—back then, they were the law. We thought we had it. What happened was, the night of the hearing, seventy-five divers show up, with their wives, and they're all wearin' red T-shirts. They got there early; they were smart. Divers are smarter than quahoggers generally. They got there early, and they had the place filled. So it came to nut-crunchin' time, the Council's hearin' all these families sayin', 'Oh, you're takin' this job away from me'—y'know, we've heard it before—and they're doin' a really good job. They said, 'Let's do a moratorium.' They grandfather everybody in, close the door, and Phil Holmes said no, so that collapsed."

It all got sorted out on the water. The violence continued for a few years, then abated. Divers like Lou Ricciarelli and Don Goebel—likable divers—helped. Some bullrakers took up diving themselves, at least for certain things. Joey Amato fucking hated divers back in the day, but now, when it comes to steamers, he puts on the gear and jumps in the water. Still, suspicions linger. Mike compares divers to quahoggers, not to bullrakers. A diver and a quahogger are two different things to him; he leaves divers out of the sacred tribe. Eventually, it all passed under the bridge, in part because not so many divers stuck with the work, and in part because bullrakers and divers came to form a unified front against the movement to introduce large-scale quahog aquaculture to Narragansett Bay. It was this battle that put Mike into the office of president of the Association.

"I got on the board," Mike says. "And this young, dynamic guy, Bob Desantis, was vice president by then, and I was like a co-vice president under him. Now, we'd had words before, him and I, at the dock, but, y'know, live and learn. Bobby took over as president; I was vice president. Well, just that spring was when they introduced the aquaculture bill; what happened was, Connecticut had done something about three years prior, and what they did was they borrowed all this money in bonds, and they had all these ancient leases that were fallow and they convinced them to put all this seed down, and they instantly turned a nascent industry into a multimillion-dollar industry. Now, we're on the decline; we're losin' fishermen right and left—it was mostly cuz of health care; it was just killin' guys—so all of a sudden we start seein' these editorials. They started an aquaculture panel, it was a big deal, and they did not allow any fishermen on the panel. All of a sudden our hair goes up.

"It turned out the divers joined us on the fight," Mike continues, "and one of the head divers, he had friends up there, and we heard the quote was, they gotta get rid of all the guys in the little boats. So we went to Senator Reed (he wasn't a senator yet, he was a congressman back then) and we asked if he could pull some strings, and he got us a chance to testify. It was really, really stressful. Bob Desantis was calling people; his wife wasn't supportive of him, he's an A-guy. He's Italian, wrapped tight—which, really, I admired, cuz sometimes you need a crazy man to get their attention.

"But what happened was, right in the springtime—I remember, cuz it was the day of a transplant—and we're headin' down to Mill Cove, Wickford, and I can see Bobby diggin' Friar's Cove. I said, 'That's weird.' So I drive over and he says, 'Oh, I want to let you know, Mike—my wife kicked me out of the house, and I resigned from bein' the president. It's all yours now!' Evidently, that day, he'd gone to a conference down in Newport that was like one of the opening conferences on this—literally showed up on his boat, in shorts, and told everybody, 'This is all the clothes I have right now, cuz my wife kicked me out, because of all the shit that you guys are doin'.' People who were there were sayin' it was like a personal meltdown; unfortunately, it was.

"So, all of a sudden," Mike says, "this all got dropped down on my lap. I had just been the vice president for, like, a year, year and a half. I got involved. Bill Harsch was our lawyer then, and he was critical to everything; he helped us meet with them. It was the most stressful period of my life—ever. They would schedule a meeting, and I would take a day out and put notes on everybody's truck at the docks, Apponaug, Warwick—y'know, it's tough gettin' guys to go out there and do stuff, especially in the summer. I'd drive all morning, and then at twelve-thirty, one o'clock, they'd call: 'Oh, Mike, we canceled the meeting.' So then you gotta call everybody. This happened two or three times—they do it on purpose is what my lawyer was saying. 'They're bustin' your balls, Mike,' he'd say.

"They did eleven version of the legislation. We had a meeting where they gave us three versions at once—it was like stacks and stacks of 'em—and back then, there was a big anti-DEM thing; the Coastal Resource Management Center was run by the legislature. They controlled it; that was their new playpen, for favors and stuff, bribes and the stuff they like to do. CRMC was the key to shoreside development—which is where the money is—so they were tryin' to do two things, one of which is to take more power from DEM.

"There was a guy," Mike recalls, "he'd be a Tea Partier now, but back then he was like a land-rights guy. He'd inherited hundreds of acres from his dad, and it was all swampland. He couldn't do shit with it—DEM wouldn't let him—and he was, like, angry with the world. These kinds o' guys . . . there was this big political push, you could tell. What happens is, they take a good idea, the right thing, and they manipulate it in a way that they'll get the most out of it. They could be part of the leaseholders for depuration—there were millions of clams behind closed lines. They had to have a bogeyman, and we were a convenient bogeyman."

Rhode Islanders, on the whole, consider their government deeply corrupt. There is ample evidence to support this perception. Former governor Ed DiPrete did a year in jail for bribery. Former Providence mayor Buddy Cianci has some national renown for doing two tours in prison, first for assault, then for bribery. Those are only the two most high-profile examples. Recently, the state rep from East Greenwich, formerly the State House minority leader, got himself arrested for DUI and possession of marijuana. He denied everything, then promptly got busted for possession again. It is also generally accepted that the state bureaucracy relies extensively on bribes and nepotism in its running of things. This is largely true.

There is also an ethnic dimension to the vilification of the State by the people who elect its officials. Providence served for a long time as the stronghold of a powerful Mafia family. Today, Mafiosi play only a small role in state affairs, mostly in protection rackets focused on strip clubs, but their continued presence, coupled with Rhode Island's WASP prejudices against Italians—which recalls the period when Italians constituted much of the legal and illegal immigrant population entering the state—keep alive the feeling that the State works like a crime family. Naturally, the State and its cronies in the local hate media blame all contemporary problems on recent waves of legal and illegal immigrants. The electorate, then, has a handy narrative that absolves voters of all complicity in any state malfeasance, while establishing that the state is mired in corruption—a narrative that makes each voter feel like an Independent Man.

For quahoggers, this situation works out pretty well. The various factions of evildoers in the state government have never reached consensus on how best to exploit shellfishing for their own personal gains. There are no Latino immigrant quahoggers, which means it's not easy to vilify diggers with anti-immigrant rhetoric, and the few legislators not given over to wickedness tend to side with the qualoggers on matters of fishery management. When it came time for the aquaculture fight, it was clear that a good number of those who were pushing for quahog farm leases expected to make big money from shoreline development. Not enough people were in on the scheme, however, and those who were not in on it found themselves able to indulge, for a while, in some entertaining fantasies about the swashbuckling quahogger.

"We had almost a hundred people up there one time," Mike says. "It was so cool. It was in May—I particularly remember Chris Hermanowski bein' there—and we all showed up. It's all these pasty-faced finance committee people, and there's these quahoggers in their T-shirts, y'know, all brown, bronzed. Spaulding, this guy from Save the Bay, he goes, 'Mike, we did a survey, and they ranked organizations and stuff, and you scored the highest of all the organizations. Save the Bay was right below you.' He goes, 'You guys were like seventy-four and we're seventy-two.' You see that a lot; you either know a quahogger: 'My uncle used to quahog'—or people think they [are quahoggers]. There was a romancing, kinda.

"And that's what they tell me: 'Y'know, Mike, you intimidated the hell out of 'em.' The whole thing collapsed at the end. We kicked their asses. I took my daughter to the State House the day of the vote, in '95; I guess she was, like, five years old. It was like the victory lap—it was just such a satisfying thing, and the wild thing is, I had nobody to tell. I got outta the hearing—I remember distinctly, it was, like, six o'clock at night, the sun was still up—and I was, like, 'I gotta tell somebody!' so I call Bob Desantis. 'Hey, Bob! Bob, we won!' And he says, 'Oh, I can't talk right now—my wife's in the other room.'

"The next day, I drove out on the water . . . You expect everybody to be, like, 'Hey!' No, the victories, they gotta be personal. If you're lookin' for a pat on the back, you're in the wrong industry, or the wrong position. That was the toughest of all the battles, and it was the first thing. I wasn't even elected then; I got elected that fall."

Since that time, Mike's diplomacy has concerned state management and market. The State is by far the easier arena. In a sense, the State is the only arena, because it is mainly through the State that the guys can change the conditions they face in the market. Deciding when guys can work and how many can work, for example, has an impact on the price of quahogs, but trying to control these variables to keep the price high is usually pointless. The Association's position is also frustrating, because the shellfishing industry relies on good management of several different sectors. Each of the Association's victories depends on a string or a network of other victories. Everything in Narragansett Bay bows to this rule, but the development of management regimes in Greenwich Bay best illustrates the point.

"Back in 1980, the Greenwich Bay area was just fallow, to use that term," says Mike. "Only part-timers used it; the full-timers were goin' out, usin' longer setups, workin' the High Banks. That's where I cut my teeth, back in the eighties, and because Greenwich was so easy to dig, and it was recreationally available, you'd go out with a recreational boat and catch; there was, like, nothin' there.

"Back in the wintertime—that's when guys didn't have great boats, lotta wooden skiffs, smaller engines, you'd get ice—basically, the biggest dealer, Finn, would lose his market, and he was getting ready to start depurating. And this is what they called the Golden Clam; they had some kind o' water system within his property that you could actually depurate the polluted clams."

Depuration means taking quahogs from polluted waters and processing them in tanks that clear them of harmful bacteria. Really, barely any machinery is necessary. Simply placing quahogs in clean water that agitates sufficiently will do the job in a few days, or a week. This makes depurating facilities fairly cheap. If the State ever allows the operation of a depurating facility—meaning, that it should allow the harvesting of quahogs from prohibited waters for purposes of depurating them for commercial sale—the population of quahoggers would collapse. You can earn a day's pay in ten minutes by working behind closure lines. Or, as Finn would have liked, a dealer could pay ten guys to get all the quahogs he needs for a day, putting all of the other guys out of work. Not only that, but water-quality standards would mean less. Why work to improve water quality to the ultra-high standards required by the shellfish trade, when the industry can just take product from bad water?

Worst of all, guys would obviously claim to be digging in prohibited waters for depuration product, then sell to non-depurating dealers. The introduction of depuration would have been a management, environ-mental, economic, and policing nightmare. But the fight over Finn's big idea did bring a real problem into the spotlight. Greenwich Bay needed a fresh approach.

"The association—and this is prior to me—back in 1979, '80—they said, no, we can't do depuration," Mike says, "so what they decided to do was turn Greenwich Bay into a management area: close it all summer, transplant into it, right, and only open it for the wintertime. Back then there were no rain closures, anything like that, and my association not only put this forward and got it through—with the dealers' blessings and stuff—but also got the money to transplant into it. We went to the legis-lative branch and basically we turned this fallow area into one of the most productive shellfish beds on the East Coast. Prior to the closure, it was the jewel; everybody was jealous of us."

Then, pollution hit. The piggishness of Rhode Islanders with regard to their own waters led to a catastrophic closure of Greenwich Bay in 1992—and that closure shows why the Association needs a whole con-stellation of management victories in order to really achieve even one. It does no good to carefully manage a set of fishing grounds into fecundity, if the people around the bay are going to shit all over the place. It has taken a long, long time to get Rhode Islanders to think of Narragansett Bay as something other than their personal sty, and it is still a struggle to get them to understand that what happens on the land affects the quality of the water. But getting the polluters on board is crucial to instituting the rules and infrastructure that make a market in wild-harvest quahogs possible.

In Greenwich Bay, some of the necessary changes came in the form of a collection of initiatives known as the Greenwich Bay SAMP—Special Area Management Plan. Among the Greenwich Bay SAMP's many action items was a program of sewer tie-ins—getting shoreline resi-dents to replace their seeping septic tanks with sewer connections. A few years after the SAMP got its way and the cities forced tie-ins, the read-ings at the mouth of Apponaug Cove became so good that the State had to open a big patch of closed water. This was the huge hot spot that Joey and a few hundred other guys would pile into, to work that December, and the spot that made the guys at the Seafood Festival—in high sum-mer, their hands numbed by ice—anxious for winter.

Jeff Grant was there at the Seafood Festival, shucking away, right next to Mike. He'd become vice president of the Association not too long before, in a way not all that dissimilar from the way Mike had become president. A big blowup over the question of how to work a super set of steamers had left Jody King on the outs and swept Jeff into office. The guys had begun to groom Jeff for the position anyway, but the dispute over how best to handle the rush on steamers had moved things along too quickly and left guys bemused, even angry. But Jeff was in it and he had to see things through. Then along came Apponaug.

Jeff is pretty wiped out by the afternoon. He got up at two in the morning to go out and get mussels for the Association's raw bar. The mussels delivered, he started shucking. Nonetheless, he perks up when he starts talking about the Apponaug opening.

"There's a line that everyone's been wanting to dig right next to, cuz it is awesome on the other side of it—just ridiculous. So this area's going to open, there's two sections that are opening: One's just a little sliver right in front of Greenwich Cove, on the south side; the bigger area is in front of Apponaug Cove, Mary's Creek area. It's going back to what it was in 1992—that was the original line, before we lost a big chunk of it in the nineties. In the nineties, we lost all of it. Then it became rain-event conditional, the last six, seven, eight years, I don't know—quite a while. The line has been progressively going, so now it's at the furthest point going in, since they've had a line. There's this tremendous resource up there that everybody knows about."

It's the same thing that happened with the steamers; it's the problem of abundance. There is going to be a gold rush in December, and the guys have to figure out how to deal with it. Ultimately, the plan became rotation: They'd divide the western half of Greenwich Bay into two areas, called, inventively, Area One and Area Two. They don't correspond to the two newly opened sections of water. They are roughly an equal division of the western bay, with Area One comprising the grounds in front of Apponaug Cove, as well as waters already open, and Area Two comprising the sliver before Greenwich Cove, as well as areas already open.

"Dividing it up," says Jeff. "Okay . . . Owen Kelly . . . This is Owen Kelly's idea. Area One will be open; Area Two will be closed. I'm gonna give you the reasoning behind doin' it: It is so good over there that we're pretty confident that, if people stick to what you can legally take and don't go crazy, you could probably double your daily limit and still catch 'em. The other part, the part we've been harvesting out of, the area that's always been open, is all undersized, all beans—tons of beans. You go there, you get a full rake, and you get fifty quahogs out of it—just ridiculous amounts of beans. So you can figure it this way: Normal winters, we get a dollar—well, this winter, we get a dollar-forty, cuz we're gettin' this big area opened up. Mike McGiveney is the one that said this, perfect example; We got a dollar-forty this winter, and we can take that forty cents and put it in the bank for next year. We're gonna let them clams grow, the beans, without people touchin' 'em, is the theory. And next year, we'll open up everywhere.

"That was the theory. This idea came up, and it went to the Association. The Shellfishermen's Association narrowly voted to approve it, it was, like, one vote—no, it was one vote, it wasn't like one vote—so when that happens, Mike McGiveney, who's the spokesperson for the shellfishing industry, is bound by the Shellfishermen's Association, whether it was one vote or twenty, unanimous, whatever, to advocate for it. It then went to the SAP—the Shellfish Advisory Panel to the Marine Fisheries Council. SAP voted unanimously to approve; people who are part of the Association, people who hate the Association, people who have no bearing—everyone who went to the SAP heard the idea and said, 'You know, that's a good idea,' and it was approved. It went to the MFC; the way everyone wanted it was for everything to open up next year. DEM has now popped their head up and said, 'We might want to look into a permanent rotation—the industry does not support that, at all, and we'll fight it, if it comes down to it.'"

There will be no shotguns in that fight; those days are done. The contemporary quahogger gets to work in the traditional way and make a decent living at it, but without having to smash up other guys' gear or slash the tires of dealers' trucks, thanks to the efforts of the quahoggers who went before him, who made certain that, work-wise, things would remain the same. Management-wise, things are pretty much the same, too, insofar as questions of management still consume guys.

Mike, Jeff, Owen, Joey, Jody, and guys like them—you can't get them to shut up about this closure line or that limit, DEM fucking up or not giving a shit, the bad surveys of the State or the good, practical knowledge of the shellfishermen. It's annoying. Whoever wants to disabuse himself of any romantic notions about the quahogger needs only to talk to one of them for five minutes on the topic of resource management. Most quahoggers are policy wonks. This phenomenon is not unique to them: It is one of the great truths of sustainable food that farmers and fishermen who work sustainably and the communities who support them must think constantly about management. The shit just never ends. Even for farmers and fishermen who work imprudently, this observation is largely true; it's just that they have narrower concerns, i.e., their own profit and nothing but their own profit.

Communities who support unsustainable food, however, have a lovely time of it. They don't have to think about anything. In fact, it is better for them not to think about what goes on with the industrial food chewing its way through their guts. Dealing with quahoggers doesn't challenge the average citizen merely because it involves coarse speech and dirty jokes and profligacy, but also because it involves one in immediate, crucial, and eminently solvable problems. Any jerk can formulate an opinion on how to run the bay, and the prospect of doing so can be quite attractive—not only because the matter is significant, but because it is obviously significant. Everybody can understand the importance of food and work. The problem is that it's so hard to have a confrontation about food and work these days.

With Mike, it's easy to fall into deliberations on how to deal with the demand side of the industry. Mike's something of an elitist, almost a snob, when it comes to quahogs and quahogging, but, because he has charm, his snobbery has appeal. He sees Rhode Island's stuff at the top of the quahog pile, and full-time, Narragansett Bay, wild-harvest bullrakers as the *nec plus ultra* of shellfishermen, possibly of working people in general. He wants consumers to know this, to recognize the value of what he and his colleagues do, and of what they provide, and his big dream is that this recognition will increase demand for Rhode Island quahogs. He believes in "the reverse Wal-Martification" of America, a move away from industrial, mass-market products to more artisan-produced goods. He wants the sustainable food movement to take notice of the quahogs of Narragansett Bay.

That's what the Rhode Island Quahog bags with the Don Bousquet logo were all about. That is, in part, what the raw bar at the Seafood

Festival is about. Mike wants people to know what is good and what is right when it comes to quahogs, because, when such principles hold sway, Rhode Island's shellfishing industry can only win. He is looking, in other words, for a way to outflank quahog aquaculture—to deliver something the farms cannot deliver, rather than compete with them on volume.

Apponaug gave a hint of how this might work. "The good thing for the dealers—and it's not so good for the guys—is because Apponaug has been left alone, fallow, for fifteen years, there's a lotta tops. A lotta guys high-graded, which I did at the beginning—which means you throw your tops over and get fifteen, sixteen, seventeen hundred count. But the dealers want the tops; they're the things that are movin'. We're gettin' a terrible price, but that's one market that's movin', because aquaculture hasn't moved into tops. Aquaculture, that's the reason why there's a strong market; the reason the prices are so low, they say, is that the Connecticut dredge boats get a lotta tops, and they're a much cheaper operation. They will catch ten thousand tops, so if they get ten cents, that's still a thousand dollars. We're doin' four, five, six, seven hundred tops—that's seventy bucks for us—so it's actually helped the dealers at that end, because a lot of production is, you know, half tops; quite a few of them have turned their machines a little tighter, if you know what I mean."

When the dealers start screwing people, it's time for the diggers to pay attention. There's a demand out there, a demand that quahog farms don't want to meet, because it takes so long to grow a quahog to topneck size. There remains the threat of the Connecticut dredge boats, but they can't last forever, because they'll wipe out the resource. The thought is tantalizing, not just to Mike, but to anyone he talks to about it. *Tops!* you may think. *Seize the fucking day!* That's the fun of dealing with the president of the Shellfishermen's Association these days—not the prospect of getting him to say something wildly stupid about union thuggery, but to get charged up about solving a problem. Before you know it, you'll find yourself using the word *incentivize*. It's embarrassing.

In the end, however, the excitable neighbor of the quahogger is not going to come up with the answers to the questions of how to keep shellfishing in Narragansett Bay sustainable. He may contribute the germ of an idea, but it's the quahoggers and the dealers and the scientists and the regulators who will figure out the details. How can the guys ever corner the tops market anyhow? Who'll see the gains? The good neighbor can help to pick the winners, which is how markets work: They are established by selecting classes of winners and then distorting the transactions to ensure that they win. But he couldn't do much to help design the system that will favor the chosen ones. It's one thing to recognize that it best serves the community to have more of the gains go to the quahoggers than to anyone else, but it's quite another thing to rig the market in such a way so as to ensure that the quahoggers do get those gains.

Thus, the good neighbor cannot discharge his responsibility to his community by virtuous consumption alone. He can't just eat chowder made from honest-to-Christ, wild-harvest, Rhode Island quahogs and call it a day, because, as things stand now, the market is rigged to favor dealers more than diggers, and restaurants more than anybody. The good neighbor also needs to tend to the quahoggers in his midst. And that's the real problem for the person who is not a part of the industry.

CHAPTER TWELVE

Old-Timers Gone

Learning was in his blood.
—H. P. LOVECRAFT, "THE WHITE APE"

I AM OF THE TWELFTH GENERATION OF HULINGS IN RHODE ISLAND. One of my great-great-uncles, a man of the fourth generation, was Captain Alexander Huling, a privateer. Once, in the late 1700s, his vessel came upon a French man-of-war in the North Atlantic. By the captain's assessment, the French ship outgunned them, and they would find no profit in attacking her. His officers hinted at gutlessness on his part. Very well, Captain Huling ordered his men to close with the man-of-war. As they came within range, his officers got a better look at the ship and concurred with the captain's initial, farsighted measure of the enemy. They conceded to him that they should turn away. The letter that tells this story continues:

> *The captain replied that they were so anxious to get a taste of the enemy's gunpowder that they should now have an opportunity. He gave the order to fire. The French ship lashed the American privateer, resulting in the death of a cook. Captain Huling's ship made its getaway, but not long after encountered a French frigate, which captured him and his crew.*

This man's blood surely coursed through my grandfather's veins. It may well run through my father's and mine. There remains in my family a tendency to prove oneself right through self-destruction. The captain had already won an admission of error from his officers, but he found himself compelled to teach his men one additional lesson on the concept of courage. To demonstrate the full injustice of his men's initial accusation against him, he delivered his ship into precisely the disaster he'd wanted to avoid. He got a man killed and made himself a pauper in a fit of righteous pique. That sounds about right for us.

These men—Captain Alexander, my grandfather, my father—twisted against themselves, and they took up work that twisted them further. My grandfather dropped out of school at age thirteen to begin working full-time. At fifteen, he was shoveling a thousand to fifteen hundred bushels of oysters a day on the oyster barons' boats. Sometime during this period, he busted his wrist when he clipped a dock, diving from the roof of a shanty. At eighteen, he broke his back in that mysterious train accident. Before World War II, he scalloped, earning two hundred dollars a day. When the Americans joined the war, he worked as a welder for Electric Boat, building submarines. He did this work intermittently for years; he worked on the *Nautilus,* the first nuclear submarine. When he bought the property where my father and I would grow up, he cut a mile-long swath through the woods for the thirteen telephone poles needed to reach the street, and he dug a twelve-foot cube hole in the ground for a septic tank—with a shovel. He retired in the 1970s; it's hard to say exactly when, because he continued to go out on the water, from time to time, until his body gave out about the time I was born. When he died in 2001, at the age of eighty-two, he could barely walk.

Upon my grandfather's death, my father dealt with the obituaries in the town paper and in the *Providence Journal.* On the phone with one of the papers, he paused to listen to a question, then said, "No, no . . . nothing like that. He wasn't a religious man." My grandfather's obituary would have no religious tones. He was a man wholly of this world. He had a deep fear of embarrassment and a deep fear of death. He came to express these fears in a certain controlled, precise wastefulness. His own father had died when my grandfather was three. As a young man, he lived perpetually in fear that he too would fall dead suddenly. When he had long exceeded his mid-thirties, the age at which his father died, he didn't consider that perhaps he had been wrong to live so afraid for so long, but continued in his fear. He expected to disappear from the world, to lose everything, every single day.

His various, self-inflicted misfortunes exacerbated this problem. He was ashamed of the risks he had taken, of the physical harm he'd done to himself. He hated that he had broken his wrist showing off on the docks. Even sixty years later, he couldn't forgive himself for it. The same was true where his train accident was concerned. He grew fat in his older years, and his big belly disgusted him—as did his crippled body. It was a great blow when he could no longer climb the stairs to his bedroom and had to convert a little den on the first floor into a place where he could sleep.

Conversely, he took great pride in his capacity for hard physical labor, and his sharp mind. One winter, he watched me shovel out his driveway and his truck and my grandmother's car, and apparently, I'd done an exceptional job that day. I'd worked quickly and steadily and got the job done well and fast. "You don' quit, do ye?" he growled, happily. "You remin' me o' myself!"

He had an ability to look at his own work objectively. At times, he appeared almost surprised at his own prowess—when considering how he'd worked on the oyster boats, for example. His impressions of himself were always filtered through what he imagined other people thought of him. He could imagine other people's amazement at the work he'd done, and so he became amazed himself. It was the same way when it came to his brains. The sharpness of his own memory impressed him. He remembered everything. He remembered Latin from the last year of his schooling. He remembered the specifications of outboard motors he'd worked on in the fifties. Cloistered in his house in the woods, he had two televisions going constantly, and a spread of newspapers and magazines before him. When people came to see him, that was how they found him: reading and watching two TVs, and very much able—and impressed that he was able—to bark about any subject on any of the media currently under his observation. His opinions impressed me: He hated George W. Bush and admired Lauryn Hill.

These two sources of pride were in conflict, however. He was embittered by the fact that he'd never finished school. His family's poverty had forced him into full-time work early. The GED came into use when he was in his mid-twenties, but to take the test would have been to admit that he had failed at school—or that his family had failed at work. His misperceptions about himself tainted his pride in his labor. It seemed to him that all of his successes had grown out of failures. He thought that if he'd been able to get his high school diploma, he never would have had to work so hard. The things in which he took so much pride and which brought him some happiness seemed not to belong to him—not entirely. He was forced into the work that he loved. That was the real tragedy of his life.

Among quahoggers—among the great body of physical laborers—he was not alone in this brand of melancholy. Many, if not most, quahoggers have the same split within them. They are genuinely in love with their work—the freedom, the independence, the challenge, the weather, the importance of it. Yet they do wonder if they could have done something else. Could things have been different? Or did their temperament, their native intelligence, their circumstances guide them inexorably into just the thing they so love to do? These are men who pride themselves on their self-mastery and their willfulness, who scorn the boss-hounded masses, the workers in the cubicles, the drones who instinctively follow the trail laid out for them. Could the quahogger, too, have been chained to his work, before he chose it for himself? They twist inside around this question, and, from time to time, their internal strife springs loose. Often, they express their quandary as self-deprecating humor. Mike McGiveney likes to say that, should quahoggers ever get a reality show, as Alaskan crab fishermen have, it would be called *The Dumbest Catch*. Ray Wyss makes the same kind of joke; just about everybody does. It's an angst common to quahoggers.

My grandfather did not deign to abuse himself in this way; he had too much pride. He would never show that kind of weakness. For him, the spring came uncoiled in acts of excess, of sublime wastefulness. He did this in both conventional and unconventional ways. Conventionally, he became a drunk for a good twenty years. He bore the trappings of the solitary drunkard—the stashes of liquor, the piles of empties, the wreckage he left in a small radius of his home. When I was young, maybe seven or eight, my father and I and our neighbor, Billy Clements, also a bullraker, put up a set of posts for our mailboxes. Three boxes and three posts in a row. I remember Billy's satisfaction with the job, after it was all done. Not so long after they went up, my grandfather got all drunk, got in his truck, went down to get the mail, and ran over Billy's post and box.

It was a minor scandal, really, but a great embarrassment to my family and me. Billy put in a new post on the other side of the road. It stung to know that Billy had had to go through the process of digging a post hole, securing the post, buying a new mailbox, and fitting it to the post, because my drunken grandfather had run over the one he'd already built with us. It shamed me to see that new mailbox of Billy's at least twice a day. My grandfather gave up drinking a few years later.

He also had unconventional approaches to dissolution. He did quite well for himself as a shellfisherman, and he had a good head for investment. When he bought his eighty acres, he had the opportunity to earn some money, or, at least, to save some money through farming. They had big gardens, chickens, goats. They even had cows up there for quite some time. But, sometimes, my grandfather handled things oddly, even perversely. For a time, they kept a flock of thirty or so sheep. Each year, my grandfather would have my father shear them. No mean task. He'd spend all day at it, shearing and being hollered at by my grandfather. When the job was done, they threw all of the wool into the woods. This is crazy, antisocial behavior: private wealth destruction. Nobody knew about it. My grandfather didn't give it away publicly; he threw it away in secret. No one benefited from it. Wool in the woods, rotting, coming apart, snagging on bullbriers, sinking in puddles. Birds must have built nests with it; mice, too, and maybe some other animals. But aside from a small charitable contribution to Nature, my grandfather's discarded wool served no purpose other than that of expressing his deep, concentrated, fuming anger at the world.

It was a healthy choice, really—healthier than drinking. Healthier than other common expressions of ill-focused anger. My grandfather was not a hitter. He screamed and yelled and often infused everyone around him with despair, but he could not abide violence. He never slaughtered any of the animals he kept; he hired someone else to do it, or he told my father to. It was always a thorn between them, that my grandfather tasked my father with the killing of animals. When a cat had an unwanted litter of kittens, it was my father who had to drown them. One of the hard truths about farming is that, no matter the harvest, the farmer must kill. All crops stain the farmer's hands with blood, whether of deer or rabbits or groundhogs or mice or, yes, kittens. You must accede to this if you are to farm—or you must find someone to do it for you.

My grandfather didn't have the heart for that side of things, but he raised my father to have it, in order to burden my father with the entirety of that unpleasant duty. There's something tyrannical about that. He made someone else carry out the killing that he didn't have the stomach for, but which his choices had made necessary. My grandfather's fear of death—or love of life—kept him from violence, but also led him to treat his son with a certain brutality. The twisted, tormented character of my grandfather's every sentiment left no part of his relationship with my father unbent. This rule held true even in the way my grandfather never laid a hand on my father.

On the morning when my grandfather died, I met my father at the hospital. I had visited my grandfather there the night before. I was the last of my family to see him alive. A little before six in the morning, I heard the phone ring. I heard my roommate answer and walk toward my door. The experience imprinted me. Even now, I hate early-morning phone calls.

I went down to meet my family. My father burst into tears when he saw me at the entrance to the hospital. He was already walking with canes of his own by then. We went into my grandfather's room. His body lay there, eyes closed, mouth in rictus, like a man in a troubled, uncomfortable sleep. Christ; we cried hard. My father reached for my grandfather's shoulder. He squeezed and rubbed it. "Dad! Dad!" he said. This was the first time I had ever seen physical affection between the two of them.

Once, several years earlier, my grandfather had fallen down in his makeshift bedroom, and he couldn't get himself back up on his small, high bed, not even with my grandmother's help. She called me, and I ran up to their house. I reached under my grandfather's arms, he grabbed my shoulders, and I hauled him off of the floor. Because of that one moment, when I helped him up, I have embraced my grandfather more than my father ever did.

"I don't even think he shook my hand, ever," my father said, years later. "Maybe at my wedding, but I don't think even then."

There's more than sadness to the way my grandfather treated my father; it was also tragic, because, on the whole, my grandfather was right. His immense anger came from the truth. He saw things clearly and never deceived himself about them. It was wrong and unfair that he had grown up poor while others had not. He had made critical mistakes, too, bad choices. These things changed the course of his life, in ways he could not bear. Perhaps, if he hadn't had to drop out of school, he could have become a scholar of Latin. Perhaps if he hadn't suffered a broken back in that foolish train accident, he could have joined the service and won a second chance at an education under the GI Bill. He didn't have to start drinking. He didn't have to indulge his kindness toward animals at the expense of his son. His regret overwhelmed him and made him bitter, but even in that wretched feeling he could find some pride: His bitterness stemmed from his rightness. He was right about himself; he was right about the world. My grandfather lived fully within this life. He had no religion, no self-deception, no sense of any world beyond this one. This doesn't mean to say that he had no solace, no reprieve from his troubles. He had his family, his land, his work, and all of the world that came to him in the newspapers and on the television. But his need to be right about his life tied him up inside. It's as if he had nothing inside of his big, powerful body but thousands and thousands of knots of corded leather. How could he reach out to his son with an inner life so balled up on itself?

Some of these things passed from my grandfather to my father and to me. Among the three of us, there was always a repugnance—in the old sense, in the logical sense—for the way each of us reflects the others. It is a fact that we have an admiration for each other, but it is also true that we fight against the desire to let this admiration lead us to be more like each other. The reflections are everywhere. We all have the same name: Raymond Earl Huling. When my great-grandfather, Ralph Augustus Huling, was young, he fought in the Philippines. One of his army buddies, a Southron, came to visit him in Rhode Island, a few years after they got back to the States. While they were walking down the sidewalk in Providence, a black man walked toward them. The Southerner knocked the black man down for walking on the same side of the street as white men. My great-grandfather helped the black man up, then turned to Southron and said, "If you wanna be friends with me, you'll never do that again." The guy changed his tune enough that my great-grandfather named his son after him, Raymond Earl. My grandfather and father both passed down the name, each hoping that his son would be like him, only better. Along with the name, they also handed down the work.

My father did not grow up with quahogging in the way that I did. My grandfather never took him out to work in the boat. He hardly took anyone out in the boat. When he did bring the family out, he kept well away from other quahoggers, because he didn't want his wife and daughters to see the men pissing over the side. But neither did he bring out his son, who, presumably, had a mind strong enough to withstand the shock of seeing a guy piss from a quahog skiff. He permitted my father to dig quahogs by himself, going so far as to procure him a skiff, a motor, and tongs, and even to replace the tongs that my precociously strong father snapped with alarming regularity. But he did not bring my father out to work alongside him, even though my father very much wanted to.

My grandfather never wanted my father to earn a living as a quahogger. He wanted my father to take advantage of the opportunities his own poverty had robbed him of. He wanted my father not to make the same mistakes he had. This didn't mean that my grandfather refused any and all material or technical support to my father when he bullraked. Quite the contrary; he gave his son all manner of equipment and advice. He just told him, while he was giving him rakes or stales or telling him where to look for quahogs, that my father would fail, that he would never, ever be able to make a living as a quahogger. Such was his manner of persuasion.

My father's approach to me was to push and pull. He took me out on the boat, encouraged me to try the work, offered to help me any way he could, and at every other turn, he expressed his deep dissatisfaction with the way his life had turned out, because he had taken up quahogging. As my grandfather did, my father loved the work. He loved the water; he loved the physical and mental challenge. It all fit nicely with his character and capabilities. My father has a hunter's eye. Even now, long years after he quit, he catches all the little details that are so essential to the task of hunting. When I show up at the house, to take him to the doctor, he says, "Did you see the big mushroom on the oak tree, near the ground—the one across the end of the driveway?" On our way out, he spots a stone, sitting solitary on the driveway's pavement. "How'd that get there?" In the parking lot at the doctor's office, he looks over a patch of grass. "Looks like they had a backhoe or something in here a couple of months ago; hey, there's a couple of washers—three of 'em! I bet we could use those."

My father knows about his hunter's way of being in the world, and he likes to think of himself as connected to other hunters, as part of a community and lineage of hunters. He has a farmer's way about him, too. The unsteadiness of fishing appeals to him, but so does the regular rhythm of farming. Plowing, fence-building, planting, weeding, picking—slow, steady, and ever-present work. Plus, his father's queasiness has served him well, with regard to some of the tougher farming jobs. When we had pigs and sheep, my father delighted in tending to them. Animals have temperaments, almost personalities; it's fascinating the way they can convey emotion. He found happiness in keeping his animals, and yet, he still had it within himself to slaughter them for our table. In this respect, the farmer is a harder man than the hunter. It's one thing to kill a strange animal, one you've never known; it's something quite different, something darker, to kill an animal you've cared for. My father was eminently well-suited for his work, whether it was farming or fishing, but he bemoaned it. The work left him exhausted, bruised his body, tore him up. Mentally, it wore on him too—not because of the stress of figuring things out, as he was always good at that, but because the work he loved had become work he needed to do. Necessity can cheapen the things we love. Love is a grand luxury, and paying the claims of vulgar needs turns a calling into a chore.

He had other talents, too. College opened his eyes. He got to play the role of the farm boy while in college. It's hard today to grasp what a signal shift took place when that huge generation of my father's became educated. Those kids did not come from book-learned homes. For many of them, as for my father, the learning available to them at college, the casual acceptance of scholarship, was a wondrous thing. He had never seen anything like it. After several years, he had acquired a taste for the Beatles and Frank Zappa, for James Joyce and Richard Brautigan. While he intermittently attended graduate classes in agriculture, he started collecting books on physics, astronomy, and the history of mathematics. He fondly remembers a period when he woke early every day in order to get back home in time to watch Bobby Fischer play chess on TV. Then my mother came along, and I came along, and he went back to shellfishing full-time.

The responsibility alone didn't drive him back onto the water. Fear and pride played their role. He was afraid to step away from the kind of work he knew—fishing and farming on a very small scale—and take up work with a wider scope. His fear had some justification. My father had very little experience working for or with other people. He had grown up alone, and, aside from a few jobs here and there, mainly gained through extended family, he had worked alone. Middle-class society requires a certain savoir faire of its prospective entrants, and my father simply had none of it. The folkways and communal knowledge of college-educated, white-collar professionals seemed mysterious to him when he encountered them at college, and they never lost their mystery. He never figured them out. My father has only once in his life filled out a job application. As an adult, he has worn a tie only once, for his own wedding. In short, he's a rube, and he knows it. He felt abashed before the gates of the middle class.

And then there was his pride. His father had told him (and kept on telling him) that there was no way to make a living quahogging. My father knew this wasn't true, and he burned with a desire—not to prove his father wrong, but to be right; to stand before his father as a man who was right, and who knew he was right. This motivation also problematized his work: You can't use something you love as a cudgel for fighting your father without beating it all out of shape. There was no beating my grandfather anyhow. Nothing could have changed his attitude toward my father—or, at least, my father could not have done anything to change things. My father lost day after day out on the water, burning up about my grandfather's insistence that he couldn't do what he was doing, instead of enjoying himself—instead of recognizing his luck, his almost singular luck, in having found work that he loved. At any rate, he was still right. For a long time, he proved himself right.

My father's ill health traces back to his decision to become a full-time bullraker. Just before he went into the hospital, for his ten-month stay, he began taking a new medicine for his rheumatoid arthritis, which is yet another of the many afflictions that occur as a result of a misguided immune system. He had arthritic growths clotting up the base of his spine, which he would need surgery to remove, but, for the meantime, the doctors gave him immunosuppressant drugs, which left him more susceptible to other diseases and disorders.

It was a blood infection that first put him in. During preoperative testing for his back surgery, a number of his vitals looked bad—his blood pressure, especially. After a week or so of trying this and that, the hospital figured out that he'd contracted a rare, tick-borne disease called behisia. They gave him medicine for it, and broad-spectrum antibiotics for another, minor infection he'd incurred. It was the latter treatment that nearly did him in. One of the deadly nosocomial (hospital) infections to have come to the fore in recent years is *Clostridium difficile*, a pathogen that infects the bowel when antibiotics wipe out the beneficial flora in the gut. *C. diff* is hospital slang for it. It is one of those antibiotic-resistant superbugs the medical profession has bred from its practice of funneling antibiotics down the gullets of any patient who peeps in its direction, and many who don't. Over the past decade or so, *Clostridium difficile* has killed thousands upon thousands of long-stay patients, especially elderly ones. My father spent twelve days in intensive care as a result of this infection, an enormous amount of time. When I was twenty, I walked around with a ruptured appendix for a full day, thinking I had food poisoning. I came within inches of dying. I spent a single night in the ICU—which tells how deep in trouble my father was.

Health care is Rhode Island's biggest industry. New England has the best medicine known to man, and yet outside of the ICU and a few random practitioners, the state's hospitals and nursing homes proved themselves utterly inadequate, incompetent, and, at times, even cruel. This is to say nothing of the massive crime against humanity that is the American health-care system. If America has any rival to the bloody ziggurats of the Aztecs, it is the hospital. The Aztecs, at least, had the good taste to have priests make sacrifices of the young and the healthy. Americans hand the knife over to the insurers, who gustily slash at the bellies of the old and sick. Between the foolishness of dispersing drugs with no thought of tomorrow and the American propensity for inflicting cruelties and indignities on its most vulnerable people, my father's long stay in the places of the sick was a hateful one. It could have been merely difficult, merely frightening. Instead, it was all of those things, along with an extended confrontation with yet another aspect of a society that has spun nearly out of control. Medicine in America is a cannibal warlord, whom we pay tribute to, rather than put on trial for crimes against humanity.

While we fought the insurance companies to secure payment for the treatments necessary to cure the illnesses the hospital gave him, the family tried to keep my father's spirits up, but the sickness and the medicine often left him fogged or even delusional. Those moments were hard. As were those when he had to suffer through some painful procedure or other—the insertion of a needle into the spine to test for meningitis, for example. To hear my father get the year wrong, to see him crunch up his face in pain was unbearable. It wasn't always unbearable in the moment, but the weight of my father's suffering would come crushing down, sooner or later.

Sobbing takes up too much time when you have doctors and nurses and hospitals and insurance companies to fight. I saved it up. It became like holding down nausea. Days would go by, weeks, even. Then it would come, and I'd walk into the bathroom—at home or at the hospital—and wait. At the hospital, I'd turn on the faucet and blend a good hot stream of water. In a few seconds, it would happen; I'd lean over the sink and the tears and the snot would come out like vomit. For about a minute or so, I'd be helpless in body and mind. Sobs would rack my whole body, and in my head, over and over again, I would think *Not my dad! Not my dad!* It would last forty-five seconds or a minute, a total loss of self, and then I would catch my breath, scrub my face with the water, towel off, blow my nose, and go out to fight with everybody who wanted not to give my father any health care—which meant everybody in the hospital, everybody in the nursing homes, everybody in every office that had anything to do with health care anywhere. Back at my apartment, the crying would take place in the shower, which was usually, but not always, loud enough to keep my wife from hearing me.

He lived. We got him home. His mind cleared, but he still has trouble remembering things. He finally had the surgery on his spine, but he suffered severe nerve damage because his illness had postponed the operation. As a result, he cannot walk. The last time I clearly remember him walking was that last night at the oyster class.

"You know," my father said, months after he'd come back home, seated in his wheelchair, the parts of a broken chain saw spread out on a table before him. "Things were just starting to get better with Grandpa when he died. I was able to talk with him better than I ever had—we were talking about doing things with land, we were talking, like real people—and then he went and died on me."

My great-grandfather's early death left my grandfather terrified of dying. Because of my grandfather's great fear, my father grew up terrified that his father would die, and he passed on that same fear to me. Along with the name, I got the fear. My father almost died on me, too—and with him almost died all of our plans to work together.

Those men inculcated an inner torment about work in me—along with the reflex to use anger and wastefulness as a means to deal with my own discord on the matter of my working life. Of course, the work I know, the work of writing, is the antipode of the one they knew. I rejected the bullrake. I rejected physical labor entirely—at least for remuneration. The opportunities that they never had or turned away from, I took advantage of. But because my understanding of work came from them—because my working rhythm echoed theirs, because I had little more savoir faire of the middle class than they'd had—I came into my work almost hankering for dissatisfaction.

Perhaps worst of all, middle-class ritual perplexes me almost as much as it does my father. The middle class—the professional classes, white-collar workers, bureaucrats, the office class—they have developed grand regalia in which they dress up their work, in order to disguise the fact that everything they do is utter luxury. In just the same way that all wealth derives ultimately from food wealth, so all work that does not produce food is actually a kind of relaxation. Nowhere is this more true than in sit-down jobs.

Few people seem to get off on the miracle of this luxury, however. I certainly don't, but neither can I take the middle-class theater seriously. Unlike my father, I have filled out job applications, but just as they would be for him, they're riddles for me. A job interview is like filling in a crossword puzzle or restoring order to a Rubik's Cube. The sheer, exuberant nothing of the work of the Information Age is mystifying; it is an overcast sky, a koan, a canvas of abstract expressionism. All of which could be marvelous, in a nihilistic sort of way, because of the Zen machismo in it—all of those business types hitting each other with sticks while crowing about efficiency, when the whole fucking establishment amounts to the same thing as the act of eating an apple while watching someone else plow a field. I've never been able to reconcile myself with that dreamy world, just as my father and grandfather could not. I have to experience the rituals of the middle class as pure rituals, not indicative or determinative of anything, which leaves me disaffected and often belligerent.

What other choice could I have made? Several years ago, I stood on the shoreline near Algiers. This was not long after a tremendous earthquake, which had displaced hundreds of thousands of people and brought down the cities of Boumerdes and Zemmouri. I stood there with a doctor, a children's physician, who had done a lot of work setting up camps for the people made homeless by the quake. We had talked about our families; I had told him that my father had been a fisherman, a fisher of *poulardes* (probably; the correct French term for a quahog is unclear). We had stopped by the shore so he could take me to a little fish stand, not far from the surf. A father and son stood behind their fish, a few small Mediterranean tuna. Past them, I could see the water.

The doctor had told me that the earthquake had done terrible things down the shore. In the midst of the tremors, the water had drawn out, farther back than anyone had ever seen a low tide go. The bottom lay revealed, horrible with fish and seaweed. The quake cracked this new ground, releasing gouts of natural gas, Algeria's principal energy resource, and, in some places, the gas ignited somehow. There's the apocalypse for you: The water became fire.

The doctor drew my attention back to the fish when he reached for one of them. He pressed his thumb on its gills and pursed his lips approvingly when blood welled up. We didn't buy, but the fisherman smiled at us as we left. The kid must have been eight or nine. Algeria has done all right over the past few years, and he will have to make decisions soon, as he's a young man by now. If he goes out on the water, he will be following his father's path, harvesting food from the site of a disaster.

From my father's and my grandfather's perspective, it is perfectly comprehensible that I made it all the way to Algeria and gabbed with a fisherman and a doctor in French and bits of broken Arabic, by a beach that had literally burned with fire a month earlier. Perfectly comprehensible. It seems like just the sort of thing that they should have been able to do—or, perhaps, were circumstantially, if not psychologically, able to do. The idea of a son or grandson venturing farther and wider than a father or grandfather ever did seems natural to them. But it is not natural to me. They have forgotten where I come from. They have missed what influence their pride in their work had on me. What am I, if I can't make a day's pay quahogging? They don't really know. Neither do I.

This doesn't mean that I regret not taking up this work I dislike so much. Certainly, my life could have been very different. Maybe I would be more satisfied. Maybe I would be happy with thick, strong hands, that horseshoe of muscle casing the bones of my shoulders and arms. Or maybe I'd be buying my first cane right about now, with a III engraved on it, to mark the continuance of a tradition. I could be spitting at the bay, cursing my choice to use it to break my body. As things stand, I'm healthy and approving enough of watermen's work to start a small oyster patch with my aged father, but there he is—crippled by the very work that has brought so much of my own life into question. There are material signs of the problem. We have cleared up much of the property. We brought in scrappers to haul away most of the machinery, all of the cars, even the old bus. But there are the oyster cages now, where an old motorcycle used to be. They are unused, waiting; they may end up as my contribution to a new layer of stuff on the land. A new era in the cycle of wasteful accumulation. The thought is maddening.

It's arguably all their fault, of course. My grandfather read a lot; my father reads enormously, and where my grandfather threw books away, my father is an obsessive collector of them. I grew up in a house swollen with books. The cellar stank of them, as they mildewed in their cardboard boxes. Every bookshelf in the house had books stacked horizontally on top of ordinary rows of books, until the spaces between the shelves were reduced to mere cracks. We stacked books in corners and against walls, gathered them in paper bags, shoved them under our beds. Even the hallways got lined with boxes of them—and boxes on top of boxes. We had three broad categories of books: highbrow, lowbrow, and instructional. We had classics and avant-garde literature, genre fiction, and textbooks and how-to books. Absolutely none of what is called contemporary literary fiction, nor any works of popular nonfiction. This was the primary stuff of my education, and it set me on my path, here, to this book.

But this is how it is going to be. Men and women like my father will take up farming and fishing in some new way, and they will raise for themselves the problems that my father knows. They will raise for everyone else the problems that I know. They will trouble themselves, their families, their communities, because the work that they do makes everyone who touches it a little crazy, prideful, scornful, generous, and, in a way that will elicit envy, satisfied. Many of them will even be happy. A good number will be drunk. Or stoned. Or adrift on some better high. Lots and lots of them will cripple themselves. They will require care and support and acceptance in a great many ways—despite the fact that, from its heart, their whole enterprise will defy the most treasured traditions and values Americans hold today. They will form a population of troublesome folk, who will work themselves raw, these new peasants—but it is either them, or it is ruination.

CHAPTER THIRTEEN

The Coin of the Fish

And when they were come to Capernaum,
they that received tribute money came to Peter, and said,
Doth not your master pay tribute?
He saith, Yes. And when he was come into the house,
Jesus prevented him, saying,
What thinkest thou, Simon?
Of whom do the kings of the earth take custom or tribute?
Of their own children, or of strangers?
Peter saith unto him, Of strangers.
Jesus saith unto him, Then are the children free.
Notwithstanding, lest we should offend them,
go thou to the sea, and cast an hook,
and take up the fish that first cometh up;
and when thou hast opened his mouth,
thou shalt find a piece of money:
that take, and give unto them for me and thee.
　　　　　　　　　　　　　　　—MATTHEW 17:24–27

. . . it is not necessity but its contrary, "luxury," that presents living
matter and mankind with their fundamental problems.
　　　　　　　　—GEORGES BATAILLE, *THE ACCURSED SHARE*

"I DON'T KNOW ONE QUAHOGGER," SAYS ALLEN HAZARD, AS HE FEEDS one valve of a quahog shell into the blade of a tile saw. "Honestly . . . I guess I would like to; if I could connect with quahoggers, that would be cool."

On his lawn, near the front deck of his house in Charlestown, he has set up his table saw, next to a milk crate filled with shells. He makes two long cuts in the shell, parallel, with about an inch between them, working from the lip of the shell toward the hinge. He snaps off the tab of shell he has made, then runs it through the saw again, to shave off a length of white shell, leaving him holding a chunk of purple. The saw has a tooth-less, circular blade, which sits in a reservoir of water that lies beneath the saw's table. Bits of shell cling to Allen's hands, to his face, and, here and there, to his amber-colored, Smith & Wesson shooting glasses. He inspects the squarish hunk of shell for a moment, then begins to apply it to the edge of the saw. He holds his left hand flat, perpendicular to the saw, crazily close, as, with his right hand, he presses the shell against the blade, delicately.

Allen's a big man; they call him Talloak. He's well over six feet, dark-skinned, long-haired and graying. He keeps his hair in a single braid that runs down his back, and he is clean-shaven, except for a dart of white hair beneath his lower lip. As he works the shell into a globular chunk, it almost disappears in his big fingertips, which hover a good millimeter or two off of the blade.

"I guess it's not even a quahogger," he says. "As much as a person that would shuck 'em and find ridiculous-colored ones that I'd like to use." On a living quahog, it's hard to detect what people—including the Narragansett and marine biologists—refer to as its wampum: the purple part of its shell. *Wampum* comes from *wampumpeag,* and refers to a white shell, the shell of the whelk. *Suckauhock* is the proper term for the purple or black shell, but by metonymy, wampum became the dominant parlance. No one knows why quahogs produce their purple coloring; not all quahogs do, and it occurs mainly on the interior of the shell. Mainly, but not entirely.

"A few of 'em bleed perfectly," says Allen, as he holds up a big chowder shell. A smudge of very dark purple stains the exterior of its shell. "That's blood," he says. "That's not dirt; this guarantees that it's got a ridiculous amount of purple in there. There's no way of seeing that and not knowin'."

Allen is a famous wampum maker. He's a Narragansett, and he learned about making wampum from his tribe first, according to tradi-tional methods, and then began experimenting on his own, with mod-ern tools.

"That's gonna be a big ol' bead," he says as he pockets the rounded shell. "I know someone who wants a Pandora bead." The Pandora is a trendy kind of glass bead, a heavily oblate sphere, almost a torus. It is decidedly not a traditional form, but that's one of Allen's aims: to stretch the medium a bit. He takes up again the quahog shell he's notched and zips it through the saw, removing the entire hinge, but in such a way as to keep its natural curve. The hinge has a fair amount of purple shot through it and it makes a pleasing arc. Allen came up with the idea of using the hinge as a base for what he calls "bear claws"—two- to three-inch-long curves of wampum, tapering to a dull point. With the hinge in hand, he heads into his workshop, a small room jammed wall to wall with crafting gear.

He sits down at his worktable, which has loads of plastic cabinets with dozens of trays in them, a small, powerful table lamp, and an inspirational photo of Julius Erving in mid-dunk hung above it. He turns on a vacuum cleaner and holds it in his left hand, along with the bead. With his right hand, he then applies a Dremel tool to the bead. Dust puffs off of the bead for the barest instant, then zips into the vacuum hose.

Allen knows about quahogging; he knows about the importance of the quahog trade for the bay; he even does a bit of scratching himself. Every Sunday, after church, when the weather's good, he heads down to Galilee and puddles around, mainly for rock crabs, but he takes quahogs and steamers, too. After he has taken the meat, he pours the quahog shells onto a largish midden just past the edge of his lawn, a pile he roots around in every once in a while, in search of good color. In a sense, in terms of tradition, Allen has the deepest connection to the quahog there can be, but he doesn't think that puts him in a position to lord it over the quahogger.

"I don't have to teach 'em anything," he says, as he sets down his Dremel tool and vacuum hose. "It's their livelihood, but a native connection that they might not know of—I'm under the impression that they do know of the native connection—is, we were the first quahoggers. They've stepped up and improved what we did." He takes out a piece of very fine sandpaper and begins rubbing the bead on it; again, the little bead is all but invisible in his hands. It's as if he's roughing up his fingers, rather than polishing the bead. "The only thing that they probably wouldn't know, and I would hope that they would like, is the rustic look that I think has always been a native reality. It's beautiful, but not feminine—although it can be feminine; it very much can be." Allen has a quite soft voice, thick with the accent of the Narragansett, which has a lot in common with the classic Rhode Island accent, but is much less harsh. He has lectured at the Smithsonian, so he knows how to address an audience, but there's not the slightest affectation in the man when he talks about wampum.

"Even in ceremonies, wampum isn't taken as an item of sacred rituals. It's to be respected, but the only way it would be touched as a sacred reality is that every Narragansett is wearing it, including the medicine man. It's just part of what we felt was going to make us look well. What man doesn't clean up before he's going to take his girl out? What girl won't spend hours and hours for her man? For what it's worth, we knew we looked good with some wampum on us, and some of the people that wear it today have it all over themselves, because it's easy to obtain, if you got the money. It's three times as easy if you make it." He pulls at his necklace, which consists of a dozen or so inch-long, cylindrical beads, drilled lengthwise, and strung on a leather cord. "This necklace is Allen Hazard's version of the original wampum beads that caused so much pain and beauty down through the years. In the Eastern nations, I'm the last one that can still make this bead. I can't imagine any quahogger looking at this and not wanting to wear one."

A few quahoggers surely would, especially among the older guys, who retain a bit of a hippie vibe and take a spiritual view of their work, but the thought of a quahogger buying wampum seems funny. He would be trading money he earned from selling quahogs for beads fashioned from quahogs—beads with, as Allen suggests, a complicated relationship with the very notion of value.

"Here's a phrase you may or may not have heard of: 'Wampum is Indian money.' Definitely no," Allen says, sitting up very straight. "To a traditional Narragansett, that's nothin' short of blasphemy. What's wampum to a Narragansett? Sacred—and if I didn't have any other opportunities in my life, I was gonna clear that up. Wampum's sacred; it ain't Indian money. When people read a book, they say, 'Oh, yeah; look at it. That was their money.' We didn't know what money was; why did we need money?

"I can explain the whole nine yards as to why it got that label, and yes, later, down through history, at the tail end of history, you could get a little ride across the ferry with a few chips of wampum—that was true—so using that as the most pathetic example I can give you, at that instant, it was Indian money, but that wasn't a Native American thing; that was a European translation, years later."

You could also pay your tuition at Harvard with it, well into the nineteenth century, and the Industrial Revolution saw actual factories dedicated to wampum production. Industrialization and capitalization vulgarize everything they touch, but the factories did not occasion the first mass production of wampum. The Eastern tribes had always made wampum at scale.

"The Narragansett were the leaders in the collection of wampum beads," says Allen. "Depending on who you talk to—and I'm sure the Pequock and the Mohegans"—this is how Allen pronounces *Pequot*—"would have something to say about this. I could be arrogant and conceited and say we were the ultimate best at it, but the truth of the matter, in my opinion, is we were the largest of the Eastern woodland nations, and just out of commonsense reasoning, when we went to the ocean—because we were hungry—we came back with twice as many quahogs as the Pequock and Mohegans. Because if we were hungry and there's ten of us, rather than five of us, who's goin' to get the most shells? Does that make us better at it than them? It's debatable. We spent hours makin' it, but not just one person; and the reason we could get more than the Pequock, again, we had twice as many people that were workin', sittin' around, talkin' about each other, actin' up—that was our pastime."

Right there is the first value of wampum: It symbolizes the success of a particular society. Even with many mouths to feed, the Narragansett had time to do things other than scratch around for food. To have a lot of wampum meant to have a fecund population and high food productivity. The Narragansett had time to spare—and making *suckauhock* did require time. The quahog is the hard-shell clam, after all, much harder to work than whelk. The purple wampum of the old days had a disk as its standard form, not the bead.

Allen still makes the old kind, now and then. He takes a flap of deer hide and sets it on his worktable. He takes up a good-size quahog shell and then works it with two pieces of antler; first, his whacking horn, a rude-looking tool; then, his cracking horn, a length of antler with two small nubs of horn set very close to each other. He breaks the shell with the whacking horn, takes a purple chip from it, and then cracks the chip into a more-uniform, more-circular shape, by fitting its edge between the nubs of the cracking horn and levering off the shell's largest projections. He places the chip on the deer hide, then assembles his drill—a bow-and-stick contraption, the kind of thing you could use to start a fire, only the stick has a prong of deer antler for its tip. He winds the stick in the string of the bow, places the tip in the center of the shell chip, and works his drill for twenty seconds or so on one side, then maybe ten on the other. He holds up the drilled shell.

Next, he takes up a foot-long stone, a sedimentary rock, with a long, straight, half-inch-wide groove down its center. He sprinkles a little sand in the groove, then abrades the edges of the disk by running them down the groove. When he's done, he has shaped a semicircular disk with a small hole in its middle. That disk was the thing you would make a strand of wampum out of, and, in the old days, they measured those strands by what the white man called the fathom. Those tribes had plenty of free time, and they used their wampum to prove it. They exchanged strands among themselves, and with other tribes, but not in the manner of mean trade.

"Now, among nations," says Allen, "you're Pequock and I'm Narragansett. I'm in your area of the woods, and I'm at the end of my hunt, and we're friends. It was common for me to go to your camp, and you would take care of me for the night, so I wouldn't have to stay out in the middle of the woods. When the morning came, there was no way I could say 'thank you' any better than to give you a string of wampum. You and I both understood the working time and the sacredness behind that wampum, and you were sayin' thank you, as well as I was sayin' thank you—sincerely. We knew we just gave each other something, so when I went on my hunt or my journey, I would have wampum to give, if I needed to. Eventually Europeans saw that; they big-time misinterpreted it. That's where the label 'Indian money' came from; the traditional pre-European wampum looked like coins."

But they were not coins. They didn't function like money at all, until long after the colonists got ahold of them. This was both because the Narragansett did not have property rights in the way the Europeans began to understand property in the late Middle Ages, and because the shell itself had a spiritual meaning that coins cannot have.

"Understand," says Allen, "the quahog's a live being—the creator made it. It has a live body, whether it's an ant, quahog, or deer. It's sacred, or the creator would never have made it, and it gave its life to us, so that we would have nourishment. And we say that about every animal that we was allowed to take. We say 'allowed to take' because we didn't go after it, like, unfortunately, fishermen do today. We went at it with prayer first, and with prayer after we got it, and we totally believed and understood that the creator led us to these quahogs. I mean, think about it—we forced ourselves into his home and took his body, and we ate his body; that's sacred. That's deep stuff. When you think about the reality o' this bein' a living being; if we could do that to a rock, there'd be no problem."

Coins are made from rocks—literally—and they have value within a system of property rights that tends to confer absolute control over things, be they parcels of land, equipment, or even slaves. When a man buys his home with coins, it becomes his castle. But to signify the passing of the responsibility of caring for, say, certain fishing grounds, with the exchange of wampum—that does not grant absolute power over those grounds. Malfeasance in the care of them could invalidate the agreement. Similarly, to give a friend some wampum after staying the night in his camp does not amount to renting a bed from him. There are two debts incurred in Allen's example, one for the guest and one for the host, and no debts repaid, if there are even debts at all. It may be best to think of the event as a mutual giving of gifts that strengthens a bond of friendship.

None of this means to say that the Narragansett did everything right, but it does help to illuminate the central problem all societies face: They produce too much wealth.

The Narragansett built up a large population over time, but not so large that they strained their resources. Far from producing too many mouths to feed, they increased their productivity to the point where they had ample time to take up pursuits other than those of hunting, gathering, or growing food. All societies have always done just the same thing, which is why all societies have always had to invent some way either to reduce their productivity, destroy their excess wealth, or both. Thus, when a society discovers that it has no need to require everyone to toil in the fields or hunt in the wilds, it goes to war or invents sport or religion or art. Well-fed groups of hunter-gatherers went down to Chauvet Cave in France and painted the walls thirty thousand years ago. Eighteen thousand years later, they built a temple at Göbekli Tepe, in Turkey. This is the same as shaping wampum, as is the lacrosse played by the Ojibwe four thousand years ago. All of these things both divert resources from food production and actively destroy excess wealth created by overproduction of food. Sometimes, these diversions become productive in their own right, as when war returns plunder or slaves, or, as in the case of the Narragansett, when sitting around drilling and sanding shells produces wampum, which can be put into use as decoration or as gifts. Faced with a superabundance of food—of quahogs, in particular—the Narragansett developed a practice that destroyed one kind of excess wealth while producing another.

There are many kinds of wealth, of course, and not even all kinds of wampum wealth are the same. When the European colonists began to produce wampum, they did so in response to conditions similar to those the Narragansett faced, albeit more intense. The colonists also had to deal with the problem of a superabundance of quahogs, and though they too resorted to wampum making as a partial solution to this problem, they did so in their own customary manner. That is, they destroyed some of the excess wealth their own high productivity of food had produced, but through practices that, in the end, returned higher gains of productivity. They turned quahogs into a form of capital. For the colonists, wampum did serve the purpose of money; it really was a kind of coin. This held true for the early Americans, following the Revolution: Because agricultural productivity was so high, a boy could quit the farm and go to work at the wampum factory, where, because he did not receive the full returns of his labor, his work would add to his society's pool of capital. The modern European—and, especially, the American—way of handling the problem of an excess of wealth results in this paradox of ever-increasing capital.

You can see it everywhere: Activities that developed to waste the energies of societies overstuffed with food, become, in America, merely new ways to deliver ever more capital. Some of the contemporary American efforts to destroy wealth make immediate sense. Professional sports, for example, provide immense and glorious spectacles, though capital has co-opted them for its own ends, and, ultimately, they produce more wealth than they destroy.

Similarly, American religion puts on a show and converts the energies of the faithful into currency. Handling rattlesnakes and drinking strychnine may constitute a more-direct method of wasting wealth than the performances of a mega-church, but it is the latter that enable the capitalist to soak up more gains.

The financialization of capital is the most puzzling of all of the ways that Americans use to destroy the wealth they have in great abundance. High finance converts wealth into esoteric forms of currency and then burns it all up, but hardly anyone ever gets to see the burning. The habit Americans have of delivering their wealth to capitalists in order that they destroy it would make more sense, if there were no metaphor. If Wall Street actually took everyone's savings and pensions and mortgages and what-have-you, converted them all into paper dollars, stacked the money in a huge pile somewhere down at the tip of Manhattan, and then literally set the cash on fire, then, at least, there'd be something near-sacred about the business. The whole thing is extremely puzzling.

What is comprehensible is how each of these solutions to the problem of wealth parallels the Narragansett's production of wampum. Every society gets to choose how it deals with its wealth, and these choices result in more or less sustainable practices. Thus, the Rhode Islander has numerous means at his disposal for trying to solve the problem the Narragansett approached through the making of wampum. For five thousand years, at least, man has had to reckon with the challenge of the superabundance of quahogs in Narragansett Bay. For perhaps a hundred and fifty years, the people who live by the bay have had the option of dealing with the quahog by simply wiping it out. They have the technology to do it. They could declare all-out war on the hard clam and, through multiple means, but primarily through dredging, they could exterminate it. They could even do so while converting the food wealth of the quahog into capital wealth. There exist precedents for such a program in Narragansett Bay in the histories of all of the fin fish that man has hunted into commercial extinction in the bay's waters, and in all of the capital produced by these extinctions. For now, the people around the bay have chosen to act through the commons, using the quahogs to provide a livelihood for a small number of its residents through trade in a market it has created, hand in hand with the federal government and the governments of other states. Rhode Island makes use of its quahog wealth in a measured way.

As a result of this decision, Rhode Island has its quahoggers to reckon with. The quahoggers occupy a peculiar position. Because they transform the bay's abundance of quahogs into a food supply, they add to the wealth of the people who live by the bay. Lots of economists like to play around with the idea of economic multipliers—the notion that some forms of economic activity have a greater impact than others. Certain kinds of wealth production deliver a value in excess of the transactions in dollars nearest to them. A multiplier accounts for this disparity in value. In the early 1990s, an economic study covering the main body of industry in Rhode Island found that quahogging had a multiplier of 4.5, the highest of any industry in the state. To this day, quahoggers will offer multipliers that range from 6 to 11 as good estimates of the real value their trade delivers to the local economy. This sort of calculation can be fun to do, but, in the end, it is always moot: Quahogging is food production, and any accounting of the true value of food production must always reach the same figure—everything. The multiplier is infinite. The value of food production is equal to the value of everything ever produced. Really, this is just an iteration of the idea that the most fundamental problem of any society is how to deal with excess wealth. It is another way of expressing one of the lessons of the story of the coin in the fish's mouth.

The parable is one of the strangest of those concerning Jesus. Primarily, the story means to explore the odd position Christ's divinity puts him in. The tax collectors come from the temple; they want him and Peter to pay the temple tax. But for Jesus to give money to the temple wouldn't make sense. He'd be giving money to himself—a novel argument for tax avoidance. Yet, he does not wish to upset the taxmen, so he needs to give them some money, while escaping the logical paradox of paying off a debt to himself. This conundrum explains why Jesus does not instruct Peter merely to catch a fish, sell it, and use the money to pay the tax. Only a medium of exchange that exists for the purpose of paying the tax, and the tax only, will solve the problem. Jesus needs miracle money.

But why trouble Peter with the work necessary to effect the miracle? Jesus could have just rolled up his sleeves and said, "Oh, Simon! I believest thou hast something behind thine ear!" and pulled out a coin. Such a resolution would have seemed like cheating. The miracles of Jesus usually work through amplification, rather than conjuration: He divides fish and loaves to feed the multitude; he doesn't just magic up more of them. Some kind of work needs to go into the production of money, even when it's only miraculous. This doesn't explain why it was Peter who got the assignment, however.

Jesus was a handyman. He could've fixed someone's roof and found a coin in the roofing—only that would have made him look like a thief. Some poor roofer could have lost the coin that Jesus found. No; the money had to come from the kind of work that Peter did: primary food production, a harvesting of natural wealth. There is work in the miracle, so it is not cheating. Fish don't need money, so it is not stealing. The logic of the miracle is satisfied.

Yet there is something more. The parable really works only because of a question it leaves unanswered about a crucial element of the story: *What became of the fish?* Jesus and Simon paid their debt in such a way that they had fish left over. What did they do with it? They could have eaten it or sold it or put it back in the water; they could have thrown it in an alley, or given it to a hungry person—or a well-fed one—or used it to instruct an aspiring fisherman on how to handle fish. Jesus could have split it into infinite pieces and fed the world forever. The point is that, as Bible stories are wont to do, the parable of the coin in the fish's mouth establishes a fundamental connection between food and wealth.

All wealth comes from food; increases in the productivity of food create the problem of how to deal with excess food; the excess calories must go to waste or deliver further wealth. In short, everything that is done, aside from food production, occurs as a result of excess food. Thus, the value of food production is both the food needed to maintain production and everything done with the excess calories.

The quahoggers of Narragansett Bay produce less wealth than would capital-intensive, machine-intensive methods of harvesting the quahog, such as dredging, but, in return for lower productivity over the short term, they preserve the resource and deliver to the people who live around the bay the interesting culture of quahogging. From the quahoggers, Rhode Islanders get food, some capital, the expectation of long-standing industry, and the opportunity to admire the quahogger.

In their daily labor, quahoggers prove admirable: in their management of their industry; in the way they've fought to keep their work sustainable; in the way they support each other in bad times. All of this is easy to admire. Further, the quahogger is a vanguard of the sustainable food movement, whether he likes it or not. By supporting quahogging, Rhode Island positions itself at the forefront of this movement, which affords Rhode Islanders the chance to admire themselves a little bit.

It would be easy to continue and even expand this opportunity for self-admiration. The easiest thing would be to eat—or even merely demand—more chowder made from the quahogs of Narragansett Bay. Not only might an increase in demand for quahogs eventually raise the price paid to the quahogger, but an increase in demand for chowder-size quahogs would also give the wild-harvest quahogger an advantage over the shellfish farmer. The wild-harvest guy can simply go and find the big quahogs that a shellfish farmer must invest years to grow. The virtuous consumer of quahogs could go even further and buy quahogs directly from quahoggers, delivering a better price on both sides of the deal. Though such bargains remain illegal for now, the penalties are fairly light, and, in any case, Rhode Islanders could use the State to create a market that allows for more-direct transactions—some kind of cooperative under the aegis of which individuals could trade quahogs for money with the full benefits of insurance.

Beyond individual demand, Rhode Islanders could move to increase collective demand: Community groups, towns, and even the State could sponsor clambakes. The festival is a proven solution to the problem of excess wealth—possibly older than sport and even religion. A good stretch of quahog festivals could keep a larger number of quahoggers working and boost their income. It is well-known that the earnings of the quahogger return to the local economy with impressive speed. Clambakes could dispense with a fair amount of quahog wealth, while feeding people and contributing to overall productivity. Rhode Islanders could also look to increase the number of quahoggers on the water throughout the whole year—first, by issuing more licenses to harvest quahogs for commercial purposes; and second, by cleaning up the bay to make more fishing grounds available. Lastly, Rhode Island could get its act together and do a better job of promoting its seafood in general, and its quahogs in particular.

On the national level, the proper action is so clear and obvious as to be banal: universal, single-payer health care. Sustainable food relies on people who perform hard manual labor, and the society that benefits from their suffering should do its best to alleviate it in the most direct way. Mike McGiveney wasn't kidding when he said that the cost of health care drove quahoggers off the water. The rising cost of insurance, insurance companies' pernicious attempts to deny care at every opportunity, and the willingness of health-care professionals to abet the insurance companies convinced many guys that the very communities they had helped to feed would throw them to the wolves once their bodies gave out after years of toil. Not only should quahoggers and all sustainable farmers and fishermen receive excellent medical care, but they should also enjoy a position of privilege, due to the sacrifices they make to deliver the most essential goods in the most responsible way.

There is a final—and more-nebulous—thing to do at the highest level, one beyond institutions of law and state. It is a matter of culture. At present, Americans turn the excess wealth provided by their extremely productive food system into all manner of destructive practices; indeed, the high productivity of their food system itself counts as a wealth-destructive practice, because of the environmental and economic damage that it does. There are healthier ways to go about delivering food at high levels of productivity and healthier things to do with all of those excess calories. There is even a compromise to be made. Alongside of war and professional sports and religious celebrations and financial disasters, Americans have resorted to another means of disposing of their extra energies, perhaps the oldest way of all: gluttony. It is the simplest solution, really; when you have far more food than you need, you can just eat it anyway. It's entirely possible that the economic and environmental benefits provided by sustainable food will not result in complete benefits to health. The food will be healthier—it won't have hormones and antibiotics and pesticides all over it—but it can still be eaten unhealthily. Even sustainable food can be a medium for gluttony. Should Americans change their food system for the better, they may still choose to remain sickeningly fat (although they may have a somewhat harder time doing so). Such an outcome should be deplored, but it shouldn't dissuade anyone from pushing for sustainable food. An excessive indulgence in excellent food may even accelerate the shift to sustainability. Those patrons of the raw bar at the Charlestown Seafood Festival, who down dozens of littlenecks on the half shell, may be doing their part for humanity.

There's always going to be a darkness to the business of producing food. Even apart from such immediately repulsive outcomes as gluttony and obesity, making food will always require the clearing of land, the killing and starvation of animals, the digging of hands into dirt, or the dunking of them into water. The hardships will never end—and, as always, the quahogger himself speaks eloquently of them, not only at the personal level, but at the global one, too.

Don Wilcox has many things to tell beyond his observations of how the best bullrakers work or how the trade in mussels happens. Don is a contemplative man; he has thought deeply about things. It is always impossible to say where a person's qualities come from, but a traumatic experience often serves as a way to make the presence of a remarkable quality more acceptable to those who do not possess it. So, if Don Wilcox is a perspicacious man and a thoughtful one, it may be comforting to imagine that perhaps he has paid for these gifts through some suffering.

"When I was quahoggin'," he says, "I wanna say I was sixteen, seventeen, maybe, and I fell overboard—February twenty-ninth, I got thrown outta my boat, off Warwick Light. The wind was blowin' hard outta the northwest, and me and Tommy, we were travelin' together, and we were goin' in between the islands, to go dig the clams, dig the quahogs, between Prudence and Patience. We were gonna go tide-diggin'. It was icin' up; I had a seventy-five-horse Johnson motor on the back of a wooden skiff, flat-bottom, and right at Warwick Light, between Shepley's and Warwick Light, Shepley's dock there, just south of Oakland Beach, the boat hooked in.

"I hit a wave, and it went in, and my stales—I had three brand-new, twenty-foot aluminum stales, brand-new, maybe two days old. I was a young kid, and I didn't tie 'em in. I saw 'em slidin' out. The boat hooked in; I mean, I was bookin'. I came to a complete stop, and the stales are goin' out, so I reached out, opened the door of the doghouse, and reached to grab the stales before they went overboard, cuz they were aluminum. And just about then, she hooked in again, threw me right overboard—and I had oil pants on.

"I went in the water and I popped my head out, and here's the boat, goin' around in a circle. The seventy-five, goin' right around in a circle there, and I'm in the middle. Tommy's long gone—he had a ninety horse at the time—and he was about near Warwick Light. I didn't know how long I was in—who knows how long I was in? A minute . . . and lo and behold, an old quahoggin' friend o' mine, Georgie Fecteau, who just died, was comin' behind us. He wasn't with us, but he happened to be comin', and he knew what had happened. He pushed my boat outta the way and got ahold of me, and he couldn't get me in the boat, I was so heavy. I couldn't pull myself—I was, like, comatose—I was just about ready to die, and he's holdin' me, and Tommy finally turned around and saw what was goin' on. He came back, and it took two of 'em to get me into the boat, and then they brought me home. Tommy brought me home in his ninety, carried me upstairs in my mother's house—you didn't go to the hospital in them days—and Georgie towed the wood skiff home. I almost bit the bullet February twenty-ninth. Georgie just died last May. Every year, I'd send him a card, thankin' him for savin' my life."

A mortal event can change a fellow; it can dull—or intensify—certain qualities in him. Maybe it's easier to think that Don can see further than other guys, because of what he went through when he was just sixteen or seventeen. At any rate, he has kept a sharp eye on precisely the things that have gone into remediating the bay, the things that so many laud as the right steps to take to keep the bay healthy, and the industries that rely on it, sustainable. He views these advances skeptically.

"The things that they're tryin' to help with are actually hurtin'," he says. "The sewage treatment—they think by puttin' the treatment plants in, they're solvin' the problem; they're actually addin' to it. When you used to shit in yer yard, you had a regular cesspool. I can remember as a kid, my grandfather bailin' the shit outta the cesspool and pourin' it on the tomato garden; it's all natural bacterias and stuff. Now they put it up through the transfer station and add all these chemicals—chlorine bleach—I don't know what it would be, if they didn't have it, but you can do an experiment.

"Take a jug of water, a quart of water, a quart paint bucket or somethin', and put some salt water in it. Put a fish in there, take an eyedropper and drop one drop of bleach or soap, drop it in that water, see how long the fish lives. And they're treatin' all the cesspools; they're killin' everything. The bay don't freeze up now like it used to, there's so many chemicals. It ain't just global warmin'—that's some of it, but I did this experiment myself, years ago. I took two glasses o' tap water—cold night, goin' down t' zero—and I put a little bit o' Joy soap in one, just a little bit, a drop; and the other, clear water, right outta the tap. I put 'em out on my back step, got up in the mornin', the clear water was froze right solid; the other one, there was mush ice in it.

"I think I read in a school book, when I was in school, that Edison—this was the guy that made lights—I think he said . . . I remember it was in a history book (if it wasn't him, it was someone, but I'm pretty sure it was Edison), he said pollution is the only thing that will wipe out mankind."

Don shifts under his shawl. A guy who goes into the water in Narragansett Bay in late February, when the water's about as cold as it gets in the year, he'll probably have a memory of that cold inside of him, like a piece of shrapnel, stuck there, for the rest of his life. But, now, Don's getting a little hot. "Man, I'm tellin' you, y'know . . . you'll get me goin' on this . . . we're killin' ourselves. We're gonna have to either evolve into another species or we're gonna decimate, and then maybe a million years from now, it'll come back."

He's exactly right.

For Don, much of the problem comes from population growth, which is, again, another thing that societies do, when their agricultural productivity increases. That is: The more food you can produce, the more children you'll have, unless you decide to do something with all of that extra food, other than feed more babies with it. Some societies do choose to expend their wealth in other ways. Most of the so-called developed world has already made that choice, and the so-called developing world is following suit.

But a decline or even a reversal of population growth won't really do the trick. It certainly isn't a guarantee that things will change for the better. Look at China: It has taken dramatic steps to check the growth of its population, while massively increasing pollution. Even more important, the finalities of the extreme long term should not assuage our fears. John Maynard Keynes was wrong when he said that the long run shouldn't trouble our thinking overmuch, because in the long run, we are all dead. The long run should matter little, because, in the long run, dead or alive, we will no longer be who we are. Of course we're going to evolve into another species; that's all that can really happen, other than becoming extinct. But so what? The important question is only what humanity will do in the interim.

Yes; as Don says, we are killing ourselves, but there is no inevitability to it—at least, not right now, or for the next few hundred years, which is the maximum radius for civilizational perception. As a society, we cannot see any further than the time in which we believe we can sustain ourselves. Within that limit, we can choose to stop killing ourselves, even with all of our numbers and all we have done to ourselves. We shall have to make sacrifices, but it is important to remember that sacrifice is a kind of luxury—even when it comes to the suffering that farmers and fishermen who do things the right way must endure. Though their friends and family and neighbors ask a great deal of them, they also grant them the luxury of a reckoning with their work, which is perhaps what they want most—to find something transcendent and permanent and real and sublime in the challenge of feeding their people.

There is a final story to relate. I have heard it a few times, but one quahogger told it particularly well. It doesn't matter if the story is true. I believe it is not, but, true or false, it expresses the final struggle, the most extreme struggle that the people who care for the quahogger must face.

"One day, several years ago—maybe Arthur Drew was out there when this conversation went on—all the old-timers were all workin' together in one spot. The subject came up about somebody passin' away. I don't remember who it was . . . and it led to guys sayin', 'Aw, I'm not goin' out like that. No, I wanna die out here, a massive heart attack on the dock, or on the water. That's it for me; that's the way I wanna go—with my boots on!' Like that, that type of thing. And the guys all drifted off, and it wound up bein' just George and Don, and George turned around to Don and said, 'It comes to dyin', if I don't die out here, if I wind up in the hospital, I want you to come and get me down in either your boat or my boat. Bring me out here, so I can go over the side.' 'Oh stop it, will you,' says Don. 'Jeez.' Georgie said, 'No ... you owe me. I'm holdin' ya to it. You gotta promise, if anythin' happens to me, you'll take me out one last time.' And why not say yes? What are the chances? 'Yeah, sure, sure, sure,' says Don. Well, George had a massive stroke. He was in the hospital, and Don went to see him, and George died tryin' to get outta bed."

Beyond the question of caring for them as they dash themselves against the stone of their work, beyond the question of how to make their work possible, and how to support them, there remains the question of how to deal with a culture that can foster stories like that. This is our reckoning.